CRIMINALIZATION, VOLUME 1

Studies in Critical Social Sciences Book Series

Haymarket Books is proud to be working with Brill Academic Publishers (www.brill.nl) to republish the *Studies in Critical Social Sciences* book series in paperback editions. This peer-reviewed book series offers insights into our current reality by exploring the content and consequences of power relationships under capitalism, and by considering the spaces of opposition and resistance to these changes that have been defining our new age. Our full catalog of *SCSS* volumes can be viewed at https://www.haymarketbooks.org/series_collections/4-studies-in-critical-social-sciences.

Series Editor
David Fasenfest (York University, Canada)

Editorial Board
Eduardo Bonilla-Silva (Duke University)
Chris Chase-Dunn (University of California–Riverside)
William Carroll (University of Victoria)
Raewyn Connell (University of Sydney)
Kimberlé W. Crenshaw (University of California–LA and Columbia University)
Raju Das (York University, Canada)
Heidi Gottfried (Wayne State University)
Alfredo Saad-Filho (Queen's University Belfast)
Chizuko Ueno (University of Tokyo)
Sylvia Walby (Royal Holloway, University of London)

CRIMINALIZATION

VOLUME 1

Politics and Policies

EDITED BY
CHIRAG BALYAN AND GARIMA PAL

Haymarket Books
Chicago, IL

First published in 2024 by Brill Academic Publishers, The Netherlands
© 2024 Koninklijke Brill NV, Leiden, The Netherlands

Published in paperback in 2025 by
Haymarket Books
P.O. Box 180165
Chicago, IL 60618
773-583-7884
www.haymarketbooks.org

ISBN: 979-8-88890-563-0

Distributed to the trade in the US through Consortium Book Sales and Distribution (www.cbsd.com) and internationally through Ingram Publisher Services International (www.ingramcontent.com).

This book was published with the generous support of Lannan Foundation, Wallace Action Fund, and the Marguerite Casey Foundation.

Special discounts are available for bulk purchases by organizations and institutions. Please call 773-583-7884 or email info@haymarketbooks.org for more information.

Cover design by Jamie Kerry and Ragina Johnson.

Printed in the United States.

Library of Congress Cataloging-in-Publication data is available.

Contents

Acknowledgments VII
Notes on Contributors VIII

1 Criminalization: An Introduction 1
   Chirag Balyan and Garima Pal

2 Politics of Criminalization 17
   Sidharth Luthra and Shubhangni Jain

3 Spaces of Assessment and Incarceration 35
   David McCallum

4 Evaluating Overcriminalization on the Basis of International Human Rights Law: The Example of Counter-terrorism Legislation 44
   Ekkehard Strauss

5 Criminalization: Reflection on Theories 71
   Chirag Balyan

6 Criminalization and the Presumption of Innocence 95
   Sébastien Lafrance

7 Democratic Erosion by Parochial Measures: A Study of Rising Criminalization of Free Speech in India 119
   Yogesh Pratap Singh

8 The Jurisprudence of Constitutional Morality and the Pathologies of Criminalization 144
   Shruti Bedi

9 Drug Laws: The Reality and Politics of Overcriminalization 163
   Alok Prasanna Kumar and Naveed Mehmood

10 The Concept of Overcriminalization in Russian Law 182
   Daria V. Ponomareva

11   Overcriminalization by Containment without COVID: Inside Kenya's
     Refugee Camps   195
       Charles A. Khamala

     Index   223

Acknowledgments

This important volume could see the day of light because of the efforts of many people. Firstly, we would like to thank contributors of this volume for their valuable chapters. We are grateful to our Hon'ble Vice-Chancellor, Prof. Dr. Dilip Ukey for his unwavering support in all our endeavours.

We are thankful to Urja Vashishth and Prakahar Tiwari for their research assistance.

We also express our gratitude to Brill for giving us the opportunity to publish this book. Particularly, we want to express our gratitude to David Fasenfest and Jason Prevost for their kind support in bringing out this volume.

Notes on Contributors

Chirag Balyan
is an Assistant Professor of Law at Maharashtra National Law University Mumbai. His area of interest is contours of criminalization, antinomies in liberal theory, and preventive justice. The title of his doctoral thesis is: "Antinomies in the Criminal Justice System: A Normative Critique of the Pre-Trial Detention Laws in India". He has recently published a book with Thomson Reuters titled, *Revisiting Reforms in Criminal Justice System in India*. He has also published a funded research project titled "Commercial Sexual Exploitation in Maharashtra: a study of public prosecutors" in collaboration with the Government of Maharashtra, India and International Justice Mission. He regularly publishes in reputed journals.

Shruti Bedi
is a Professor of Law at the University Institute of Legal Studies (UILS), Panjab University (PU), Chandigarh. She is the Co-ordinator for the Department of Law at University School of Open Learning, PU, Director for Centre for Constitution and Public Policy, UILS, PU and also a TEDx speaker. She has authored two books and co-edited four books including a Festschrift in honour of Professor Upendra Baxi in addition to publishing numerous articles in national and international journals, blogs, books, newspapers etc. She has lectured at universities in England, Canada, Vietnam, Indonesia and Brazil.

Shubhangni Jain
is a psychologist and psychology educator. Clinical Psychology being her specialization, she has been associated with various hospitals and institutes in research, counselling as well as academic roles. She holds a Ph.D. in Clinical Psychology. Her thesis on 'Moderating Role of Emotional Maturity and Social Support in Treatment Outcome among Women with Conversion Disorder' and other research papers have been published in various national and international journals as well as presented at renowned conferences.

Charles A. Khamala
is a Senior Lecturer in law (since 2016) and Academic Leader of Criminal Justice and Security Management at Africa Nazarene University Law School, Nairobi. Prior to this, he lectured at Kabarak University Law School. He holds a Ph.D. in Law from the Université de Pau et des Pays de l'Adour (2015), LL.M. (2006), LL.B. (1990) and Postgraduate Diploma in Law (1992). He has practised

as an advocate of the High Court of Kenya for 29 years and is Listed Counsel of the International Criminal Court, member of the Association of Defence Counsel Practising before International Courts and Tribunals, and on both the African Court on Human and Peoples' Rights' and UN's Ombudsperson to the ISIL (Da'esh) and Al-Qaida, Legal Aid Schemes. He was a Fondation Maison des Sciences de l'Homme Themis Lauréate (2023), joint Platform Magazine's C.B. Madan awardee (2020), served at the Law Faculties of KU Leuven (Visiting Scholar, 2018) and Rhodes University (Andrew W. Mellon Post-Doctoral Fellow, 2016). His doctorate Crimes against Humanity in Kenya's Post-2007 Conflicts is published by Wolf Legal Publishers (2018). Besides serving the Criminal Justice Committees of the EALS (2023–4) and LSK (2018–22), he is Kenya's Director General on the International Forum on Crime and Criminal Law in the Global Era (since 2018), and sits on six Editorial Boards of journals in Africa, Asia and the US. He is widely published in peer-reviewed journals on international criminal law, criminal law and procedure, corporate and white collar crime, and human rights.

Alok Prasanna Kumar
is Co-Founder and Lead, Vidhi Centre for Legal Policy, Karnataka. (India). His areas of research include judicial reforms, Constitutional law, urban development, and law and technology. He graduated with a B.A. and LL.B. (Hons) from the NALSAR University in 2008 and obtained the BCL from the University of Oxford in 2009. He writes a monthly column for the Economic and Political Weekly and has published in the Indian Journal of Constitutional Law and National Law School of India Review apart from media outlets such as The Hindu, Indian Express, Scroll, Quint and Caravan.

Sébastien Lafrance
is Fellow of the Central Asian Legal Research centre at Tashkent State University of Law, Uzbekistan. Adjunct professor at Jindal Global Law School, India. Adjunct professor at Universitas Airlangga, Indonesia. Adjunct lecturer at Ho Chi Minh City University of Law, Vietnam. Former part-time professor at Civil Law Faculty, University of Ottawa, Canada (2010–2013). Crown Counsel (Prosecutor) at the Public Prosecution Service of Canada in the Competition Law Section since 2013. LL.M. / Master's in Law (Criminal Law) (with Honours / Merit List) at Laval University; LL.B. / Law at Université du Québec à Montréal; B.Sc. / Political Science at University of Montreal. Former clerk for the Honourable Marie Deschamps of the Supreme Court of Canada (2010–2011) and is also in-house counsel at the Law Branch of the Supreme Court of Canada (2011–2013). Former clerk for the Honourable Michel Robert, Chief

Judge of the Quebec Court of Appeal (2008–2009). He has published book chapters and articles in Australia, Canada, France, India, Indonesia, United Kingdom and Vietnam.

Sidharth Luthra

is a senior advocate at the Supreme Court of India. In July 2012, he was appointed as the Additional Solicitor General of India at the Supreme Court and represented the union and various state governments in matters relating to fundamental rights, electoral reforms, criminal law and policy issues. He is a member of the Delhi State Legal Services Authority for the past 6 years. He is a resource person and teaches at the Delhi Judicial Academy. He is the Vice President of the Indian Criminal Justice Society and sits on the advisory boards of the legal journals – Delhi Law Times and the Delhi Reported Judgements.

David McCallum

is an Emeritus Professor in the Centre for International Research on Education Systems (CIRES), Victoria University. He was previously Head of the Humanities and Social Sciences Discipline Group in the College of Arts & Education at Victoria University (2014–2017). He is the author or co-author of four books and over 40 articles in the research field of history of human sciences and a member of the Sociological Association of Australia and the International Sociological Association.

Naveed Mehmood

is a Senior Resident Fellow with the Criminal Justice Team at Vidhi Centre for Legal Policy. His work focuses on decriminalization of India's legislative landscape and reimagining India's approach towards Crime & Punishment. Previously, Naveed has worked on criminalization of drug use and evaluated the government response to increasing violence against women. Naveed holds an undergraduate degree in law from National University of Law, Punjab and a master's in law from Tata Institute of Social Sciences, Mumbai.

Garima Pal

is an Assistant Professor of Sociology at Maharashtra National Law University Mumbai, who continues to make significant contributions to the fields of Criminology, Victimology, and Human Rights. Holding a Ph.D. focused on "Drug Abuse and Alcoholism and the Role of Rehabilitation Centers in Uttarakhand," she has established herself as a versatile and interdisciplinary scholar. Her professional journey is marked by notable positions, including her role as a Research Associate at the Institute of Social Sciences, New Delhi, and a Project Coordinator at NLU Delhi for projects funded by prestigious bodies like the Indian Council of Social Sciences Research, the Ministry of Home Affairs, and the National Commission for Women. Her recent authorial works include "The Palghar Report: Status of Project Affected Families in Palghar," published by Mohan Law House, and "Hate Crime in India," published by Springer Nature. She has also co-authored "Bhartiya Nyaya Sanhita 2023" with Whiteman and Co.

Daria V. Ponomareva

Ph.D. in Law, is Deputy Head of the Department of Legal Practice. Graduated with honours Kutafin Moscow State Law University (MSAL). Over a number of years Daria had been working for the Ministry of Justice of the Russian Federation (central office) specializing in the sphere of recognition and enforcement of foreign judgments in Russia. In addition Daria is an expert in the area of energy law, legal regulation of genomic research. At the present time alongside with legal practice she is a Deputy Head of the Department of Practical Jurisprudence of Kutafin Moscow State Law University (MSAL). Daria is engaged in a number of scientific projects dedicated to digital law. Daria is an author of a number of articles published in such journals as "Actual Problems of Russian Law" and "International Legal Courier".

Yogesh Pratap Singh

is a Professor of Law at National Law University Orissa and presently on lien to serve as the Vice-Chancellor of National Law University Tripura. He received his LL.M. from National Law School of India University (NLSIU), Bangalore and LL.B. from the University of Allahabad. His doctoral thesis entitled "Contribution of Dissenting Opinions of Indian Supreme Court Judges to the Indian Legal System: A Critical Evaluation" is recognized as a significant contribution to the understanding of voting patterns of judges in the Supreme Court of India. This work was later published as book entitled "Judicial Dissent and Indian Supreme Court: Enriching Constitutional Discourse" by Thomson Reuters.

Ekkehard Strauss

currently teaches and researches at the Berlin School of Economics and Law on the topics of police and security management, international human rights protection and international conflict management. His professional focus lay on assisting international organizations, governments, private companies and civil society in developing strategies, institutions and processes to monitor and respond to risk factors for crises, conflict and instability. Previously, he has been the Senior Human Rights Officer to the UN Resident and Humanitarian Coordinator in Jordan. He has also served in different functions with OHCHR in both Geneva and New York, as well as further afield. His doctoral thesis concerned the prevention of human rights violations by international organisations.

CHAPTER 1

Criminalization: An Introduction

Chirag Balyan and Garima Pal

The breadth of criminal law has been a persistent topic of concern in academic discourse. Scholars have frequently highlighted the perception that existing criminal statutes are overly expansive and in need of refinement. The extensive use of criminal law for various social regulation purposes raises significant concerns regarding its appropriate scope and boundaries. The pervasive tendency to resort to criminalization for addressing societal issues as a default choice indicates a need for evaluating the proper extent of criminal law's application. While it's essential to establish boundaries in any legal domain, this necessity is particularly pressing in criminal law due to its profound impact on individuals' freedoms, economic status, and even lives, emphasizing the importance of delineating its appropriate limits.

But, to complain of over-criminalization is premised on some normative standard as to the appropriate limits of criminalization. For criminal law philosophers interested in theorizing criminal law each claim presented in the preceding statement requires scrutiny. It is obvious to ask – what is 'over' and how much is 'over' in over-criminalization? Can the claim of over-criminalization empirically and normatively be substantiated? Talking of 'normative' standards, where should one look for normative philosophy – conception of state, constitution, moral philosophy (if so which school), criminal law as a self-contained institution or something else?

Then one can talk about what entails criminalization. It is just a legislative action of defining offences or it is an inclusive 'process' or an 'institution' in which criminal law manifests itself in practice? Even the term 'limit' is not free from contention as it raises both political and normative questions such as can the legislative power to create criminal law be limited? There are of course constitutional limitations but the nature of enquiry there is limited to violation of fundamental rights and due process. Again, this doesn't mean that constitutional guarantees can't be used to check excessive use of criminal law. The States governed by the Constitution and the rule of law permits the deprivation of liberty or even life through the due process of law. Likewise, international conventions on human rights justify the use of criminal law to safeguard human rights. The criminal law in this sense has its normative justifications in the constitutional law and human rights instruments.

The Indian Supreme Court's interpretation of morality as constitutional morality rather than public morality has been used to strike down offences which were immoral according to the public but not the constitution. Similarly, equality protection in the Indian constitution has been used to invalidate criminal laws which were found to be arbitrary and vague. There are ample other innovations of the Indian Supreme Court to check overcriminalization including those resulting from pre-trial detentions. The systematic account of the Indian Supreme Court's role in curtailing overcriminalization is not possible here. Moreover, constitutional courts invalidate a criminal law or administrative action when a lot of harm is already caused by an unjust criminal law when enacted by legislature and enforced by criminal justice functionaries like police and prosecutors. Therefore, a constitutional limit to criminal law is not a substitute for normative theory of criminal law which must be utilized in law making as well as law enforcement. It is noteworthy that the constitutional and human rights laws which have right to life and liberty at their heart provide for the deprivation of the same with the same stroke.

Further, it is obviously not practical to answer all these claims here, suffice is to say that the bulk of academic literature has come to one consensus that there is 'no consensus' (Balyan, 2020). The editors of one of the extensive contemporary works on criminalization stating about challenge in building a theory of criminalization notes "that our early ambition to work towards a normative theory of criminalization was soon replaced by a more realistic ambition to work towards a clearer understanding of the complex range of normative questions that bear on the various processes of criminalization involved in a modern system of criminal law." (Duff, Farmer, et al. 2013). In their subsequent work they note, "the grail of grand theory is illusory." (Duff, Farmer, et al. 2014, 6).

However, one point which every scholar would admit is that there should be less of criminal law, and it should be used not as a default option but as a 'last resort' (Husak, 2004) (Ashworth, 2000). Further, academic cleavage on these issues should not deter us from finding answers to these hard questions. For, more than the end result it is the academic discourse which is important as it shows that our conscience as a society is still awake to practical problems our criminal law is causing. George Fletcher has pertinently noted that the fundamental concepts of criminal liability have mainly been formulated by scholars rather than being shaped solely by judicial rulings (Fletcher, 2007: 91). However, in contemporary legal discourse, scholars' involvement in defining the limits of criminalization is inadequately acknowledged, possibly owing to scholarly modesty or the constrained scope of political legitimacy typically associated with legal scholars.

1   Criminalization

Within the domain of criminal law, the selections made by legislatures of the definition of offenses within the Special Part of a criminal law is significant. According to Moore the central question for the theory of criminalization is to ask: In what instances can the legislative body lawfully designate certain behaviours for prohibition and subsequent punitive measures? (Moore, 1997: 639). Criminalization from this view involves determining which actions, conducts or behaviour warrant criminal status and the reasoning behind such classification within legal frameworks. It explores the justification for punitive measures within liberal states, covering theoretical and procedural aspects (Farmer, 2024). This includes the process of criminalizing specific behaviours or groups and the functioning of the justice system.

But, Lindsay Farmer argues, theories concerning the process of criminalization ought to devote greater attention to understanding what qualifies a law as criminal, encompassing its distinct features and objectives. To formulate a normative theory on criminalization – identifying behaviours appropriate for regulation through criminal law – it becomes essential to offer a more nuanced exploration of the essence, purposes, and desired outcomes of criminal law (Farmer, 2014: 81).

Generally, wrongs have been justified to deal with criminal sanction on the ground of harm, wrongfulness, public nature of wrongs, seriousness, immorality, social welfare, protection of legal goods (*Rechtsgüterschutz*), and so on. Each ground has its strengths and weaknesses. But none of them by itself offer a comprehensive account on what may or may not be criminalized. These factors however do contribute to understanding the 'purpose or aim of the criminal law'.

For example, the harm principle has for considerable time occupied the central space in criminalization discourse so as so that when United States prepared its Model Penal Code, one of its stated objects was to "to forbid and prevent conduct that unjustifiably and inexcusably inflicts or threatens substantial harm to individual or public interests.". The discourse on harm principle, as articulated by John Stuart Mill, justifies state intervention in criminalizing acts is *only* justified if it aims "to prevent harm to others". It serves as a restrictive measure, limiting criminal law to actions directly harming individuals. The term harm in Mill's philosophy is morally loaded and raises more normative questions than it answers. Joel Feinberg further develops this principle, rejecting legal paternalism and moralism as sufficient grounds for criminalization (Fienberg, 1990). Fienberg's version of harm principle justifies criminalization of conduct if it is "effective in preventing (eliminating, reducing) harm to persons other than the actor and there is probably no other means that is equally effective at no greater cost to other values." (Feinberg, 1984: 26) Further, Feinberg's explanation of the notion of harm encompasses only setbacks to interests that are deemed wrongful, and wrongs that result in setbacks to interests (Feinberg, 1984: 36).

While discussion on issues around harm principle have not been devoid of merit, an examination of the burgeoning expansion of criminal law (Ashworth, 2000: 225), evident in the proliferation of possession and inchoate offenses, alongside the adoption of hybrid civil/criminal measures, reveals a discernible diminution in the potency of the harm principle (Dubber, 2005: 118).

Simester and von Hirsch have emphasized the importance of wrongfulness alongside harm in justifying criminalization. They argue that criminalization requires conduct to be morally wrong (Simester and Hrisch, 2011: 22). This proposition is not free from controversy for there is hardly any agreement about what constitutes morality.

Since criminal law is the legitimate way to 'punish', criminalization theories have also focussed on justification of criminal law based on justification of punishment. So, the question can be framed as: when is it appropriate for the State 'to punish' by labelling wrongs as crimes? Since punishment is the strongest censure which the State can use against an individual, it is pertinent to examine the circumstances when imposing punishment is legitimate. Also, equally important is to ask why is the State justified in punishing? Is it to deter, or retribute, or reform, or for something else? As most of criminal laws are created with the State logic to deter offending, such laws are criticized on account of failure of the State to show that criminal laws really deter. Those who insist on retribution as the aim of the punishment have not adequately answered what justifies criminalization of non-serious wrongs, regulatory offences, and disproportionate punishments. On more normative grounds theory is criticized for not adequately justifying rationale for deserved hard treatment. (Tadros, 2011) claims that it is barbaric to assume that inflicting suffering can be good. Further, assigning individuals the label of "offenders" through condemnation exacerbates their societal alienation and diminishes their prospects for envisioning personal redemption in the future (Lacely and Hanna, 2015).

At a very fundamental level it is suggested that a person should be punished only for a wrongful act committed with the guilty mind. This has raised questions about legitimacy of punishment when it is imposed by law without the 'act' requirement. So, legitimacy of punishment for instances such as: possession, preparation, attempts, abetments etc. comes into question. Further law which punishes an individual for merely having an 'ill intention' stands on a troubled footing. Similarly, cases wherein the law punishes an individual for only committing an act without requiring the proof of fault requirement or *mens rea* requirement (strict liability offence) have raised many curious debates about such law's legitimacy. Even within this, there are concerns about use as well as scope of negligence and recklessness to impose criminal liability. Then, there are a large number of preventive offences which are criminalized not for the 'act' but based on prediction or propensity of the person to commit such an act. These preventive offences have also generated rich literature arguing for their justification in the criminalization theory and in particular how the consequences of preventive turn in criminal law can be balanced with traditional rights of the accused.

Then there are also normative questions about the subject of criminal law viz. 'an individual'. Can criminal law decide to punish an individual who is not able to act as a rational and free agent? How can the criminal law be framed so that it respects liberal theory of criminal law? And if this is ensured, is liberal theory of criminal law an adequate response to poststructuralists which claim that it fails to disregard 'otherness', 'colonialism', and 'marginalization of poor and vulnerable' through instrumentality of criminal law? And what about the contradictions and antinomies which liberal theory of criminal law generates by universalizing the conception of justice? Critical realists such as Alan Norrie would argue that criminal law is real and emergent which is shaped by the history, social structures, and politics (Norrie, 2005). Then there is also a critique of the entire western criminal law scholarship by those who propound 'southern criminology'. The chief proponents of this school notes that southern criminology is "primarily concerned with the careful analysis of networks and interactions linking South and North which have been obscured by the metropolitan hegemony over criminological thought." (Carrington, et al. 2015).

It is important to recognize that criminalization discourse must be put in – globalized vis-à-vis localized perspective, historical vis-à-vis contemporary standpoint, colonial vis-à-vis decolonial thought, accused centric criminal law vis-à-vis victim centric criminalization, and authoritarian vis-à-vis liberal trends. The criminalization project must recognize the plurality of conceptions of criminal law. This necessitates an examination of criminal law which recognizes the differences in form, place, and structure (McSherry, et al. 2009: 4).

A proper theory of criminalization must address all these questions. However, on each of these questions there is a wide cleavage of opinion. While this is so, it is not surprising that even the term criminalization has no uniform understanding. Therefore, in the next part, we intend to develop the meaning of criminalization which is used in this book.

But before doing so it is important to recall what (McSherry, et al. 2009) noted in the introduction of their edited work. They stated, "Legal scholars do not represent a homogenous caste, and the chapters in this collection reflect some of the scholarly diversity of opinion as well as the general concern that criminal law is moving in new and dangerous directions. While there may be many different 'futures' for the criminal law, a focus on present developments give rise to real concerns as to the present direction of travel. In identifying such changes and by seeking to understand them in the context of deeper social developments, this collection seeks to contribute to debate about how matters will and ought to proceed."

We completely resonate with this statement. The legal scholars are not a representation of 'homogenous caste', and they should not be. The law can only progress amongst the plurality of thoughts and perspectives which are contextualized in space and time. In this framework, the primary aim of our work is to give voice to southern criminal law scholars on the matters of criminalization. We intend to contextualize the criminalization debates in the stories, narratives, and conditions of the global south.

2 Extended Meaning of Criminalization

While criminalization may involve legislative or judicial procedures, it often extends beyond formal legal changes to encompass enforcement practices of police and prosecutors. Defining crimes and defences may not significantly impact sentencing outcomes; instead, it primarily empowers prosecutors to shape the criminal justice system. Accordingly, the function of defining crimes and defences in determining criminal punishment is often overestimated. Instead of primarily influencing sentencing outcomes, their main purpose is to grant authority to criminal justice functionaries, who wield substantial influence in shaping the criminal justice system (Stuntz, 2001). Thus, Erik Luna called for a shift in focus from principled criminalization to principled enforcement (Luna, 2000: 515). But the editors of "Criminalization: The Political Morality of the Criminal Law" regard the role of law enforcers, as well as judges in applying or interpreting criminal law as a proper concern of normative theory of criminalization (Duff and Farmer, et al. 2014: 2–3).

William Stuntz has argued that expansive scope of criminal law can be attributed not only to penal populism, and political ideology of the government but also to institutional design and incentives. Power is divided among legislators, prosecutors, and judges, but rather than checking each other, there's tacit cooperation between prosecutors and legislators, resulting in broader laws.

Criminal law is not just one event, i.e. the law created by the legislature. It is an ongoing process which is constantly shaped by various institutions and factors such as criminal justice functionaries including law enforcers and courts, public opinion, and government's endeavour to sustain its hegemony. Criminal law is shaped by multiple competing values of all these actors.

For example, as a political institution, criminal law can be seen as a political response to social as well as political problems. This political response can be manifested in myriad ways including creating new crimes, expanding the definition of new crimes, escalation of punishments, targeted enforcement of certain crimes specially to stifle dissent and suppress political rivals or even ideologies. Money plays an important role in electoral politics. Election campaigning requires significant expenditures. A government in power can use its extensive powers under economic and taxation laws to target wealthy politicians of the opposition parties and which in turn could adversely affect the financing of elections of the opposition parties. This is the most direct way to use criminal law to tackle political issues. An indirect way could involve using sedition law or even terrorism laws to suppress and stifle the political dissent and ideologies on account of national interest and security.

The criminal law can also be used to woo a particular class or community. It can be used to communicate to a community that we care about you. For example, in India a legislation was enacted Muslim Women (Protection of Rights on Marriage) Act, 2019 to criminalize triple *talaq* – a particular kind of Muslim divorce. This legislation as claimed by many is to garner the Muslim women vote bank. In another move, which is allegedly made to garner the vote bank of marginalized communities, Indian parliament in 2018 amended the Scheduled Castes and the Scheduled Tribes (Prevention of Atrocities) Act, 1989 to allow police officers to register the criminal case without any preliminary enquiry and make arrests without any approval. It also took away the power of the court to grant anticipatory bail in such matters. While instant *talaq* and atrocities of Dalits is a grave social problem, there can also be a political framing of the same issue in terms of using criminal law to attract the vote banks. While both Triple *talaq* law and Atrocities Act was meant to address concerns of the minorities, governments also enact criminal laws which are populist so as to woo the majoritarian sentiment. For example, in the majority of the northern Indian states cow slaughter is criminalized with some states prescribing imprisonment up to 10 years and fine up to half a million Indian rupees (The Indian Express, 2016). Since cows are considered as holy animals amongst the Hindus, these laws are alleged to woo the Hindu community. This also illustrates how political ideologies or beliefs can shape the content of the criminal law. The same logic of wooing a political vote bank can also be used to decriminalize certain offences. For example, the Jan Vishwas (Amendment of Provisions) Act, 2023 enacted by Indian parliament in order to attract the business community either decriminalized or reduced the harshness of seventy-two laws which prescribed criminal punishments. Thus, the political nature of criminal law leads to both over-criminalization and decriminalization.

A normative theory of criminalization thus must be able to speak about such antinomies which criminal justice produces. Thurgood Marshall in his opinion in *Powell v. Texas* noted that "[t]he doctrines of actus reus, mens rea, insanity, mistake, justification, and duress *have historically provided the tools for a constantly shifting adjustment of the tension between the evolving aims of the criminal law and changing religious, moral, philosophical, and medical views of the nature of man*. This process of-adjustment has always been thought to be the province of the States." (emphasis supplied). While we can debate if we should call these concepts as tools or something else, or about the adequacy of these *tools* in the process of adjustment, and as well as the role of the State in it (Bilionis, 1998: 1302); it is important to emphasize 'nature of criminal law' as a constant process which is contingent on history, society, politics as well as changing nature of man and human existence. In the words of MacCormick, "Criminal law is always and inevitably expressive, or perhaps it is better to say constitutive, of a prevailing social morality adopted and enforced by the state" (MacCormick, 2007: 211). According to this perspective, criminal law reflects and shapes societal morality through legal institutions. This connection between law and morality influences the concept of public wrong and may affect criminal law content. MacCormick speaks of criminal law as a moral voice through which society expresses its disapprobation of conduct mediated through the institutions of law.

Recognising criminal law as a reflection of its institutional form is an endeavour to systematically reconstruct an interpretation of the essence and structure of criminal law within specific temporal contexts. In particular it entails, exploring its development, encompassing habits, customs, theories, and practices that shaped it. This endeavour necessitates an acknowledgment of the inherent constraints of theory, given that criminal laws are fundamentally grounded in institutional realities. Consequently, as the institutional landscape evolves, so must our comprehension of criminal law.

The aim of this work is to look at the overall aim of the criminal justice system. We are not very much concerned about how the criminal justice system deviates in various countries. They obviously deviate. We rather argue for the normative basis of creating criminal laws. The criminal law should not be the result of vagaries of political whims and public opinion.

As you must have seen from the tone of this introduction, we are more interested in raising complex questions than just finding answers. Obviously, there would be answers. But questioning the criminal law and its practices itself serves an important function.

Though we wanted to title our work 'over-criminalization', we didn't want to have a prejudiced thought of 'over' before delving into the criminalization arena. India is itself a country of diversity and plurality. We hope that this cultural tradition is also reflected in this work. In bringing this work we acknowledge that while there is a drive to push the boundaries of criminal law, there is also a movement in our country (and elsewhere also) to reduce criminal laws to enhance ease of living and ease of doing business.

These developments from political prism tells us that Indian polity is committed to keep average citizens out of the criminal law framework. But, at the same time those who are indulged in crimes against the State, economic offences such as money laundering, national security offences, offences against women and children will receive hard treatment to an extent that even their homes can be bulldozed into the dust or as someone may call as 'bulldozing of the criminal law' itself. The average citizen of the country legitimizes bulldozing of homes of accused and the government in turn gives such citizens incentive by decriminalizing offences which are regulatory in nature or are simply immoral. This creates a divide of 'we versus them' ultimately resulting in the denuding of citizenship of certain categories of accused having certain social and political affiliations. So, these emergent and real societal and political realities which reveals the tension between over-criminalization and decriminalization. These tensions manifest in a way that one supports the other. Therefore, understanding of term criminalization in its extended form also requires understanding of decriminalization, over-criminalization, and under-criminalization.

In 'Politics of Overcriminalization', Sidharth Luthra and Shubhangni Jain talk about overcriminalization driven by political motivations, public opinion, and the morality of those in power, and the problems created by the same. Taking the examples of the anti-conversion and liquor-prohibition laws in the Indian states of Uttar Pradesh and Bihar (respectively), the authors point out how legislations based on public morality are often violative of constitutional morality, and disregard established principles of criminal law (presumption of innocence, punishment proportional to the crime, etc.). Referring to the criminalization of Triple-*Talaq* (*Talaq-i-biddat*) in India, the authors highlight how political (and moral) considerations run the risk of redundant criminal laws, often doing more harm than good to those the laws are supposed to benefit. The authors, with the help of the *Nirbhaya* judgement (on the 2012 gang rape case in the Indian capital of Delhi), highlight that even the judiciary is not immune to public pressures. To curb the menace of overcriminalization, the authors argue in favour of a more evidence-based and scientific method of criminalization.

In 'Spaces of Assessment and Incarceration', David McCallum examines the historical and contemporary governance of vulnerable children in Australia through the lens of Michel Foucault and Norbert Elias's theories. He stresses on how societal norms and power dynamics influence the construction of deviance, leading to the criminalization of behaviors that may not inherently be criminal. By tracing the evolution of governance arrangements and the development of disciplinary mechanisms, the chapter sheds light on how certain populations, such as Indigenous peoples and marginalized children, have been disproportionately targeted by criminal justice systems. The analysis offered by David McCallum deepens our understanding of how structural factors contribute to the overcriminalization of certain groups, reflecting broader issues of social inequality and systemic injustice. Furthermore, it underscores the importance of adopting a critical perspective on legal and social policies to address the complexities of criminalization and overcriminalization in contemporary society.

The liberal critique presented by David challenges the notion of the 'abstract individual' by questioning the applicability of liberal principles, such as individual freedoms and equal worth, to the lived realities of governance, particularly concerning vulnerable populations like Indigenous peoples and marginalized children. This critique highlights how theoretical liberalism often fails to account for the complexities of power dynamics and historical contexts, leading to the reinforcement of oppressive structures and thereby demonstrates the "internal malleability of liberal theory", and how it might be leveraged to advance authoritarian agendas by contravening prevalent or orthodox interpretations (Ramsay, 2006).

In 'Criminalization and International Human Rights Standards', Ekkehard Strauss takes an international human rights law perspective to look at overcriminalization. He relies upon international human rights conventions like ICCPR to set standards (which, when breached, would lead to overcriminalization). Due to their sensitive nature, instances of overcriminalization arise specifically in cases of counterterrorism and emergency legislations, more so when the said legislations are vague and all-encompassing in nature. To prevent the same, the author concludes by providing certain suggestions, like using the necessity and proportionality test, staying within the bounds of international law while enacting legislations, not using broad and vague terms, etc.

In 'Overcriminalization and the Presumption of Innocence in Canada and India – A Theoretical, Practical and Comparative Approach', Sébastien Lafrance undertakes a holistic study of overcriminalization, its causes, and its relationship with the presumption of innocence and burden of proof. He critically analyses the different definitions of overcriminalization, as well as the different approaches towards presumption of innocence and the burden of proof. Taking the examples of Indian and Canadian laws, he comments how outdated laws (which can no longer be enforced) should not be included as examples of overcriminalization. Lafrance explains how giving way to moral considerations in criminal law could be problematic by referring to the fictitious "criminalized onion". In conclusion, the author mentions the substantive dimension of the presumption of innocence, which (as of now, in its rudimentary stage) serves as a protection against overcriminalization.

In 'Democratic Erosion by Parochial Measures: A Study of Rising Criminalization of Free Speech in India', Prof. (Dr.) Yogesh Pratap Singh talks about the rising instances of criminalization of free speech in India over the past few years. This is done by the misuse of certain legal provisions like criminal defamation and sedition laws. The author criticises the misuse of anti-terrorism laws like the National Security Act and the Unlawful Activities Prevention Act. He questions the validity of such laws on account of their unrestricted area of operation and their disregard of the established principles of criminal law (bail as the norm, presumption of innocence, etc.) The author concludes by suggesting changes to the specified laws in order to make them more compatible with the freedom of speech and expression enshrined in Article 19(1)(a) of the Indian Constitution. He also suggests repealing draconian colonial laws like criminal defamation and sedition.

In 'The Jurisprudence of Constitutional Morality and the Pathologies of Criminalization', Shruti Bedi talks about the interplay of constitutional and criminal law, and how the latter should be framed (in a democracy) keeping in mind the principles of the former. Bedi points to the increasing trend of criminalization in India (criminalization of triple *talaq*, failure to abide by corporate social responsibility, etc.) and highlights the problems posed by overcriminalization (including overburdened justice delivery mechanism, amongst others). Talking about the drawbacks of different schools of criminalization (paternalistic, morality, and harm principle), the author concludes that the decision of criminalizing or de-criminalizing any act should be guided by constitutional morality (not public/popular morality), in order to avoid overcriminalization and the misuse of the criminal laws.

In 'Drug Laws – The Reality and Politics of Overcriminalization', Alok Prasanna Kumar and Naveen Mahmood Ahmad effectively argue that decriminalization of drug consumption and a more empathetic approach towards drug addicts is the way to tackle the drug menace. They analyse the historical development of drug laws in India and note how the colonial outlook towards drugs (specifically opium) was more accommodative of local practices/beliefs than the laws of independent India. The latter disproportionately come to the detriment of the marginalised section of society and the most vulnerable stakeholders (the addicts). The authors take the examples of the Indian states of Maharashtra and Punjab to drive the point across. They also examine the impact of political considerations on the real-life enforcement of drug laws. Observing the difficulties created by the strict quantification of drugs into small, intermediate, and commercial quantities and the dubious adjudication process, the authors conclude that the most efficient manner of dealing with this problem is to have a public health approach aimed at a complete rehabilitation of the addicts.

Another important feature of modern criminal law is *increased regulation*. Regulation encompasses the deliberate and sustained endeavour to influence the conduct of individuals according to specific standards or objectives, with the aim of achieving broad outcomes. This process involves various mechanisms such as establishing standards, gathering information, and modifying behaviour (Black, 2002). Regulatory criminal laws, which pertain to strategic planning in professions like employers, doctors, veterinarians, and public officials, are primarily preventive in nature, focusing on minimizing risks rather than addressing past harm. Scholars like Ashworth and Zedner have expressed scepticism towards regulatory criminal law, viewing it as an undesirable addition to traditional criminal law (Ashworth and Zedner, 2008: 40). These regulatory offences usually impose liability for omissions (as contracts to 'acts'), don't require proof of fault element, and impose reverse burden on the accused. Daria V. Ponomareva picks up this theme of regulatory offences in her chapter titled, 'Criminalization and Constitutionality in Russia', where she firstly introduces the general features of the Russian criminal law and then goes on to note that the economic sphere is experiencing a rise in criminalization, where minor infractions are unjustly treated as serious crimes, leading to inefficiencies in the legal system and discouraging innovation in business practices. Legislative reforms and clearer guidelines for law enforcement are proposed to address overcriminalization in economic activities, particularly in currency regulation and control. She maintains that despite recent amendments aiming to mitigate the burden on businesses, challenges remain in effectively applying existing laws and balancing the need for regulatory oversight with fostering a conducive environment for entrepreneurship.

Indeed, there is a debate amongst the philosophers about classification of regulatory offences as 'criminal' and the nature of 'administrative penalties' which may be imposed for such regulatory offences in lieu of the punishment. For example, Victor Tadros argues that penalties aim to redistribute benefits and burdens, not to deter, ensuring that violators bear the costs, not victims (Tadros, 2010: 174). Whereas, the alternative view is that administrative penalties lack the element of formal censure.

In fact, the Indian government in order to improve ease of living as well as ease of doing business, notified Jan Vishwas (Amendment of Provisions) Act, 2023 which has decriminalized 183 provisions under 42 Central (Federal) legislations. In a strict sense, this law doesn't not entirely decriminalize 183 provisions. What it does is that it has substituted punishment of imprisonment with fine or penalty. Since a fine also counts as a punishment one can say that there is no complete decriminalization. Also, there are provisions where both imprisonment and fine has been done away with and on the other side, there are also provisions where both have been kept but offences have been made compoundable i.e. they can be settled by the parties.

From the gamut of regulatory offences then we move to the gamut of what Ashworth and Zedner labels as 'preventive justice'.

Charles Khamala sheds light upon the conditions of Somali (and other) refugees inside Kenya's refugee camps, specifically during the COVID 19 times in his chapter, 'Overcriminalization by Containment without COVID: Inside Kenya's Refugee Camps'. Noting that the orders preventing the movement of refugees from the camps were brought forth by the Cabinet Secretary for Internal Security (and not his Health counterpart), Khamala brings attention to the covert objective of the order (uprooting Somali refugees from Kenya apparently in order to curb terrorism). Khamala argues that attempts to relocate refugees from urban areas back to border camps, the imposition of caps on refugee numbers within Kenya, the use of administrative orders such as the closure of refugee camps to curtail the rights and movement of refugees, and the use of blanket refouling orders, which rely on guilt by association rather than individual criminal responsibility, undermines fundamental principles of common law and contributes to the overcriminalization of refugees.

The author critically analyses the Kenyan policies implemented in the name of 'public health' and 'security' to criminalize the refugees against the backdrop of normative theory of overcriminalization. He points out the problems created by forced quarantine and compulsory testing and concludes by denouncing the policy, particularly when less restrictive measures (face masks, testing, etc.) were available to deal with the problem.

Bibliography

Ashworth, A. (2000) "Is the Criminal Law a Lost Cause?" 116 *Law Quarterly Review:* 225.

Ashworth, A. (2008) "Conceptions of Overcriminalization." *Ohio State Journal of Criminal Law*, 5: 408–425.

Ashworth, A. and Horder, J. (2013) *Principles of Criminal Law*. New York: Oxford University Press.

Ashworth, A., and Zedner, L. (2008) "Defending the Criminal Law: Reflections on the Changing Character of Crime, Procedure, and Sanctions." *Criminal Law and Philosophy*, 2(1): 21–51.

Baker, D. J. (2016) *The Right Not to be Criminalized: Demarcating Criminal Law's Authority*. London: Routledge.

Balyan, C. (2020) "Overcriminalization in India." In: Balyan,C., et al. (eds) *Revisiting Reforms in the Criminal Justice System in India*. Gurgaon: Thomson Reuters, 306.

Bilionis, L. D. (1998) "Process, the Constitution, and Substantive Criminal Law." *Michigan Law Review*, 96: 1269.

Black, J. (2002) "Critical Reflections on Regulation." *Australian Journal of Legal Philosophy*, 27: 1.

Carrington, K., et al. (2015) "Southern Criminology." *The British Journal of Criminology*, 57 (1): 1–20.

Chan, Cheong-Wing, et al. (2011) *Codification, Macaulay and the Indian Penal Code: The Legacies and Modern Challenges of Criminal Law Reform*. London: Routledge.

Duff, R. A. (2007) *Answering for Crime*. Oxford: Hart Publishing.

Duff, R. A. (2018) *The Realm of Criminal Law*. New York: Oxford University Press.

Duff, R. A., et al. (2013) *The Constitution of the Criminal Law*. New York: Oxford University Press.

Duff, R. A., et al. (2014) *Criminalization: The Political Morality of the Criminal Law*. New York: Oxford University Press.

Farmer, L. (2024) "Criminalization and Decriminalization." In: Gless, S., et al. (eds) *Elgar Encyclopedia of Crime and Criminal Justice Vol. 1*. Elgar Online: Edward Elgar Publishing. Available at: https://doi.org/10.4337/9781789902990.criminalization.decriminalization Accessed on March 01, 2024.

Farmer, L. (2014) "Criminal Law as an Institution: Rethinking Theoretical Approaches to Criminalization." In: Duff, R. A., et al. *Criminalization: The Political Morality of the Criminal Law*. New York: Oxford University Press.

Feinberg, J. (1984) *The Moral Limits of the Criminal Law 1: Harm to Others*. New York: Oxford University Press.

Feinberg, J. (1985) *The Moral Limits of the Criminal Law 2: Offense to Others*. New York: Oxford University Press.

Feinberg, J. (1989) *The Moral Limits of the Criminal Law 3: Harm to Self*. New York: Oxford University Press.

Fienberg, J. (1990) *The Moral Limits of the Criminal Law 4: Harmless Wrongdoing*. New York: Oxford University Press.

Fletcher, G. (2007) *The Grammar of Criminal Law*. New York: Oxford University Press.

Gardner, J. (2008) *Overcriminalization: The Limits of the Criminal Law*. Notre Dame Philosophical Reviews. Available at: https://ndpr.nd.edu/reviews/overcriminalization-the-limits-of-the-criminal-law/ Accessed on December 01, 2021.

Gray, J. (1991) *J.S. Mill On Liberty*. London: Routledge.

Hall, L, and Glueck, S. (1958) *Cases on the Criminal Law and its Enforcement*. St. Paul: West Publishing.

Hart Jr., H. M. (1958) "The Aims of The Criminal Law." *Law And Contemporary Problems*, 23: 401–441.

Hart, H. L. A. (1968) *Punishment And Responsibility: Essays in The Philosophy of Law*. New York: Oxford University Press.

Huda, S. S. (1902) *The Principles of the Law of Crimes in British India*. Calcutta: Butterworth.

Husak, D. (2004) "The Criminal Law as Last Resort." *Oxford Journal of Legal Studies*, 24(2): 207–235.

Husak, D. (2008) *Overcriminalization: The Limits of the Criminal Law*. New York: Oxford University Press.

Lacely, N., and Hanna, P. (2015) "To Blame or to Forgive? Reconciling Punishment and Forgiveness in Criminal Justice." Oxford Journal of Legal Studies, 35 (4): 665–696.

Luna, E. (2000) "Principled Enforcement of Penal Codes." *Buffalo Criminal Law Review*, 5: 515.

MacCormick, N. (2007) *Institutions of Law: An Essay in Legal Theory*. New York: Oxford University Press.

McSherry, B., et al. (2009) *Regulating Deviance The Redirection of Criminalization and the Futures of Criminal Law*. Oxford: Hart Publishing.

Moore, M. S. (1997) *Placing Blame*. New York: Oxford University Press.

Norrie, A. (2005) *Law and the Beautiful Soul*. London: GlassHouse Press.

Norrie, A. (2009) "Citizenship, Authoritarianism and the Changing Shape of the Criminal Law." In: Mcsherry, B., et al. (eds) *Regulating Deviance: The Redirection Of Criminalization And The Futures of Criminal Law*, 13–34. Oxford: Hart Publishing.

Norrie, A. (2014) *Crime, Reason and History*. New York: Cambridge University Press.

Prime Minister's Office. (2022) "English rendering of PM's address at Joint Conference of Chief Ministers and Chief Justices of High Courts". *Press Information Bureau*. Available at: https://www.pib.gov.in/PressReleseDetail.aspx?PRID=1821534 Accessed on December 01, 2022.

Ramsay, P. (2006) "The Responsible Subject as Citizen: Criminal Law, Democracy and the Authoritarian State." *Modern Law Review*, 69(1): 29.

Ripstein, A. (2006) "Beyond the Harm Principle." *Philosophy and Public Affairs* 34: 215.

Simester, A. P., and Hrisch, A. (2011) *Crimes, Harms, and Wrongs: On the Principles of Criminalization*. Oxford: Hart Publishing.

Simons, K. W. (1996–97) "When is Strict Criminal Liability Just". *Journal of Criminal Law & Criminology*, 87: 1075.

Stuntz, W. J. (2001) "The Pathological Politics of Criminal Law". *Michigan Law Review*, 100 (3): 505–600.

Tadros, V. (2010) "Criminalization and Regulation." In: R.A. Duff, Lindsay F., S.E. Marshall, Massimo R., Victor T. (eds) *The Boundaries of the Criminal Law*. New York: Oxford University Press.

Tadros, V. (2011) *The Ends of Harm: The Moral Foundations of Criminal Law*. New York: Oxford University Press.

The Indian Express. (2016) "Beef row: Where it is illegal and what the law says". (July 27, 2016) *Indian Express*. Available at: https://indianexpress.com/article/india/india-news-india/beef-madhya-pradesh-video-cow-vigilantes-gau-rakshaks-2938751/. Accessed on June 01, 2021.

Wootton, B. (1981) *Crime and the Criminal Law: Reflections of a Magistrate and Social Scientist*. London: Stevens.

Yeo, S., and Wright, B. (2011) *Codification, Macaulay and the Indian Penal Code: The Legacies and Modern Challenges of Criminal Law Reform*. London: Routledge.

CHAPTER 2

Politics of Criminalization

Sidharth Luthra and Shubhangni Jain

1   Introduction

Scholars of criminal law have propounded theories on criminalisation and punishment which ought to guide the lawmakers in enacting the law. T.B. Macaulay who drafted the Indian Penal Code, 1860 was influenced by the philosophy of Jeremy Bentham. (Chang, Wright, and Yeo, 2011).

Bentham, the founder of modern utilitarianism, argued that the general object of laws ought to be to augment total happiness of the community and therefore, as far as may be, to exclude everything that subtracts that happiness i.e., the mischief. Though punishment itself is mischief, it should only be imposed as far as it promises to exclude greater mischief (Bentham, 1823/2000: 134, Ch. XIII: Cases Unmeet for Punishment).

Bentham stipulated four instances where punishment should not be imposed:

> Where it is groundless: where there is no mischief for it to prevent;
> Where it must be inefficacious: where it cannot act so as to prevent the mischief.
> Where it is unprofitable, or too expensive: where the mischief it would produce would be greater than what it prevented.
> Where it is needless: where the mischief may be prevented, or cease of itself, without it: that is, at a cheaper rate.
> BENTHAM, 1823/2000: 134, Ch. XIII: Cases Unmeet for Punishment

John Stuart Mill argued that the state can interfere in the actions of a person only when they harm others i.e., the *"Harm Principle"*. An individual's own good, either physical or moral, is not a sufficient warrant for state interference (Mill, 1859/2009: 18–19, Ch 1: Introductory). An individual has complete sovereignty over himself and therefore, acts harming oneself (he refers to those as self-regarding actions) cannot be punished and especially interfered with on the grounds of public morality. Public morality cannot be codified into laws for there are many who consider as an injury to themselves any conduct that they have a distaste for (like a religious bigot) (Mill, 1859/2009: 141–158, Ch 4: Of Limits to the Authority of Society over the individual).

An exception to the *"harm principle"* is the principle of legal paternalism which in criminal law refers to the use of criminal sanctions to penalise those who harm or attempt to harm themselves (Von Hirsch, 2008). H.L.A. Hart, although criticising the principle of Mill with regard to non-interference of state with self-regarding conduct, contended that criminal law cannot be used merely to enforce public morality and that paternalism needs to be distinguished from moralism. His view was that it cannot be assumed that if law is not designed to protect one man from another, the only rationale behind it would be to enforce a moral principle (Hart, 1963: 30–34, Paternalism and the enforcement of morality).

Joel Fienberg calls legal paternalism a preposterous doctrine but with a caveat that it cannot be entirely rejected. He argues that a weak form of paternalism would be justified when the state has the right to prevent self-regarding harmful conduct when it is substantially non-voluntary or when temporary intervention is necessary to establish whether it is voluntary or not. Non-voluntary conduct would mean that no normal person would voluntarily choose or consent to the kind of conduct in question, nor should it be a ground for detaining a person until the voluntary character of his choice can be established (Feinberg, 1971).

Andrew Von Hirsch argues that limited paternalism or weak paternalism (as Fienberg calls it) warrants state intervention of some kind but does not justify state intervention by means of criminal law. Penal sanctions with its deprivations and censure would not promote the interests of the person harming himself or herself. After all "In cases of severe punishment for supposedly self-damaging behavior such as drug abuse, this argument is manifestly correct: how could a drug user's own interests be fostered through infliction of the lengthy terms of confinement that drug laws (especially of the American variety) prescribe?" (Von Hirsch, 2008).

Yet despite the doctrines above, human conduct is often criminalized, and penalties enhanced ostensibly for public welfare which actually reflect political considerations. Such penalisation and criminalization are based on morality of the majority or of the governing party or often due to media uproar. Such laws are inadequately planned without data to support them and entail significant social and other costs to society.

Measures introduced without coherence in penal philosophy or clarity in the object to be achieved by criminalisation, are abhorrent to the rule of law. Whether it be legislative actions (such as the Bihar

Prohibition law (Bihar Prohibition and Excise Act, 2016) or the criminalization of Triple Talaq (Muslim Women (Protection of Rights on Marriage) Act, 2019: sec. 4)) or the judicial interpretation in the Nirbhaya judgement (*Mukesh v. State*, 2017) which accepted society's cry for justice as a basis for death penalty, such legislations or precedents are merely representative of public discourse and pressure and can constitute oppressive measures while harshly curtailing liberty.

2   The Uttar Pradesh Anti-conversion Law

In *Rev. Stainislaus v. State of* M.P. (1977), the Supreme Court upheld the Madhya Pradesh and Odisha (then Orissa) laws criminalizing conversion by force, allurement or fraud and the Right to Freedom of Religion under Article 25 of the Constitution. The *Uttar Pradesh Prohibition of Unlawful Conversion of Religion Act 2021* ostensibly introduced to protect religious freedom guaranteed under Article 25 of the Constitution (Uttar Pradesh Unlawful Conversion of Religion Act, 2021) provides for draconian criminal law sanctions curtailing liberty and rights guaranteed under Article 20(3) of the Constitution antithetical to freedom of choice.

The Uttar Pradesh Prohibition of Unlawful Conversion of Religion Act 2021 was part of the election agenda for the Uttar Pradesh State Assembly Elections, 2022. The then State Government Manifesto for the 2022 Uttar Pradesh State Assembly Elections included punishing love jihad with ten years imprisonment and with one lakh fine (*Bhartiya Janata Party, Uttar Pradesh*, 2022).

The Uttar Pradesh Prohibition of Unlawful Conversion of Religion Act 2021 proposes to curtail what is now termed "*love jihad*" and Section 3 of the Act prohibits conversion by fraud, misrepresentation, allurement, undue influence, or coercion and conversion by solemnization of marriage on account of these factors.

Section 5 makes contravention of Section 3 punishable. The problematic provisions, however, of the Uttar Pradesh Prohibition of Unlawful Conversion of Religion Act 2021 are Sections 4 and Section 12.

Like many legislations, Central or State, there is a reverse burden provision which is increasingly being used in legislative drafting in criminal law. Section 12 is an all-encompassing provision which reverses the burden and thereby nullifies the presumption of innocence which is part of Article 21 (Constitution of India, 1950: Art. 21) and reads as under:

The burden of proof as to whether a religious conversion was not effected through misrepresentation, force, undue influence, coercion, allurement or by any fraudulent means or by marriage, lies on the person who has caused the conversion and, where such conversion has been facilitated by any person, on such other person.

Even the celebrated decision of *Noor Aga v. State of Punjab* (2008), while interpreting provisions under the Narcotics and Psychotropic Substances Act 1985 (sec. 35, 54), the Supreme Court held that prior to shifting the burden of proof upon the accused, certain foundational facts will have to be proved by the prosecution:

> 58. Sections 35 and 54 of the Act, no doubt, raise presumptions with regard to the culpable mental state on the part of the accused as also place the burden of proof in this behalf on the accused; but a bare perusal of the said provision would clearly show that presumption would operate in the trial of the accused only in the event the circumstances contained therein are fully satisfied. An initial burden exists upon the prosecution and only when it stands satisfied, would the legal burden shift. Even then, the standard of proof required for the accused to prove his innocence is not as high as that of the prosecution. *Whereas the standard of proof required to prove the guilt of the accused on the prosecution is "beyond all reasonable doubt" but it is "preponderance of probability" on the accused.*

Contrary to establishing foundational facts, Section 12 of the Uttar Pradesh Prohibition of Unlawful Conversion of Religion Act 2021 requires only to prove conversion which per se is not illegal. The law presumes the guilt of the accused at the very instance of conversion without the requirement of establishing the link between the facts of the case and the criminalized act of religious conversion. The absence of proving the foundational fact of non-consensual conversion is contrary to *Noor Aga v. State of Punjab* (2008) and hence, unconstitutional for being violative of the presumption of innocence.

Noor Aga v. State of Punjab (2008) further states that the burden upon the accused cannot be a legal burden but an evidentiary burden. However, in case of Section 12 of the Uttar Pradesh Prohibition of Unlawful Conversion of Religion Act 2021, the burden is legal as what is required to be proved cannot be said to be within the special knowledge of the accused or something the prosecution would find difficult in proving.

This becomes insidiously problematic when we look at Sections 4, 7 and 11 of the Uttar Pradesh Prohibition of Unlawful Conversion of Religion Act 2021.

Since Section 4 of the Uttar Pradesh Prohibition of Unlawful Conversion of Religion Act 2021 empowers any person, parents, siblings or persons related by blood to register a FIR for a breach of the law, it will have the effect of bringing havoc in the personal lives and the privacy of individuals which is now recognized as a fundamental right in *K.S. Puttaswamy v. Union of India & ors.* (2017). This is a blow to personal autonomy protected by the law in *K.S. Puttaswamy v. Union of India & ors.* (2017). Similarly, in *Shafin Jahan v. Asokan K.M.* (2018), the Supreme Court held that no fetters could be placed on a woman over the age of eighteen years on her choice of where to reside and whom to reside with. The Supreme Court in *Shakti Vahini v. Union of India*, (2018), a case of honour killing, recognised the right to marry a person of one's choice.

Upon a mere act of conversion through marriage, any person can be prosecuted and arrested upon a complaint of a family member. This becomes harsher since the offences under the Uttar Pradesh Prohibition of Unlawful Conversion of Religion Act 2021 are non-bailable and cognizable. Section 11 of the Uttar Pradesh Prohibition of Unlawful Conversion of Religion Act 2021 makes other persons i.e., "(a) every person who does or omits to do any act for the purpose of enabling or aiding another person to commit the offence, (b) every person who aids or abets another person in committing the offence and (c) any person who counsels, convinces or procures any other person to commit the offence", also culpable for the offence. What ensues is that even family members could be arrested and their liberty curtailed notwithstanding whether the conversion was lawful or unlawful.

Unfortunately, there is no analysis that has been done to showcase the justification of reverse burden of clauses and that it leads to higher convictions or prevention of crime. Regardless, higher convictions can be deceptive as the reverse burden of proof clauses often leads to wrongful convictions.

3 The Female Vote Bank and the Bihar Prohibition and Excise Act, 2016

In March, 2013, widespread protests erupted in the State of Bihar by women demanding a ban on alcohol. Going by the catchphrase, *"Humari aabroo ki keemat pe sharab ka dhandha nahi chalega."* (Alcohol cannot be sold at the cost of our honour) (Vatsyayan, 2019), the women demanded a ban on alcohol which according to them was the reason behind domestic violence and poverty.

The State Assembly elections were in the year 2015 and hence, a ban on alcohol soon became a poll promise to woo female voters (Mishra, 2015).

Following massive protests by women and social activists against alcohol addiction, when the Grand Alliance of Rashtriya Janata Dal, Janata Dal (United) and Indian National Congress came to power in 2015 in the State, they enacted the Bihar Prohibition and Excise Act 2016. The Bihar Prohibition and Excise Act 2016 was symbolically enacted on Gandhi Jayanti, October 2, 2016, the birth anniversary of Mahatma Gandhi who had called for a ban on alcohol on several occasions (Gandhi, 1948).

Section 13 of the Bihar Prohibition and Excise Act 2016 prohibits manufacture, bottling, distribution, transportation, collection, storage, possession, purchase, sale or consumption of any *"intoxicant"* or *"liquor"*. What is astounding is that the term *"intoxicant"* defined under Section 2(40) of the Bihar Prohibition and Excise Act 2016 also covers within its definition *"medicinal preparation"* as defined under the Medicinal and Toilet preparations (Excise Duties) Act 1955 [sec. 2(f)].

Section 39 of the Bihar Prohibition and Excise Act 2016 provides for a punishment of a minimum eight year up to ten years to a chemist, druggist, apothecary or a keeper of a dispensary, for allowing *inter alia* any medicine or medicinal preparation which has been declared by the State Government to be an intoxicant to be consumed on his business premises by any person. The person who consumes such intoxicant would be punished with a term not less than five years but which may extend to seven years and with fine, which shall not be less than one lakh rupees which may extend to ten lakh rupees.

Prior to the enactment of the Bihar Prohibition and Excise Act 2016, a Circular dated 17.03.2016 of the Excise Commissioner, Bihar was issued wherein the circular informed all Collectors-cum-District Magistrates in the State that henceforth the licenses granted under the Medicinal and Toilet Preparations (Excise Duties) Act 1955 shall not be renewed nor new licenses be issued and thus, prohibited manufacture and sale of all medicines containing alcohol in the State. This circular was challenged before the High Court of Patna.

The High Court vide its judgment dated 27.10.2016 (*Shree Baidyanath Ayurved Bhawan Pvt. Ltd. v. State of Bihar*, 2016) struck down the circular as unconstitutional. The High Court held that the State cannot prohibit manufacture, sale or distribution of medicinal preparations containing alcohol and it can only place reasonable restrictions on the same.

The High Court relied upon the judgment of the Supreme Court of India in *Khoday Distilleries Ltd. v. State of Karnataka*, a Constitution Bench judgment which held that the State cannot absolutely prohibit trade or business in medicinal and toilet preparations but can only impose reasonable restrictions under Article 19(6) of the Constitution. The same mischief is now being created by the Bihar Prohibition and Excise Act 2016. Thus, the definition of *"intoxicant"* under Section 2(40) to the extent it includes medicinal preparations is in contravention of the afore-said judgments as also unconstitutional for being violative of Article 19 (Constitution of India, 1950: Art. 19).

The unlawful import, export, transport, manufacture, possession and sale, etc. is made punishable under Section 30 of the Bihar Prohibition and Excise Act 2016. The punishment under this provision was a minimum sentence of ten years which may extend to imprisonment for life and with fine not less than one lakh rupees but which may extend to ten lakh rupees. The enhanced punishment for conviction for an offence under the Bihar Prohibition Act after previous conviction is twice the punishment provided for the first conviction (Bihar Prohibition and Excise Act, 2016: sec. 53).

By the 2018 Amendment to the Bihar Prohibition and Excise Act 2016 (sec. 53), for first time offenders, the punishment under Section 30 was reduced to not less than five years and fine of not less than one lakh rupees and for second and subsequent offenders, not less than 10 years and fine of not less than 5 lakh rupees. Though the amendment gives relief to first time offenders, however, the fine of 1 lakh rupees and 5 lakh rupees is harsh especially when the offenders are mostly from the poor and marginalised class.

Section 38 of the Bihar Prohibition and Excise Act 2016 provided for penalty for possession or knowledge of possession of intoxicant with minimum punishment of 8 years but which may extend to 10 years and fine which may extend to 10 lakhs. This provision was omitted by the Bihar Prohibition and Excise (Amendment) Act 2018 (sec. 10).

The Bihar Prohibition and Excise Act 2016 also made family members liable for possession of intoxicants by any other member of the family. The explanation to Section 30 as well as Section 38 defined possession as:

> possession by any family or member of that family and includes the knowledge of possession where any member of a family or the family itself know that such possession is illegal, whether it is in his or her own possession or with some other member of the family.

Thus, the mere knowledge by a family member or the possession of alcohol by another member of the family was by itself punishable with a minimum sentence of 10 years.

To put it in perspective, an alcoholic struggling with an addiction if found in possession of a bottle of alcohol would be punished for a minimum sentence of 10 years. So will the family which too is struggling at the hands of the addiction of the family member would be punished with 10 years minimum instead of getting medical and rehabilitative assistance.

It was only within 2 years of the passing of the Bihar Prohibition and Excise Act 2016 that these provisions punishing the adults of a household had to be omitted [Bihar Prohibition and Excise (Amendment) Act, 2018: sec. 3].

Even otherwise, an innocent consumer of alcohol cannot be punished with a minimum punishment of 10 years solely due to criminalization of a conduct on the farcical idea of what is right and what is wrong of the ruling party in the State. It is unfortunate that the consumption of alcohol which ought to be regulated is being prohibited and punished. Needless to say, since then there have been changes in governments in the State with different alliances forming governments, but the prohibition law in Bihar remains in force.

Mill argued that liberty of a person cannot be illegitimately curbed by censuring self-regarding conduct on the basis of the morality of the majority and morality of those who impose these censures. Public morality cannot be codified into laws for there are many who consider as an injury to themselves any conduct that they have a distaste for (like a religious bigot) (Mill, 2009: 141–158, Ch. 4: Of Limits to the Authority of Society over the individual).

The Bihar Prohibition and Excise Act 2016 and the punishment prescribed under the Act are a perfect example of the mischief pointed out by Mill perpetrated by vote bank politics. So much so that the State Government refused to provide compensation to families who lost family members due to consumption of spurious liquor as they were "sinners and not Indians" ("'Those Who Drink Are Mahapaapi, Not Indians': Bihar CM Nitish Kumar," 2022).

Another argument made by Mill was that society has the means of "bringing its weaker members up to its ordinary standard of rational conduct" which should not be done by waiting for the individual to do something irrational and then punishing them morally or legally for it (Mill, 2009: 139, Ch. 4: Of Limits to the Authority of Society over the individual).

The Supreme Court (*Navtej Singh Johar v. Union of India*, 2018) has held that the only morality that has a place in our society is constitutional morality i.e., assurance of certain minimum rights, essential for free existence of every member of society. The Court noted that "We are aware of the perils of allowing morality to dictate the terms of criminal law. If a single, homogeneous morality is carved out for a society, it will undoubtedly have the effect of hegemonising or "othering" the morality of minorities."

Besides, a blanket ban on alcohol cannot be considered to be an adequate response to domestic violence. What is required is regulation of liquor consumption and sale in the State and other socio-economic reforms rather than a blanket ban on alcohol consumption.

The inefficacy of the Bihar Prohibition Act can be seen from the statistics by the National Family Health Survey-5 (2019–2020) (*National Family Health Survey (NFHS-5), India, 2019–21*, 2021: Bihar) which are as under:

a. Enacted with the aim of curbing spousal violence, the spousal violence rates remain as high as 40.6% in Bihar, only the second highest in the country.
b. Although the report states that spousal violence is the least in households where the spouse doesn't consume alcohol, it still remains as high as 34%.
c. Furthermore,
    i. 39% of ever-married women in the age group of 18–49 have experienced physical violence committed by their husbands;
    ii. 8% have experienced sexual violence committed by their husbands;
    iii. 17% have experienced emotional violence committed by their husbands;
    iv. 36% of ever-married women report having been slapped by their husbands;
    v. 15% pushed, shaken, or having something thrown at them, or having their arm twisted or hair pulled;
    vi. 13% being punched with a fist or something that could hurt her;
    vii. 9% report being kicked, dragged, or beaten up;
    viii. 3% said that their husband tried to choke or burn them on purpose;
    ix. 1% have been threatened or attacked with a knife, gun, or any other weapon;
    x. 6% of ever-married women aged 18–49 report that their husbands physically forced them to have sex even when they did not want to; and
    xi. 4 % report that their husbands forced them with threats or in any other way to perform sexual acts they did not want to perform.

The Bihar Prohibition Act has created various problems in the State:
a. It has led to the creation of liquor mafia in the State who sell alcohol at double the rate. As it turns out, now men spend double the amount on liquor (Malhotra, 2022) on the same limited income leading to further poverty. As observed by the Patna High Court in *Niraj Singh v. State of Bihar* (2022):

"The prohibition has, in fact, *given rise to unauthorized trade of liquor and other contraband items. Liquor is freely available.* The draconian provisions have become handy for the police, who are in tandem with the smugglers. Innovative ideas to hoodwink law enforcing agency have evolved to carry and deliver the contraband."

b. The High Court in *Niraj Singh v. State of Bihar* (2022) noted that the availability of illegal liquor was possible only due to the involvement of the state machinery including state tax officials, police officers and excise officers. It observed that the smuggling of alcohol is being done through stolen vehicles, fake number plates and chassis numbers. E-way bills were being generated subsequent to the seizure of the vehicle and alcohol transported in the garb of GST goods or in transport vehicles which were registered outside the State and were being allowed to enter the State without being intercepted or being checked.

c. Scathing observations were made against the investigating agencies that they only prosecute the drivers, cleaners, labourers instead of acting against the smugglers or gang operators. Bystanders or passers-by who have no connection with the smuggling are prosecuted. The only persons prosecuted are daily wagers who are often the sole bread earners of the family.

d. A disastrous repercussion of the illegal alcohol trade is that alcohol is being sold without any quality check leading to hooch tragedies. The High Court in *Niraj Singh v. State of Bihar* (2022) also observed that post-prohibition, hooch tragedies have increased in the State.

e. Data supplied to the High Court in *Niraj Singh v. State of Bihar* (2022) showed that 3,48,170 cases were lodged, and 4,01,855 arrests were made under the Bihar Prohibition and Excise Act 2016 until October 2021. Hundreds of persons languish in jail under the Act awaiting trial leading to loss of livelihood and in turn, increase in poverty. The Bihar Prohibition and Excise Act 2016 earlier punished not only the one committing the offence but all adults of the household who are bread earners, thus pushing them further below the poverty line.

f. The High Court in *Niraj Singh v. State of Bihar* (2022) noted that the alcohol ban was leading to a sharp rise in the consumption of drugs and persons addicted to them. It noted as below:

"The data shows that before 2015, there were hardly any case related to drugs, but post 2015, the same has alarmingly surged. What is more worrying trend is that most addicts are as young as 10 years and below 25 years of age. *The statistics shows that the addiction for ganja charas/ bhang has shooted up post prohibition.*"

g. The state continues to lose out on revenue which could have been used for welfare schemes including schemes to empower women. In 2015–2016, the state excise revenue was Rs. 31,417.5 million which fell to 464 million in 2016–2017 (*State Finances: A Study of Budgets of 2017–18 and 2018–19*, 2018).
h. The Bihar Prohibition and Excise Act 2016 also led to an increase in the burden on courts in deciding bail applications and trials.
i. The Supreme Court vide order dated 23.02.2022 (*Sudhir Kumar Yadav v. State of Bihar*, 2022). observed that the trial Court and the Patna High Court are both being crowded by bail applications to an extent that at some stage 16 judges of the Patna High Court are hearing bail matters and asked the State Government for steps taken in terms of court infrastructure and manpower required to deal with the litigation arising from the Bihar Prohibition and Excise Act 2016. Only after the Supreme Court took note of this issue were the Special Courts constituted under Sections 83 of the Bihar Prohibition and Excise Act 2016 by way of the Bihar Prohibition And Excise (Amendment) Act, 2022 (sec. 17).
j. The State's affidavit, contents of which were produced in order dated 24.08.2022 of the Supreme Court acknowledged that a total of 3,78,186 cases have been registered as of 11.05.2022 and trial has commenced in only 1,16,103 cases. Trial is concluded in only 2473 cases leading to the acquittal of 830 accused and conviction of 1643 accused persons (*Sudhir Kumar Yadav v. State of Bihar*, 2022).

To make matters worse, the Bihar Prohibition and Excise Act 2016 provides for certain other stringent provisions such as,

i. Offences under the Act are non-compoundable (*Bihar Prohibition and Excise Act*, 2016: sec. 55);
ii. Section 32 provides for reverse burden of proof in certain cases;
iii. Under Section 75, any officer under the Act may ask any person to undergo breath analysis tests and or/such other medical tests. The provision while permitting officers under the Bihar Prohibition and Excise Act 2016 to conduct medical tests, compels the individual to submit himself to such tests or else it shall be presumed to have committed an offence under Section 37 of the Act. The provision makes these reports admissible in evidence and thus is in the teeth of the Right to remain silent and against self-incrimination under Article 20(3) of the Constitution;

iv. Section 76 make the offences under the Act as cognizable and non-bailable except for first time offenders under Section 37 and 54;
v. Section 76(2) excludes the application of Section 438 CrPC i.e., anticipatory bail to arrest of a person accused of having committed an offence under this Act;
vi. Section 77 allows the Excise Commissioner or Collector or any excise officer or police officer not below the rank of Assistant Sub Inspector, to require any person or any establishment deemed reasonably connected with any unlawful handling of any liquor or intoxicant to furnish to him such information as he may specify. This too is violative of Article 20(3) of the Constitution as it infringes upon the Right to remain silent and Right against self-incrimination.
vii. Section 37 provides for a penalty for consumption of liquor. Whoever consumes liquor or intoxicant or is found drunk or under influence of any intoxicant within any premises or outside shall be arrested immediately and produced before an Executive Magistrate (and not a judicial Magistrate). There is no provision for sentencing and Section 37(1) merely states that a person will be released upon payment of penalty as maybe notified by the State Government. If the offender does not pay the said penalty, he/she shall be liable for simple imprisonment for one month. The proviso further gives power to the State Government to prescribe additional penalty or imprisonment in case of repeat offenders.
viii. Section 37 doesn't lay down the quantum of penalty and the procedure required to carry out the proceedings, which has been left to the executive conferring unfettered and arbitrary discretion.

An instance of loose and casual draftsmanship is the framing of Rule 12A of the Bihar Prohibition and Excise (Amendment) Rules, 2022. Rule 12A(2) provides that for release of vehicles, conveyance etc., the penalty shall be 50% of the latest insured value of the vehicle, conveyance etc and be assessed by the insurance company. This penalty is not only disproportionate but also differential. A person caught drinking in a car with a value of 2 lakhs, she/he would pay 1 lakh rupees whereas a person caught in a car worth 30 lakhs would pay 15 lakhs penalty.

The judiciary imposes different punishments for the same offence however, that is based on facts and circumstances of the case and other relevant factors. This judicial discretion is backed by statutory sanction. However, Rule 12A is based on the extraneous element of the kind of vehicle that one possesses.

The Act punishes offenders with excessive fine. The State legislature has failed to consider that fines cannot be onerous especially since a vast majority of the population in Bihar lives in poverty. As per the Niti Aayog report of 2021, 51.91% of the population was multidimensionally poor, the highest in the country (*National Multidimensional Poverty Index Baseline Report*, 2021). In this context, the High Court of Patna in *Niraj Singh v. State of Bihar* (2022) observed that "It has been found that the labourers earning paltry daily wages were slapped with large fine they could not afford and had to take loans that push them further into the death."

Bentham stipulated "cases unmet for punishment" amongst which one of the case was "Where, on the one hand, the nature of the offense, on the other hand, that of the punishment, are, in the ordinary state of things, such, that when compared together, the evil of the latter will turn out to be greater than that of the former." (Burns and Hart, 1996): 137, Ch. XIII: Cases Unmeet for Punishment) The Bihar Prohibition Act fits in this criterion.

4 Society's Cry for Justice and Capital Punishment

The judiciary too has not been immune to law-making on the basis of public perception.

While laying down guidelines for sentencing, the Supreme Court in *Bachan Singh v. State of Punjab* (1980) had held that public opinion could have no role in sentencing and that the judges were inept in understanding public opinion. However, years later the Supreme Court in *Mukesh v. State* (2017) invoked collective conscience or society's cry for justice to grant death sentence to the Nirbhaya rape and murder accused based on public perception/media trial. Thus, setting a bad precedent of sentencing based on public outcry.

This is when the above case fell in the category of rarest of rare, even dehors the principle of *"collective conscience"* or *"society's cry for justice"*.

The Supreme Court in *Santosh Kumar Satishbhushan Bariyar v. State of Maharashtra*, (2009) had held that the equal protection clause enshrined in Article 14 of the Constitution is applicable to sentencing. Thus, public opinion or outcry has no place in granting death sentences in a country which guarantees equal protection in matters of sentencing. In doing so, the courts may dilute its role as an arbiter, while losing objectivity.

5 Criminalizing *Talaq-e-Biddat*

The Supreme Court in *Shayara Bano v. Union of India* (2017) declared the practice of *talaq-e-biddat* as unconstitutional.

On June 21, 2019, the Muslim Women (Protection of Rights on Marriage) Bill 2019 was introduced in the *Lok Sabha* as it was felt that the judgment of the Supreme Court as well as the assurances of the All India Muslim Personal Law Board had failed to deter the practice of triple *talaq* [Muslim Women (Protection of Rights on Marriage) Bill, 2019].

The Muslim Women (Protection of Rights on Marriage) Act 2019 ("Muslim Women Protection Act") was enacted on July 31, 2019. The ostensible purpose of the Muslim Women Protection Act was "ensuring the larger Constitutional goals of gender justice and gender equality of married Muslim women and help subserve their fundamental rights of non-discrimination and empowerment" [Muslim Women (Protection of Rights on Marriage) Bill, 2019]. The first year anniversary of the Muslim Women Protection Act was celebrated as the 'Muslim Women Rights day' by the government (Ray, 2020).

The Muslim Women Protection Act criminalizes triple *talaq* or *talaq-e-biddat* ostensibly to protect Muslim women [Muslim Women (Protection of Rights on Marriage) Act, 2019: sec. 4]. Yet the Act does little in this regard.

The Muslim Women Protection Act under Section 3 makes the act of *talaq-e-biddat* as void and illegal. It reads as under:

> Any pronouncement of talaq by a Muslim husband upon his wife, by words either spoken or written or in electronic form or in any other manner whatsoever, shall be void and illegal.

The declaration of triple *talaq* as void and illegal is redundant as the said practice has already been declared unconstitutional in *Shayara Bano v. Union of India* (2017) which is a declaration of law as per Article 141 of the Constitution.

Section 4 of the Muslim Women Protection Act criminalised the act of *talaq-e-biddat* and makes it punishable for a term which may extend to three years and with fine.

In our opinion, criminalizing the act is contrary to the interests of Muslim women and the judgment of the Supreme Court in *Shayara Bano v. Union of India* (2017). The Supreme Court held the practice of triple *talaq* as unconstitutional as it was instant and irrevocable and left no room for reconciliation; however, prosecuting the husband for the act will also prevent any reconciliation efforts between the husband and wife, thus creating the same mischief.

The 'harm' principle originally articulated by Mill, argued, "the only purpose for which power can be rightfully exercised over any member of a civilised community, against his will, is to prevent harm to others." He further argued that only actions which violate the legal rights of others should be the subject of legal sanction (and public condemnation) (Mill, 2009: 18, Ch. 1: Introductory). Since, triple *talaq* can no longer repudiate a marriage after being declared void by the Supreme Court, its pronouncement would have no effect, harmful or otherwise or violate a legal right. Therefore, the need for criminalizing the same does not arise especially since it may prevent rehabilitation efforts detrimental to the woman defeating the rights recognized by the Supreme Court (*Shayara Bano v. Union of India*, 2017) of Muslim women.

The Muslim Women Protection Act gives disproportionate coercive powers to the State in that the pronouncement of triple *talaq* is a cognizable and non-bailable offence [Muslim Women (Protection of Rights on Marriage) Act, 2019: sec. 7(a)], therefore the police may arrest a husband for the offence of pronouncing triple *talaq*, without a warrant. Such power may be exercised, not just on the information given by a Muslim woman herself, but 'by any person related to her by blood or marriage.' [Muslim Women (Protection of Rights on Marriage) Act, 2019: sec. 7(a)] Having been arrested, he must wait for the Magistrate to hear his wife and determine whether there are reasonable grounds to release him on bail [Muslim Women (Protection of Rights on Marriage) Act, 2019: sec. 7(c)].

If anything, the Muslim Women Protection Act enacted (purportedly) to protect Muslim women is likely to cause more harm to them. If husbands are in custody or convicted then it may also divest the woman and her children of their financial security and put them at the mercy of hostile family members. The estrangement may also compromise on a happy conjugal life.

The Act amounts to punishing abandonment by a husband but is limited to only one community. If abandonment or desertion is to be considered a criminal wrong warranting coercive action and curtailing of liberty then all such acts are to be made punishable notwithstanding the religion of the party involved and even the gender of the party.

The Act, however, is nothing more than a political gimmick casting the practices of a minority community as problematic and in need of a legal solution while acting as saviours of Muslim women.

Policy making is an evidence and data based method of law-making. However, in India, it often stems from public and media perception, voter appeasement and a very primitive sense of morality of the ruling party. The Supreme Court in its order dated 24.08.2022 (*Sudhir Kumar Yadav v. State of*

Bihar, 2022) noted that no legislative impact study was ever carried out prior to the introduction of the Bihar Prohibition and Excise Act, 2016. Similarly, no Muslim group was consulted prior to criminalizing triple *talaq* ("No Muslim Groups Consulted Over Triple Talaq Law: Govt," 2017). These supposed reforms were nothing but big ticket reforms based on voter impulses. Such reforms, although often appease and please sections of the public have irreversible social and economic impact and dilute constitutional safeguards.

Bibliography

Bachan Singh v. State of Punjab, 2 SCC 684 (1980) Supreme Court, India.
Bihar Prohibition And Excise (Amendment) Act (2022).
Bihar Prohibition and Excise (Amendment) Act, No. 8 of 2018 (2018).
Bihar Prohibition and Excise Act, No. 20 of 2016 (2016).
Burns, J. H. and Hart, H. L. A. (1996) *The Collected Works of Jeremy Bentham: An Introduction to the Principles of Morals and Legislation.* Oxford: Clarendon Press.
Constitution of India (1950).
Feinberg, J. (1971) "Legal Paternalism". *Canadian Journal of Philosophy*, 1(1), 105–124.
Gandhi, M. K. (1948) *Key To Health.* Ahmedabad: Navjivan Publishing House.
Hart, H. L. A. (1963) *Law, Liberty, and Morality.* Stanford: Stanford University Press.
Hirsch, A. V. (2008) "Direct paternalism: Criminalizing self-injurious conduct." *Criminal Justice Ethics*, 27(1): 25–33.
K. S. Puttaswamy v. Union of India, 10 SCC 1 (2017) Supreme Court, India.
Khoday Distilleries Ltd. v. State of Karnataka, 1 SCC 574 (1995) Supreme Court, India.
Legislative Assembly Election Manifesto. (2022) "Lok Kalyan Sankalp Patra." *Bhartiya Janata Party, Uttar Pradesh.* Available at: https://www.bjp.org/files/election-manifesto-documents/UP_Lok_Kalyan_Sankalp_Patra-2022%20%281%29_0.pdf Accessed on March 01, 2024.
Malhotra, S. (2022, March 08) "Why Bihar's liquor ban isn't working". *The Mint.* Available at: https://www.livemint.com/politics/policy/prohibition-makes-for-a-heady-cocktail-in-bihar-11646757792102.html. Accessed on March 01, 2024.
Medicinal and Toilet Preparations (Excise Duties) Act, No. 16 of 1955 (1955).
Mill, J. S. (2009) *On Liberty.* Waiheke Island: The Floating Press. (Original work published 1859).
Ministry of Health and Family Welfare, Government of India. (2021) "National Family Health Survey (NFHS-5)". *International Institute for Population Sciences.* Available at: http://rchiips.org/nfhs/NFH S-5 Reports/Bihar.pdf. Accessed on March 01, 2024.

Mishra, S. (2015, September 16) "Bihar polls: Nitish Kumar promises liquor prohibition." *Business Standard*. Available at: https://www.business-standard.com/article/politics/bihar-polls-nitish-kumar-promises-liquor-prohibition-115070901044_1.html Accessed on March 01, 2024.

Mukesh v. State, 6 SCC 1 (2017) Supreme Court, India.

Muslim Women (Protection of Rights on Marriage) Act, No. 20 of 2019 (2019).

Muslim Women (Protection of Rights on Marriage) Bill (2019). Available at: https://prsindia.org/files/bills_acts/bills_parliament/2019/Muslim%20women%20(Protection%20of%20Rights%20on%20Marriage)%20Bill,%202019.pdf. Accessed on March 01, 2024.

Narcotics and Psychotropic Substances Act, No. 61 of 1985 (1985).

Navtej Singh Johar v. Union of India, 10 SCC 1 (2018) Supreme Court, India.

Niraj Singh v. State of Bihar, SCC Online 3473 (2022) Supreme Court, India.

NITI Aayog. (2021) "National Multidimensional Poverty Index Baseline Report." *NITI Aayog*. Available at: https://www.niti.gov.in/sites/default/files/2021-11/National_MPI_India-11242021.pdf. Accessed on March 01, 2024.

"No Muslim groups consulted over triple talaq law: Govt." (December 20, 2017) *The Indian Express*. Available at: https://indianexpress.com/article/india/no-muslim-groups-consulted-over-triple-talaq-law-govt-4992054/. Accessed on March 01, 2021.

Noor Aga v. State of Punjab, 16 SCC 417 (2008) Supreme Court, India.

Ray, M. (July 31, 2020) "BJP marks anniversary of passage of triple talaq law as Muslim Women's Rights Day, Union ministers hail PM Modi." *Hindustan Times*. Available at: https://www.hindustantimes.com/india-news/bjp-marks-anniversary-of-passage-of-triple-talaq-law-as-muslim-women-s-rights-day-union-ministers-hail-pm-modi/story-0r04MBT23QUiYpkQAla8IK.html. Accessed on March 15, 2021.

Reserve Bank of India. (2018) "State Finances: A study of Budgets of 2017–18 and 2018–19". *Sangita Misra*. Available at: https://rbidocs.rbi.org.in/rdocs/Publications/PDFs/0SF201718_FULL6EE17CFBD8004287A0CD4FDB0632AFE8.PDF. Accessed on March 01, 2024.

Rev. Stainslaus v. State of M.P., 1 SCC 677 (1977) Supreme Court, India.

Santosh Kumar Satishbhushan Bariyar v. State of Maharashtra, 6 SCC 498 (2009) Supreme Court, India.

Shafin Jahan v. Asokan K. M., 16 SCC 368 (2018) Supreme Court, India.

Shakti Vahini v. Union of India, 7 SCC 192 (2018) Supreme Court, India.

Shayara Bano v. Union of India, 9 SCC 1 (2017) Supreme Court, India.

Shree Baidyanath Ayurved Bhawan Pvt. Ltd. v. State of Bihar, SCC OnLine 5243 (2016) Patna High Court, India.

Sudhir Kumar Yadav v. State of Bihar, SLP (Crl.) No. 1821 of 2022 (2022) Supreme Court, India.

"Those who drink are mahapaapi, not Indians': Bihar CM Nitish Kumar". (March 31, 2022) *The Indian Express*. Available at: https://indianexpress.com/article/cities/patna/bihar-cm-nitish-kumar-alcohol-prohibition-bill-assembly-7845644/. Accessed on March 15, 2023.

Uttar Pradesh Unlawful Conversion of Religion Act, No. 3 of 2021 (2021).

Vatsyayan, S. (May 15, 2019) "Alcohol Prohibition In Bihar: A Policy Analysis." *Movendi International*. Available at: https://movendi.ngo/blog/2019/05/16/alcohol-prohibition-in-bihar-a-policy-analysis/. Accessed on March 15, 2020.

CHAPTER 3

Spaces of Assessment and Incarceration

David McCallum

1   Introduction

The writings of Michel Foucault and Norbert Elias, and concepts of 'governing through freedom' and 'conduct/conduction/habitus' have for decades been thoroughly explored throughout the social sciences. Here, the works are brought to bear on a study of how governing vulnerable children and young people in Australia can be considered as 'histories of the present' (Nietzsche 1983; Elias 1994; Barry, Osborne and Rose 1995; Foucault 2008; Garland 2014). The study seeks to examine historical material that relates to the present related to the ongoing aftermath of the occupation of lands, and the accompanying destruction of Australian Indigenous peoples deaths and First Nations children from early and also present colonising periods. The study is grounded in the relations between knowledge and power, informed more particularly to Foucault's published lectures on *Security, Territory, Population* (2007) and *The Birth of Biopolitics* (2008), and also in the ways in which forms of liberal governing seeks to define the nature and scope of freedoms in populations through the practices of the human sciences. Liberal political reason accepts that governing involves reflection on governing practices rather than simply asserting a power, or as Donzelot (2008: 122) put it, 'recognising that truth is told elsewhere than at the centre of the State' ... there is no freedom that is not produced, that is not to be constructed, and this construction takes place through interventions by the State'.

As a start, we might assume that all kinds of governing takes its initial pulse from the production of knowledge in the human sciences, including knowledge of population through the production of statistics (the 'science of state'), the making up of categories of persons and their capacities (or freedoms) for self-governing, and the knowledge produced in technologies of administration that are then applied to those parts of the population considered unable to govern themselves, and hence needing to be managed (Hacking, 1986). Categories of person are dependent upon and are the products of historically distinctive practices and techniques. Elias extended and elaborated on core sociological problems of the management of conduct: of how people became enmeshed in ever more extensive webs of interdependence and developed mechanisms of habitual self-restraint; of how societies are formed on networks of interdependencies or 'figurations' as part of their organisation; of how social life is characterised by socially and historically specific forms of habitus. Finally, Elias sought to break from structuralist accounts of the relations between psychic structure, bodily experiences and social relations that became, in turn, a characteristic precondition of specifically liberal forms of governing or self-governing (Elias, 1994 [1939]).

It is one thing to commit to the liberal principle of equal worth of all individuals. However, it is quite another to equate liberalism in academic political theory with liberalism as a 'powerful historical phenomenon' (Hindess, 2004). So, while theoretical versions of liberalism may be wedded to claims about individual freedoms and equal worth, these claims do not necessarily reflect 'actually existing liberalism', such as the versions of liberal rule under forms of imperialism and other versions of 'authoritarian liberalism' (Hindess, 2008). Claims concerning freedom under liberalism are often qualified by a further claim that such freedoms are not possessed at birth but are acquired through discipline and moral progress, and that liberal governments might sometimes aim to assist in the moral development of members of subject populations. Further, this historical argument might also entail a coming-to-terms with a Euro-centric 'developmental view of humanity' and acknowledgement by such nineteenth century liberal theorists as J.S. Mill or Alex de Tocqueville that non-Western peoples were 'not yet ready for self-government' (Hindess, 2009). The developmental story among educated Europeans comprised the view that humanity was divided into societies and that these could be ranked along a development spectrum, with Western Europe at the top. In addition, among these 'more advanced' societies, some people – the educated and prosperous minority – have advanced further than the rest.

2 Knowing the 'Neglected' and 'Criminal' Child

Evidence in the case of children taken from the mid-nineteenth century was a problem of how to govern such an important area of life on such an extensive scale. Rationalities of governing children were taking form throughout the following half-century, focussed on the maturation of children services, and public policy favoured family intervention and monitoring; this to the point where a quarter of all children born in the state of Victoria would be notified for suspected child abuse or neglect during their childhood or adolescence (Victorian Department of Human Services, 2003: vi). The 'civilizing' of children was given over to familial relations, or what could be called the modernist family project (Donzelot, 2008; Wyness, 2013).

The answer can be looked for in the kind of governance arrangements set in place which, although seeming to fail to relieve poverty and health issues, nevertheless did achieve some success in developing the production of knowledge of poor families and children. It established a governance relation, and mapped out a domain of population in the same moment. A rationality of 'securitisation of populations' may not of itself produce poverty relief and a reduction of family violence but it built a grid for assessing the 'habits and mode of living', as the first legislation for establishing a Children's Court described it (Victoria, 1906), of that part of the population whose performance in a range of life circumstances might be regarded as problematic. Governing agencies set about reforming their approaches to problem populations in response to the failure of earlier policies of policing and institutional placement. The Victorian Neglected and Criminal Children's Act (1864) established barrack-style institutions for both categories of children, but the so-called Industrial Schools quickly filled with poor children (Jaggs, 1986). At the same time, these agencies also failed to promote the 'family principle' of providing a 'patriarchal, homely, and affectionate' environment (Victoria, 1872).

Policing reformed the practice of identifying the 'habitual criminal' through improved detection such as photography and finger-printing, but also through the tracking of parents and children that also reformed the methods of parents' maintenance payments. An important relay from the 1890s was the 'Children's Depot', a clearing house for both the 'neglected' and 'offending' children used to observe children before they were relocated. After the Depot (in the next century relocated from central Melbourne courts to Parkville, now a juvenile prison), it was 'habit', 'habitual', or alternatively what we could describe as 'habitus' that came under the gaze of the agencies and was its object of knowledge. This 'coercive normalisation' (McCallum, 2007) gauged within the children's courts from the early 1900s, and their auxiliaries in the children's court clinics after 1947, extended that gaze through linkages between courts and police, then the charity workers and probation officers, and after that the newly found psychological expertise, expanded the number of families and children under various kinds of organised oversight and supervision. The carving out of each element of this domain of the 'conduct of conduct' was accompanied by the threat of prison (ibid: 118).

There are already plenty of studies which show evidence of a pattern of relations that seem to correspond to the notion of 'conduct of conduct' explored by Foucault in his *Security, Territory, Population* lectures (2007), in which he takes philosophical advantage of the two meanings of the concept of conduct:

Conduct is the activity of conducting (*conduire*), of conduction (*la conduction*) if you like, but it is equally the way in which one conducts oneself (*se conduit*), lets oneself be conducted (*se laisse conduire*) and finally, in which one behaves (*se comporter*) under the influence of a conduct as the action of conducting or of conduction (*conduction*) (ibid: 193).

Although Foucault has attracted most attention in those parts of his lectures to the rise of studies of governmentality, it is also clear that his immediate move to 'revolts of conduct' and the concept of counter-conduct provides a rich source of enquiry into power relations that previously was less valued (Davidson, 2011: 25). To govern an individual or group is 'to act on the possibilities of action of other individuals', or 'to structure the possible fields of actions of others', which presupposes that power acts on a certain field of possibilities. Foucault's work on power and freedom is highly suggestive about how we go about theorising the governing '…of children, or souls, of communities, of families, of the sick', of anything; and also has to do with necessary relations between the how power works, and the practice of freedom: '(p)ower is exercised only over free subjects and only insofar as they are "free"' (Foucault, 1994: 341–2). It is not so much a face-to-face confrontation of power and freedom but a much more complicated interplay, in that freedom may well appear as the condition for the exercise of power. Where there is no freedom there is no relationship of power. So, for example, slavery is not a power relationship but rather a physical relationship of constraint.

Over such a broad historical canvas, it is not possible to provide detailed evidence here of the minutiae of relations of power that are invested in the family/child/government nexus. However, one such historical example of the specificity of powers relations examined as conduct of conduct, and of the necessary relations between power and freedom, is provided in early 20th century attempts in Australia to govern the habitual criminal through indeterminate sentencing, a system which in turn devolved as a method for assessing child criminality. Modelled on the provisions of the UK Prison Act (1898) and the Prevention of Crime Act (1908), this began as a program for adult prisoners heralded in the Royal Commission into Victoria Police in 1906, as an economical method of keeping trace of the habitual criminal. Locating these offenders was an inefficient use of police resources, dependent on photographic and physical measures of offenders stored in the central police files. The Chief Commissioner of Police laid out a classificatory system whereby it was possible to recognize the habitual criminal in quantifiable terms: 'on his third conviction, you would have fair evidence that he is going to live a life of crime' (Victoria, 1906; para 1253). It offered a program of reform in which the criminal came to know, keep trace, and act on his own habit: 'so a man knowing the system as he would from having it put before him while in gaol, and knowing that he was determining his own fate, would naturally get out of the more serious class, and go down to the other' (Victoria, 1906: para. 1253). The chief of prisons lauded the economy of indeterminate sentencing as it had the effect of 'creating the desire on the part of those who may be affected by its provisions to go beyond its reach' (Victoria, 1906b). Adult prisoners given an indeterminate sentence were held at the Governor's pleasure, while children could be detained until the age of 18, at which point they could be transferred to an adult prison.

3 Children, and 'Counter-conduct'

But what of 'counter-conduct', a theoretical variant of the concept of resistance? Foucault describes counter-conduct as 'struggle against the procedures implemented for conducting others', and a term quite different from 'misconduct' or the actions of a 'dissident' (Foucault, 2007). Counter-conduct enters power relations as a relation of force, in any social configuration, pattern of behaviour, bodily gesture, a certain attitude, a way of life (Davidson, 2011: 29). Based on analysis of anti-pastoral communities in the Middle Ages, Foucault draws out both political and ethical components of counter-conduct – resistance to the need for a shepherd in organised religion, and also 'a whole new attitude', way of doing things and attitude' 'a whole new way of relating to ... civil life'. At that time, Davidson emphasises Foucault's remarks on what makes homosexuality, for some at least, so disturbing – the homosexual 'way of life' being much more than just a sexual act, that puts into play 'relations in the absence of codes or established lines of conduct', 'affective intensities', 'forms that change' (ibid: 33).

A demonstration of the case for counter-conduct caught in specific power relations might be found in Carrington's (1993) ground-breaking study of the social processes that criminalize children, particularly girls and Aborigines, once these children enter the welfare and justice systems. According to Carrington (1993: 111), most conduct that ends up in the Children's Court is in vital respects no different from that observed outside the legal system. They are behaviours routinely managed by teachers and parents without recourse to the law: truanting, parental defiance, shop-lifting, sexual promiscuity, fare evasion and 'offensive behaviour'. Often these behaviours are the starting point of a police intervention that in turn takes the form of a court hearing. But in the specific context of the welfare and justice systems, a complex web of governmental technologies ostensibly to save children from 'bad families' produced what Carrington called a 'delinquency manufacturing process' (1993: 1). Court proceedings shift quickly from considering the nature of the offence to the nature of the child. Even in the small number of contested cases, judgments about what to do with the child slide between strictly legal considerations and the 'manner, character and family' of the child. Conduct, or more specifically counter-conduct – 'a pattern of behaviour, bodily gesture, a certain attitude, a way of life' – rather than events described in law, are drawn into relations of force and enjoined in struggle.

Thus, girls appearing in court on welfare matters were more likely to receive a custodial sentence than those appearing on criminal offences. Sentencing was based on the logic of 'preventative intervention' rather than judicial logic. 'Deficit discourses' were utilized in the identification of pre-delinquency, and such a classification seemed to be sufficient to justify the committal of welfare cases to institutions. 'Deficiencies' were held to be located in the individual children or their families, so that children and families were held responsible for school failure. Cultural differences and marginality were criminalized, and family poverty translated into family pathology. Because pathologies are calculated in these discourses as 'deviations from the specificity of the norm', they have an intense criminalizing effect on social marginality. Reports presented to the Court show the use of a range of deficit discourses – moral, psychological, social – in coming to an assessment about individual girls studied in the survey. They then had practical effects on the way children were chosen, placed and punished by juvenile justice and child welfare authorities alike (ibid: 127).

Similarly, in child protection in the UK, Parton (1991) shows that in the 'grey areas' outside of the gaze of the court, where the work is done on sifting out children and families at 'high risk', disciplinary mechanisms became central and defined the day-to-day practice of child services. High risk is a description of the 'habit', 'habitual' and 'habitus' of children under the newly implemented risk management strategies. Parton's study deals with a politics of these knowledges and the problem of the professional groups surrounding them in the UK at the height of the New Right agenda in the late 1970s and 1980s, where the notion of dangerousness became the yardstick for allocating scarce government resources (ibid: 203). From this period, rather than being simply one of a range of children's services, child protection became the main priority of social work. In Australia, it was during this period that medicine relinquished its grip on specialist knowledge of family life, passing the baton to professional social work. Child protection in the UK became embroiled in these politics, and policy shifted towards establishing a clear demarcation between a care system and a voluntary system of children's services for children in need. This policy direction was adopted later in Australia, with new legislation from 2005 introduced in both Victoria and New South Wales (Victorian Department of Human Services, 2002; Government of New South Wales, 2008).

The spaces described in Carrington's and Parton's research could be seen as elements of a genealogy of a space in the late 19th century called the 'children's depot'. The spaces allow a gaze onto the child that was to determine the 'disposal' of the child – industrial school or reformatory school, 'boarding out' (out of home care) or residential care, or prison (juvenile justice facility). The object of knowledge was 'habits and mode of living' which for the purposes of this paper I have chosen to adopt the term conduct: 'dispositions, attributes, capacities, habit, bearing, comportment, manners, gesture' (McFall, Du Gay and Carter, 2008).

4   Conclusion

In the space of a century of attempts to govern families and children, population became an important object of knowledge. Science entered the room of governing, and was required to provide an impartial assessment of children broadly on a scale of 'normality'. One interpretation of these historical events is to take seriously the challenges to social work and its knowledge of populations as instances of counter-conduct – as a refusal of the ways in which conduct of individuals and populations would be governed. This interpretation would need to also take seriously evidence of the governing actions of science itself as the determinant of normal life, normal growing up, and also a corollary, the functioning of science in legal determinations of normal families. Such an interpretation adds weight to arguments about the critical role of bio-politics, as distinct from sovereign power and civil rights, in furthering or limiting children and their families' participation in decisions about their upbringing.

Bibliography

Apology to the Stolen Generations. (2022) Deadly Story. Available at: https://deadlystory. com/page/culture/history/Apology_to_the_Stolen_Generations. Accessed on July 01, 2023.

Barry, A., Osborne, T., & Rose, N. (1996). *Foucault and Political Reason: Liberalism, Neo-Liberalism and Rationalities of Power.* London: UCL Press.

Carrington, K. (1993) *Offending Girls: Sex, Youth and Justice.* Sydney: Allen and Unwin.

Davidson, A. (2011) "In praise of counter-conduct". *History of the Human Sciences*, 24(4): 25–41.

Donzelot, J. (2008) "Michel Foucault and liberal intelligence". *Economy and Society*, 37(1): 115–134.

Elias, N. (1994 [1939]) *The Civilizing Process*. Basel: Oxford: Blackwell.

Foucault, M. (1994) "The Subject and Power". In: J. D. Faubion (ed.) *Michel Foucault – Power: the Essential Works of Foucault*, Vol. 3. London: Penguin, 327–348.

Foucault, M. (2007) *Security, Territory, Population*. Lectures at the College de France 1977–1978 (Trans. G. Burchell), Basingstoke: Palgrave MacMillan.

Foucault, M. (2008) *The Birth of Biopolitics*. Lectures at the College de France *1978–1979* (trans. G. Burchell) Basingstoke: Palgrave Macmillan.

Gannoni, A. and Bricknell, S. (2019) "Indigenous deaths in custody: 25 years since the Royal Commission into Aboriginal Deaths in Custody". *Statistical Bulletin no. 17*. Australian Institute of Criminology. Available at: https://www.aic.gov.au/publications/sb/sb17.

Government of New South Wales (2008) "Special Commission of Inquiry into Child Protection Services in New South Wales". State of New South Wales. Available at: https://www.nsw.gov.au/sites/default/files/2023-07/Volume-1-Special-Commission-of-Inquiry-into-Child-Protection-Services-in-NSW.pdf.

Hacking, I. (1986) "Making Up People". In: Heller, T., et al. (eds) *Reconstructing Individualism: Autonomy, Individuality and the Self in Western Thought*. Stanford: Stanford University Press.

Hindess, B. (2001) "The Liberal Government of Unfreedom". *Alternatives*, 26(2): 93–111.

Hindess, B. (2004) "Liberalism: What's in a Name?". In: Larner, W. and Walters, W. (eds) *Global Governmentality: Governing International Spaces*. London: Routledge.

Hindess, B. (2009) "Liberalism and History". Keynote Address, *Foucault: 25 Years On*, University of South Australia.

Hindess, B. (2008) "Political Theory and 'Actually Existing Liberalism'". *Critical Review of International Social and Political Philosophy*, 11(3): 347–352.

Jaggs, D. (1986) *Neglected and Criminal: Foundations of Child Welfare Legislation in Victoria*. Melbourne: Centre for Youth and Community Studies, Phillip Institute of Technology.

Marchetti, E., et al. (2021) "Listening to Country: A prison pilot project that connects Aboriginal and Torres Strait Islander women on remand to Country". *Current Issues in Criminal Justice*, 34(2): 155–170.

McCallum, D. (2007) "Coercive Normalization and Family Policing: The limits of the 'psy-complex' in Australian penal systems". *Social and Legal Studies*, 16(1): 113–129.

McFall, L., et al. (2008) *Conduct. Sociology and Social Worlds*. Manchester and New York: Manchester University Press.

Nietzsche, F. (1983) "On The Uses And Disadvantages Of History For Life". In: Stern, J. P. (ed) *Untidy Meditations* (Trans. R. J. Hollingdale). Cambridge: Cambridge University Press.

Parton, N. (1991) *Governing The Family: Child Care, Child Protection and The State*. Basingstoke: Palgrave Macmillan.

United Kingdom (1898) Prison Act.

United Kingdom (1908) Prevention of Crime Act.

Van Krieken, R. (1991) *Children And The State. Social Control And The Formation Of Australian Child Welfare*. Sydney: Allen and Unwin.

Victoria (1864) Neglected and Criminal Children's Act.

Victoria (1872) First Report of the Royal Commission on Industrial and Reformatory Schools and the Sanitary Station. Melbourne: Victoria.

Victoria (1906) Children's Court Act.

Victoria. (1906a) "Report of the Inspector General of Penal Establishments and Goals for the Year 1905". *Victorian Parliamentary Papers*, Vol. 2. Acting Government Printer.

Victoria. (1906b) "Royal Commission on the Victorian Police Force". *Victorian Parliamentary Papers*, Vol. 1 (xiii). Acting Government Printer.

Victoria (2005) Children, Youth and Families Act.

Victorian Department of Human Services (VDHS). (2002) "An Integrated Strategy For Child Protection And Placement Services". *Community Care Division*, VDHS, Melbourne. Available at: www.dhs.vic.gov.au. Accessed on March 01, 2024.

Victorian Department of Human Services (VDHS). (2003) "Protecting Children: The Child Protection Outcomes Project, Final Report of the Victorian Department of Human Services". *Community Care Division*, VDHS, Melbourne.

Wyness, M. (2013), "Children, Family and The State: Revisiting Public and Private Realms". *Sociology 48(1)*: 59–74.

CHAPTER 4

Evaluating Overcriminalization on the Basis of International Human Rights Law: The Example of Counter-terrorism Legislation

Ekkehard Strauss

1   Introduction

The enactment of criminal law is a political decision that is often caused less by the use of technological innovation to commit new crimes than the public outrage that followed media coverage of tragic events. The legislatures do not use a principled approach. In this paper, I will argue that, in order to identify and measure overcriminalization on the basis of a normative theory, international human rights law should be integrated.

The perceived threat of international terrorism has led to the passing of standardised counterterrorism laws with similar structural features despite varying conditions within countries (Alston & Goodman, 2013: 387). This chapter seeks to contribute to political decision making as to whether a behaviour should be criminalized altogether and, in the affirmative, which rules should be applied for its implementation in order not to become excessive. Overcriminalization can occur with regard to international human rights law in the space between the obligations to use criminal law to protect human rights and the obligation to justify any limitation of its application. A similar methodology may be used to expand the analysis to other contexts. To go further with this thesis, first, I will explain what overcriminalization is and the concept of overcriminalization. Thereafter, I will examine the various sources of international law which mandates countries to enact a criminal norm. Also, I will examin the limitations created by international law to enact criminal law to punish certain conducts especially when such conducts are protected by human rights instruments. Human rights and criminal law have an interesting interface. Criminal law infringes liberty – a cherished human rights value. Human rights instruments often require enactment of criminal law to protect human rights. Thus, if a criminal law intended to safeguard human rights law is not framed properly, then the same law could be a source of human rights violations. I will argue that States should not use the shield of international human rights law to create broad and vague terrorism laws.

2   Concept of Overcriminalization

In a national context, overcriminalization refers to the perceived overuse of criminal law as a means to influence human behaviour. Concern arises from the assumption that criminal law is not simply one of a range of techniques available to governments for regulating the conduct and activities of people. Criminal law carries with it particular social, moral and legal significance for its link with punishment. Punishment involves severe restrictions on liberty, in particular imprisonment, and only serious wrongdoing can be a sufficient justification for this serious limitation of human rights. Criminal law implies that such conduct should not happen and, in this regard, criminal law serves a preventive function. At a procedural level, it authorises law enforcement officials (e.g., police and prosecutors) to take action to prevent such conduct from occurring and to pursue those who are reasonably believed to have committed crimes so as to bring them to court with a view to conviction and sentence. Based on this definition, a concept of overcriminalization has to consider both criminal procedure law and the substantive law of criminal offences.

Most concepts of overcriminalization start from the general functions of criminal law. On this basis, overcriminalization is measured by the expansion of substantive criminal law and the rise in the use of punishment (Husak, 2008). In the USA, the discussion is dominated by the application of the principle of strict liability. This introduces a qualitative element to the review, which is further reflected in different categories of overcriminalization (Smith, 2013: 537 et seq.). A finding on overcriminalization is also influenced by the justification of punishment and the relationship of infliction of sanction and imposition of stigma.

The idea that the penal system only intervenes when a crime has been committed or attempted and that sanctioning of the criminal is according to the commission of the crime and can actually be attributed has been extended by the introduction of endangerment law as new interpretations of the familiar classical function of criminal law. The growing preoccupation of governments with risk, danger and the prevention of harm raised the possibility of overcriminalization with a view to the core function of prevention. The criteria considered as risk factors are related to undefined individuals, e.g. the prisoner, the foreign gangs, etc., i.e. certain risk populations that are now predicted to be dangerous or harmful to general security. Consequently, risk factors are the reason for intervention through criminal law. The spectrum of possible addresses of criminal law is expanded to e.g. being a foreigner, lack of discipline in prison, acquaintance with criminals, refusal of therapies, all coded as possible sources of harmful events in the future (Böhm, 2011).

Overcriminalization occurs as well, where the severity of the punishment is no longer a function of the crime, i.e. when punishment is disproportionate and exceeds what the offender deserves. This includes categories of crimes for a conduct which, in the opinion of large parts of the population, does not deserve censure at all, e.g. homosexuality, prostitution or abortion, or if aggravating circumstances are not apparent from the law itself, e.g. terrorism or violent extremism, and it is unclear, how the aggravation corresponds to ordinary crimes, e.g. murder or assault. Analysis based on the degree of punishment should distinguish the elements of crime from the legal consequences of the norm.

An important function of criminal law is to guide behaviour. The police are only dealing with a fraction of the infringements of criminal law. Most transgressions are reported by citizens based on their belief that criminal law is just (Husak, 2008: 32). The scope of criminal law provides law enforcement agencies with increased powers to arrest, search and apply surveillance techniques and leads to a constant increase of caseload of criminal courts with negative consequences for their ability to ensure the rule of law (Krey & Windgätter, 2012: 579 et seq.). Those who might take criminal law seriously, may be frustrated by the criminalization of previously lawful and even commendable behaviour, even though this impact is difficult to prove empirically (Husak, 2008: 12). A similar result can be caused by excessive discretionary powers left to the police and the prosecution by the law. This raises questions of overcriminalization through very broad offence definitions.

Another element of the core functions of criminal law is the requirement of fault and culpability as reason for punishment. Overcriminalization may occur, when offences are based on complicity in an act or the membership in an organisation, e.g. in the context of extremism or terrorism. Preparatory crimes and endangerment offences, e.g. in the context of terrorism and organised crime, are considered in this regard. As far as preparatory crimes remove the conduct requirement in favour of a proof of purpose, concerns of overcriminalization arise with regard to the risk of extracting confessions, the presumption of innocence and the punishment of thoughts. Similar concerns are raised by the related offences of solicitation or incitement in the context of terrorism. Depending on their content, crimes of possession of certain items considered dangerous in abstract, e.g. narcotics, child pornography, without need of proof of a particular purpose may raise concerns of overcriminalization if expanded.

Since the specific limitations to criminal law are the same under international human rights law and national constitutions, it can be concluded that the core functions of criminal law considered in human rights law are the same as in national law. In addition, any limitation of human rights of an individual, including criminal sanctions, needs to be justified.

International criminal law establishes individual criminal responsibility for grave violations of international human rights that constitute international crimes. Genocide, war crimes, crimes against humanity and aggression are international crimes punishable independent of national criminal law. However, States can exercise jurisdiction on the basis of universality. The international concern for these acts are based on the recognition that grave crimes threaten the peace, security and well-being of the world (Rome Statute of the International Criminal Court, 1998: Preamble, para 3). The most recent and comprehensive catalogue of international crimes, reflecting customary international law to a large extent, can be found in art. 6–8 of the ICC Statute (Schabas, 2004: 26 et seq.). The general function of international criminal law is somewhat different from national criminal law and is left out of the present review.

3 International Obligations to Use Criminal Law

3.1 *Explicit Obligations*

3.1.1   Explicit Obligations in International Human Rights Treaties
Several human rights treaties include an obligation to declare certain acts as offences punishable by law. In addition, the International Covenant on Civil and Political Rights, 1996 (ICCPR) envisages in some articles certain areas where there are positive obligations on States to address the activities of private persons or entities by law. The following review will be limited to the ICCPR and the Convention on the Elimination of Racial Discrimination, 1965 (CERD) with a view to their relevance in assessing the compliance of criminal law enacted in the context of counterterrorism with international human rights law.

According to Art. 20 II of ICCPR, incitement to discrimination, hostility or violence shall be prohibited by law. However, the norm is not applicable to non-violent acts of racial or religious discrimination but rather to prevent the public incitement of racial hatred and violence within a state or against other states or people, because it was a historical reaction to the Nazi racial hatred campaigns ("General Comment No. 11", 1983: Art. 20, para 2).

According to the Human Rights Committee (HRC), states are obliged under Art. 6 I ICCPR to set appropriate laws in place to protect life from all reasonably foreseeable threats, including those from private persons and entities ("General Comment No. 36", 2019: Art. 6, para 18). The HRC considers that

States should take measures not only to prevent and punish deprivation of life by criminal acts, but also to prevent arbitrary killing by their own security forces. States have scope to fulfil their obligation to protect the right to life by law. Therefore, a violation can only be assumed when legislation is non-existent or substantially insufficient. For instance, if a country were to grant impunity for murder and manslaughter this would be a violation of Art. 6 I ICCPR. The deprivation of life by the authorities of the State is considered a matter of utmost gravity. Therefore, the law must strictly control and limit the circumstances in which a person may be deprived of his life by such authorities (Joseph & Castan, 2013: 167). A violation was found in an excessively wide definition of self-defence, e.g. a general statutory presumption of justification for the police force when they are taking part in operations to repress certain types of offences (Suarez de Gueterro v. Colombia, 1982: para 13.3.).

The standard way to ensure the protection of the right to life is to criminalize the killing of human beings. Purely disciplinary and administrative remedies cannot be deemed to constitute adequate and effective remedies within the meaning of article 2 III ICCPR in the event of an alleged violation of the right to life. The HRC placed emphasis on criminal law remedies for State killings (Joseph & Castan, 2013: 179). It has been confirmed in numerous cases that the ICCPR contains no independent right to see a person prosecuted, however, it seems that the duty to investigate alleged violations of the ICCPR in good faith may occasionally entail a duty to prosecute a certain person (Bautista de Arellana v. Colombia, 1993). The positive right to life includes a duty to prevent and punish killings and disappearances by private actors. States must refrain from deporting, extraditing or otherwise transferring individuals to countries where there is a personal, real and imminent threat that their right to life will be violated ("General Comment No. 36", 2019: para 30).

Art. 2 I lit. d CERD requires states to prohibit and bring to an end racial discrimination, including by legislation. This obligation is specified in art. 4 lit. a and b CERD to declare incitement to racial discrimination and related acts an offence punishable by law. According to the Committee, criminal law is not always the most suitable means and should be limited to particularly grave cases, which can be proven beyond reasonable doubt ("General Recommendation No. 35", 2013: para 12). States are obliged to provide effective legal protection in criminal law, in particular by initiating prosecution measures if suspicion of a violation are substantiated, with a margin of appreciation. The obligations of international law should be understood as minimum standards and States are granted a wide scope for shaping and assessing the corresponding legislation (Angst & Lantschner, 2020: Art. 4, para 73 et seq.). Art. 5 lit. b CERD requires States to eliminate any racial and related discrimination, inter alia, in respect of the right to security of person and calls for protection by the State against violence or bodily harm, whether inflicted by government officials or by any individual, group or institution. The comprehensive protection of citizens against the use of violence and bodily harm requires protection through criminal law ("General Comment No. 35", 2014). The effective protection and remedies in Art. 6 I CERD must also have a criminal law dimension ("General Recommendation No. 31", 2005).

In the context of explicit treaty obligations to pass criminal law to protect human rights, overcriminalization may occur, where acts become punishable by law, which fall outside the scope of the respective treaty provision. Where the treaty obligation is explicit only with regard to legislation in general, the use of criminal law may be excessive with regard to the general functions of criminal law.

3.1.2   Explicit Obligations in International Terrorism Conventions

Since 1963, the international community has developed 19 international treaties to combat specific acts of terrorism, e.g. the hijacking of aircraft, mostly in response to particular events. These conventions demand states to take different action against an agreed scope of terrorist acts, but most of them include an obligation to criminalize certain behaviour and co-operate with other States in intelligence sharing, mutual legal assistance, asset freezing and confiscation and extradition, without an agreement on a definition of terrorism (OSCE Office for Democratic Institutions and Human Rights 2007: 22). In their preambular paragraphs, most conventions refer to the purposes and principles of the United Nations, which include the promotion of human rights, and to the right to life, liberty and security of the person (International Convention against the Taking of Hostages, 1979).

In the context of counterterrorism treaties, there is a risk of overcriminalization as far as they lead to the punishment of behaviour that can be considered legitimate violence. In addition, the obligation to criminalize separates the act from terrorism, which remains undefined, and thus opens the possibility of including motives, e.g. travelling abroad with a terrorist intent, political opposition etc., not justifying the declaration as crime [*Report of the Special Rapporteur on the Promotion and Protection of Human Rights and Fundamental Freedoms While Countering Terrorism*, 2018 (hereinafter "A/73/361, 2018"): para 31].

3.1.3   Explicit Obligations in Security Council Resolutions

The Security Council passed several resolutions containing an obligation under Chapter VII of the UN Charter to criminalize certain terrorist acts, the financing of terrorism and the justification, glorification and incitement of terrorism without defining the keyword of terrorism ("Resolution 1373", 2001; "Resolution 1624", 2005; "Resolution 2178", 2014). These resolutions include the obligation to criminalize acts, such as travelling abroad with a terrorist intent, which has no other basis in international law. At the same time, the obligation of States to implement Security Council resolutions sidesteps the balance between ratification, effectiveness test and sovereignty, which is important to ensure national protection of international human rights without overreach (A/73/361, 2018: para 31, 43). The prerogative of the national human rights system is replaced by an alternative system of legislation by the Security Council, which may undermine the national legislative process, including the participation of civil society, respect of the principle of necessity and determining the legal, political, social and cultural effect.

It is not clear whether the Special Rapporteur of the UN Human Rights Council on the promotion and protection of human rights and fundamental freedoms while countering terrorism (Special Rapporteur) ("Special rapporteur on Counter-terrorism and Human Rights", 2022), in this context, suggests a general proportionality analysis by the Security Council and participation of civil society before passing resolutions (A/73/361, 2018: para 32).

3.1.4 Explicit Obligations in the United Nations Global Counter-Terrorism Strategy (GCTS)

In the GCTS, all UN Member States agreed to a common strategic and operational approach to fighting terrorism (United Nations Global Counter-Terrorism Strategy, 2006). States sought a balanced approach between declaring terrorism unacceptable in all its forms and manifestations and to take practical steps, individually and collectively, and accepting human rights as the fundamental basis of the fight against terrorism. In principle, States recognize that compliance with human rights is necessary to address the long-term conditions conducive to the spread of terrorism, and that effective counter-terrorism measures and the protection of human rights are complementary and mutually reinforcing goals (Parker, 2019). The GCTS itself does not provide general criteria for a requirement to adopt criminal law.

However, in the most recent 7th review of the GCTS, States reaffirmed that any acts of terrorism are criminal and unjustifiable (United Nations Global Counter-Terrorism Strategy: Seventh Review, 2021: Preamble, 1). In the same document, States stressed the importance of the development and maintenance of effective, fair, humane, transparent and accountable criminal justice systems based on respect for human rights and the rule of law, due process and fair trial guarantees and called on States to continue efforts to combat terrorism through national legislation (United Nations Global Counter-Terrorism Strategy: Seventh Review, 2021: 4). They reiterated the obligation of States to criminalize acts related to the funding of terrorism, providing detailed descriptions of such acts. They should be defined as serious criminal offences in domestic laws and regulations and the punishment should reflect the seriousness of such terrorist acts, to ensure effective, proportionate and dissuasive criminal sanctions. In the resolution, States are urged to establish as criminal offences under their domestic law the illegal manufacture, possession, stockpiling and trade of small arms and light weapons, including their diversion to unauthorized recipients (United Nations Global Counter-Terrorism Strategy: Seventh Review, 2021: 5) and calls upon States to ensure the criminalization and prosecution of terrorism offences in accordance with their obligations under international law (United Nations Global Counter-Terrorism Strategy: Seventh Review, 2021: 12).

3.1.5 Explicit Obligations in the Context of Emergencies

A state of emergency can be a cause of overcriminalization as far as it triggers particular criminal offences or the application of special rules in criminal procedures.

International human rights law recognizes the permissibility of certain restrictions on certain rights and freedoms during emergencies and enables governments to take necessary measures consistent with international obligations. Restrictions must meet certain conditions, i.e. they must be necessary, the least restrictive alternative, proportional between means and clearly stated objectives, and consistent with other fundamental rights and non-discriminatory in purpose and practice. Restrictions are conceptually narrower than derogation and were designed to meet specific objectives to a specific extent and for certain democratically justifiable purposes. Restrictions may be viewed as having a less severe effect on the protection of human rights than derogation [*Report of the special rapporteur on the promotion and protection of human rights and fundamental freedoms while countering terrorism on the human rights challenge of states of emergency in the context of countering terrorism*, 2018 (hereinafter, "A/HRC/37/52, 2018"): para 8].

It is generally recognized that terrorist acts and the actions of terrorist organisations can create necessary and sufficient conditions to activate the threshold of emergency under international law, subject to the requirements of legality, proportionality and non-discrimination. Random acts of terrorism though may not reach the necessary thresholds or pose the scale of threat sufficient to activate emergency powers under national and international law.

The Special Rapporteur recalled that international law requires States to use ordinary law if emergency measures are not strictly necessary (A/HRC/37/52, 2018: para 1). Overreaction by governments can ratchet up the levels of violence and confrontation as well as undermine the broader fight against terrorism and inadvertently bolster the conditions conducive to terrorism. The Special Rapporteur recalled that when emergency powers are misused, overused, and misapplied, the consequences for the rule of law, accountability and transparency are devastating (A/HRC/37/52, 2018: para 8). The Special Rapporteur developed criteria for the use of emergency procedures to prevent overcriminalization which will be reviewed in the context of limitations, below at 5.2.3.

3.2   Implied Obligations to Use Criminal Law

3.2.1   Implied Obligations in General Treaty Obligations

Where an obligation is not explicit in requiring the adoption of criminal law, such obligations could be implied from the general obligation to give effect to the respective treaty obligations and with specific rights.

Every international human right includes general obligations for States regarding its implementation, i.e. the obligation to respect, protect and ensure (fulfil) (De Schutter, 2010: 242 et seq.). These obligations include the passing of national legislation and its implementation. The obligation to protect requires the State to ensure that human rights are respected also among private individuals, including enabling their security, which is itself broadly defined. More specifically, this duty is recognized as part of States' obligations to ensure respect for the right to life and the right to security of person. States are obliged to take reasonable and effective measures to secure the safety, security and the right to life of persons within their jurisdiction, including from terrorism. One possibility to ensure this protection is by criminal law, building on its general functions.

The HRC did not establish general criteria for the obligation to protect and ensure human rights through criminal law. However, the HRC clarified that positive obligations of States to ensure ICCPR rights will only be fully met if individuals are protected against violations by state agents and against acts committed by private persons or entities. A failure to ensure rights as required by art. 2 ICCPR may violate this obligation, e.g. if a State does not take appropriate measures or exercise due diligence to prevent, punish, investigate or redress the harm caused by acts of private persons or entities, including through criminal law. In this context, the HRC refers to the interrelationship between the positive obligations imposed under art. 2 ICCPR and the need to provide effective remedies in the event of breach under art. 2 III ICCPR ("General Comment No. 31", 2004: para 8).

In some views on individual complaints and in concluding observations to periodic reports the HRC addressed the relationship between the general obligations in art. 2 ICCPR and specific treaty rights. The most relevant statements will be addressed, following the Committees perspective, in the context of implicit limitations to the use of criminal law, below.

Based on the wording of art. 12 III and 18 ICCPR, three conditions have been defined for general limitations to human rights. First, any interference with a right should be prescribed by law (condition of legality). Second, it must be justified by the pursuance of a legitimate aim (condition of legitimacy). Third, the interference must be limited to what is necessary for the fulfilment of that aim, which means that it must be appropriate to pursuing the objective, and that it may not go beyond what is required in order to effectively achieve that aim – or, at a minimum, that all the interests involved should be carefully balanced against one another (condition of proportionality) (De Schutter, 2010: 288 et. seq.). In order for an interference with a protected right to be proportional, the measure creating the interference must be appropriate to the fulfilment of the legitimate aim pursued (a condition referred to as 'appropriateness' or 'rational connection'), and it must not go beyond what is strictly required by the need to achieve that aim, i.e. it must be necessary to attain the objective justifying the interference (condition of 'necessity' or 'minimal impairment').

According to art. 9 I ICCPR, everyone has the right to liberty and security of person. This reference to an individual right to security of person must be distinguished from references to national security as one of the legitimate aims for which certain rights may be restricted, as provided for by arts. 12 III, 13, 14 I, 19 III lit. b, 21, and 22 II ICCPR (Scheinin, 2020: para 3). The HRC clarified that the right to personal security obliges States to protect individuals from foreseeable threats to life or bodily integrity from any governmental or private actors. States must take measures to prevent future injury and retrospective measures, such as enforcement of criminal laws, in response to past injury ("General Comment No. 35", 2014: para 9). In its views in the case of Delgado Páez v. Colombia the HRC stated that both the location of the phrase as a part of a paragraph and the travaux préparatoires suggested that the right to security arises in the context of deprivations of liberty. However, as the right to security is mentioned separately both in art. 3 of the Universal Declaration of Human Rights (UDHR) and art. 9 ICCPR, it cannot be the case that States can ignore known threats to the life of persons under their jurisdiction, just because he or she is not arrested or otherwise detained (Delgado Páez v. Colombia, 1990: para 5.5). However, if State obligations in respect of the right to security of person were given broad application, for instance in the field of police powers, this might be misunderstood as legitimising far-reaching interferences with individual human rights (Scheinin, 2020: para 22).

A restriction on the freedom of association is justified by art. 22 II ICCPR if it is provided by law, serves a purpose mentioned in the norm, and if it is necessary in a democratic society to achieve one of these purposes (Belyatsky v. Belarus, 2007: para 7.3). This does not include restrictions on associations which peacefully promote political ideas in opposition to the government as they are regarded as a cornerstone of a democratic society (Belyatsky v. Belarus, 2007: para 7.3).

The CERD Committee did not provide a general interpretation of state party obligations deriving from art. 2 CERD.

3.2.2 Explicit Obligations Based on Derogation

The adoption of criminal law with a risk of overcriminalization may occur, when general obligations or specific treaty provisions are permanently or temporarily suspended.

Derogation allows the suspension of certain international human rights in a situation that constituted a threat to the life of the nation, as provided for in different human rights treaties, including art. 4 ICCPR (A/HRC/37/52, 2018: para 40). The interpretation of the respective treaty provisions is guided further by the Paris Minimum Standards of Human Rights Norms in a State of Emergency, developed by the International Law Association, and the Siracusa Principles on the Limitation and Derogation Provisions in the International Covenant on Civil and Political Rights ["Siracusa Principles on the Limitation and Derogation Provisions in the International Covenant on Civil and Political Rights", 1984 (hereinafter, "Siracusa Principles")]. Only derogable rights may be subject to limitations by criminal law. Non-derogable rights cannot be limited or suspended, regardless of the extent or the source of the crisis faced by the State. There is some variance across treaties on what constitute non-derogable rights. The HRC stressed that even derogable rights cannot be derogated from at will; derogable rights which also constitute peremptory norms of international law are effectively non-derogable in emergencies. Moreover, the HRC stated that derogation from certain rights could never be proportionate (for example, hostage taking, arbitrary deprivation of liberty, deviation from the principles of fair trial) ("General Comment No. 29", 2001). Thus, criminal procedures contrary to these rules may amount to overcriminalization.

A historic interpretation of the respective treaty provisions clarifies that States were aware of the challenges of terrorism, insurrection, internal armed conflict and collective violence at the time of drafting the ICCPR. Derogation from certain treaty obligations in emergency situations is legally distinct from restrictions allowed in normal times. The Special Rapporteur recalls in this regard that where possible and appropriate, ordinary law should be used to regulate political challengers. States could supplement, if necessary, the ordinary law through the application of human rights-based limitations or restrictions. Even as new methods and means of terrorism have emerged in recent decades, the language of derogation is sufficiently broad and encompassing to address new challenges and new contexts (A/HRC/37/52, 2018: para 9).

The adoption of measures by a State derogating from treaty obligations is conditioned by different requirements. Derogation from the provisions of the ICCPR must be of an exceptional and temporary nature. Before a State invokes a derogation, two fundamental conditions must be met, i.e. the situation must amount to an emergency, which threatens the life of the nation, and the State must have officially proclaimed a state of emergency (De Schutter, 2010: 513 et. seq.).

With regard to derogation for counterterrorism, the Special Rapporteur recalls that treaty provisions have given rise to a substantial amount of jurisprudence from international bodies on when a derogation is justified, what kinds of measures and in what degree are justified, as well as oversees State reporting and notification ("General Comment No. 29", 2001). State obligations are no different whether the threat emanates from terrorism, natural disaster or war (A/HRC/37/52: para 28). Derogation requires that the scale of threat be exceptional and affect the State's fundamental capacity to function effectively, and impact the State's core security, independence and sovereignty (A/HRC/37/52: para 12). An essential requirement for measures derogating from the ICCPR is that they be limited to the extent strictly required by the exigencies of the situation. Courts interpret this requirement as applying to the duration, geographical coverage and material scope of the state of emergency and any measures of derogation in accordance with the principles of legitimacy, proportionality and necessity (A/HRC/37/52: para 11). A further principle is that the existence of an emergency and the modification of legal regulation affecting the exercise of human rights be public and notified (A/HRC/37/52: para 21).

On the basis of these criteria, the Special Rapporteur appears to suggest that overcriminalization occurs, when emergency legislation is introduced beyond these limitations. The Special Rapporteur suggested in this context non-discrimination-based benchmarking of emergency legislation, without providing details of such a test (A/HRC/37/52: para 28c). In practice, emergency statutes have been absorbed into the ordinary legal framework, including counterterrorism legislation, which normalised the exception (A/HRC/37/52: para 16).

4   Prohibition of and Limitations to the Use of Criminal Law

4.1   Explicit Limitations

Other human rights norms prohibit the use of criminal law to sanction certain behaviour.

Art. 11 ICCPR aims at protecting against imprisonment as a punishment for the inability to fulfil a contractual obligation. This right is non-derogable.

Art. 15 ICCPR limits the application of criminal law to acts constituting an offence prior to their commitment.

Art. 6 II ICCPR establishes rules for the application of the death penalty. It follows from article 6 III – VI ICCPR that States parties are not obliged to abolish the death penalty totally. Art. 6 II ICCPR allows for the imposition of the death penalty only for the most serious crimes. In several cases, the HRC tried to define a list of crimes falling within the definition of the ICCPR. Some crimes could be serious enough to allow the death penalty even if they injured no one, such as 'bombing of busy quarters, destruction of reservoirs, poisoning of drinking water, gassing in subway stations and probably espionage in war-time'. This is because some crimes 'create a grave danger which may result in death or irreparable harm to many and unspecified persons', and should thus be severely punished regardless of their ultimate consequences. The HRC has also confirmed offences that cannot be punished by the death penalty without violating article 6 ICCPR. i.e. treason, piracy, robbery, traffic in toxic or dangerous wastes, abetting suicide, drug trafficking, drug-related offences, property offences, multiple evasion of military service, apostasy, committing a third homosexual act, embezzlement by officials, theft by force, 'abduction not resulting in death', stealing cattle, illicit sex, crimes of an economic nature, adultery, corruption, 'vague offences related to internal and external security', political and economic offences, and 'crimes that do not result in the loss of life' (Joseph & Castan, 2013: 190).

4.2   Implied Limitations

Implied limitations of the use of criminal law to protect human rights derive from the general obligations to give effect to international human rights at the national level.

The Special Rapporteur developed general criteria for the assessment of the compliance of national law with obligations deriving from international human rights norms and their application in a concrete case. On this basis, the Special Rapporteur made specific findings regarding the overcriminalization related to counter-extremism, preparatory measures and the Internet.

As a basis for any evaluation, the Special Rapporteur used the risk of terrorism according to the Global Terrorism Index as a basis for a review of national criminal law ("Visit to Uzbekistan", 2022: para 7). In cases of a low threat level, a criminal justice approach is most likely to provide redress in a human rights compliant way and to close the impunity gap for international crimes ("Visit to Uzbekistan", 2022: para 18). Any national risk assessment, as a basis for passing criminal law, should be undertaken based on evidence gathered from direct consultations with civil society and community-based organisations ("Visit to Uzbekistan", 2022: para 34). The impact of legislation is examined through an empirically based assessment of the scale of misuse of the respective measures ("Impact of Measures to Address Terrorism and Violent Extremism on Civic Space and the Rights of Civil Society Actors and Human Rights Defenders," 2019: para 1–3, 12). The impact of national legislation is considered on the basis of findings of human rights treaty bodies in the light of the general functions of criminal law.

The Special Rapporteur used the principles of legality, legal certainty and proportionality to evaluate compliance of penal legislation with international human rights obligations. In general, the Special Rapporteur stresses that conduct criminalized as terrorist offences must be truly terrorist in nature, require specific intent and is restricted to activities with a genuine link to the operation of terrorist groups and acts ("Visit to France," 2019: para 30). However, no criteria are provided that could be applied to the definition of terrorism for the purposes of this test, e.g. the definition of transnational terrorism by the United Nations Special Tribunal for Lebanon (*Interlocutory Decision on the Applicable Law: Terrorism, Conspiracy, Homicide, Perpetration, Cumulative Charging*, 2011) as basis for identifying core elements to distinguish acts of terrorism from criminal acts (Saul, 2012: 79, et. seq.).

Regarding the wording of offences, the Special Rapporteur evaluates national legislation against the general definitions of key terms, e.g. gender, terrorism, incitement to terrorism and incitement to hatred, by UN human rights treaty bodies and other UN bodies ["Human Rights Impact of Counter-terrorism and Countering (Violent) Extremism Policies and Practices on the Rights of Women, Girls and the Family," 2021 (hereinafter, "A/HRC/46/36, 2021"): para 3], including the Security Council ("Visit to Kazakhstan", 2020: para 14). In the absence of globally agreed definitions, e.g. terrorism, violent extremism, radicalisation, the Special Rapporteur observed a general risk of national law criminalizing acts, which are protected by international human rights law, including freedom of expression, privacy, peaceful assembly and religious belief and expression, the right to a fair trial, the right to leave and return to one's country and the right to family life (A/HRC/46/36, 2021: para 4). The national definition must not anticipate solutions that are scientifically unjustifiable or controversial, but, while quoting from scientific studies (A/HRC/46/36, 2021: para 22), there seems to be no general standard for a sufficient scientific basis (A/HRC/46/36, 2021: para 28). The effectiveness of some regulations may be difficult to measure in the absence of semantic and conceptual clarity, e.g. regarding a predictive relationship between radicalisation and terrorism ["Human Rights Impact of Policies and Practices Aimed at Preventing and Countering Violent Extremism," 2020 (hereinafter, "A/HRC/43/46, 2020"): para 12, 16]. Such provisions are incompatible prima facie with the principles of proportionality and necessity (A/HRC/43/46, 2020: para 12). The criminalization of extremist thought and belief as perceived precursor of terrorism is a paradigm shift from the differentiation in criminal law between violent and non-violent actions ("Visit to Kazakhstan", 2020: para 24). The lack of engagement with civil society in drafting national or international regulations indicates a lack of determination of their legal, political, social and cultural effects.

The application of criminal law is guided by the same general limitations and, in addition, specific human rights obligations with a view to its enforceability and sanctions character. Human rights treaties provide for limitations of the application of each right and counterterrorism measures, including through criminal law, have been part of the scope of application of human rights treaties. As a consequence, counterterrorism measures are subject to a general human rights test as established by the practice of human rights treaty bodies, international and national courts and which has been widely accepted by States.[1]

Regarding criminal procedure law, respect for the general principles of a fair trial could prevent overcriminalization. The Special Rapporteur stated with regard to the role of expert evidence in criminal cases involving religious extremism or the production, dissemination or storage of religious materials that their opinion must be possible to challenge. The use of such expertise was evaluated against the principle of the separation of powers in criminal procedures and the equality of arms (A/HRC/43/46, 2020: para 45). Based on the application of these standards and the fairness of proceedings, exceptional rules for terrorism trials, e.g. regarding the access to evidence, can be dismissed according to Art. 14 ICCPR ("Visit to Kazakhstan", 2020: para 38). The Special Rapporteur also applied a proportionality test based on the threat level of terrorism to the allocation of resources to counter-terrorism on the basis of the number of offices ("Visit to Kazakhstan", 2020: para 43), which may indicate

---

1 See above 4.2.1.

the frequency and depth of counter-terrorism related measures, which, if based on criminal law, could lead to overcriminalization.

4.2.1   Implied Limitations Regarding Counter-extremism Measures

Regarding counter-extremism measures, the Special Rapporteur refers to the general evaluation of the risk of applying poorly defined concepts in legislation [*Report of the Special Rapporteur on the Promotion and Protection of Human Rights and Fundamental Freedoms While Countering Terrorism*, 2016 (hereinafter, "A/HRC/31/65, 2016"): para 21]. This raises concerns regarding the principle of legality as contained in Art. 15 CCPR. States should ensure that they do not have a negative impact on civil society's rights to freedom of association, expression, assembly and privacy and that the principles of necessity, proportionality and non-discrimination are respected (A/HRC/31/65, 2016: para 22).

For the offence of incitement to terrorism to comply with international human rights law, the crime must be limited to conduct that is truly terrorist in nature; must restrict freedom of expression no more than is necessary for the protection of national security, public order and safety or public health or morals; must be prescribed by law in precise language and avoid vague terms such as "glorifying" or "promoting" terrorism; must include an actual (objective) risk that the act incited will be committed; should expressly refer to intent to communicate a message and intent that this message incite the commission of a terrorist act; and should preserve the application of legal defences or principles leading to the exclusion of criminal liability by referring to "unlawful" incitement to terrorism. The Special Rapporteur recalled the statement of the Secretary-General that laws should only allow for the criminal prosecution of direct incitement to terrorism, that is, speech that directly encourages the commission of a crime, is intended to result in and is likely to, result in criminal action. A model offence of incitement to terrorism was also provided ("Ten Areas of Best Practices in Countering Terrorism," 2010: para 29–32).

Regarding measures that criminalize preparatory offences to terrorism and measures that focus on countering the appeal of, or preventing individuals from being drawn into, terrorism, the Special Rapporteur evaluated national law against obligations from specific human rights, in particular measures that target specific individuals or groups based on a determination that they are particularly at risk of violent extremism can be discriminatory and stigmatise various minority, ethnic, religious or indigenous groups (A/HRC/31/65, 2016: para 36f). In this context, the Special Rapporteur stressed that simply holding or peacefully expressing views that are considered extreme under any definition should never be criminalized, unless they are associated with violence or criminal activity (A/HRC/31/65, 2016: para 38). In referring to the findings of the HRC, the elements of "praising", "glorifying" or "justifying" terrorism must be clearly defined and liability cannot be based on the content of the speech, rather than the speaker's intention or the actual impact of the speech (A/HRC/31/65, 2016: para 39).

The Special Rapporteur expressed concern at the offence of "apology for terrorism" for its unjustified interference with the freedom of expression ("Visit to France", 2019: para 29). The concern is partly based on the fact that 85 percent of cases related to terrorism in France are based on this provision. Apart from the absolute numbers, the Special Rapporteur is concerned at the equation of apology with "positive moral judgement" and the uncertainty caused by the broad wording of the law, which enabled overreach. The penalty appears disproportionate as well. The proposal to apply the Rabat Plan of Action to prevent overreach could serve as a general instrument to evaluate and prevent overcriminalization in this context.

4.2.2   Implied Limitations Regarding the Use of the Internet

The Special Rapporteur refers to the findings of the HRC that repressive legislative measures to block, filter and ban specific content or entire websites on the Internet should not be generic but content-specific and independent judicial recourse must be available. Laws that allow executive authorities to block websites may not comply with this requirement in the absence of any initial judicial control or ex post facto judicial recourse (A/HRC/31/65, 2016: para 49).

Regulations of mass surveillance through automated data mining algorithms without any prior suspicion related to a specific individual or organisation can be evaluated for overcriminalization on the basis of the detailed criteria developed by the Special Rapporteur (*Report of the Special Rapporteur on the Promotion and Protection of Human Rights and Fundamental Freedoms While Countering Terrorism*, 2014: para 7, et. seq.). In addition, these considerations allow us to draw some general conclusions on the evaluation of criminal law.

The Special Rapporteur refers to the findings of the United Nations High Commissioner for Human Rights that international human rights law provided a clear and universal framework for the promotion and protection of the right to privacy, including in the context of mass surveillance ("The Right to Privacy in the Digital Age," 2014: para 47). Consequently, the regulations of States in general and their application in a specific case must comply with the requirements of art. 17 CCPR. The Special Rapporteur refers to the core principle of interdependence of all human rights, when underscoring the character of the right to privacy as enabling and supporting a range of other rights (A/HRC/46/36, 2021: para 11). An analysis can be carried out regarding the necessity and proportionality of the regulation and the compliance of the activities of law enforcement agencies with international human rights law. First, there must be an articulable and evidence-based justification for mass surveillance. Since the use of mass surveillance techniques effectively eliminates the right to privacy within the internet as an individualised proportionality analysis is impossible. As a consequence, the State must provide a meaningful public account to allow the public to balance the social interest in the protection of online privacy and the tangible benefits for counter-terrorism and law enforcement. According to the Special Rapporteur, the legislative process provides an opportunity for a transparent debate of the balance of privacy and security. Second, while the prevention, suppression and investigation of terrorism clearly is a legitimate objective to interfere with the right to privacy, the legislation justifying such interference must be of a particular quality. The wording of the legislation must be accessible, clear and precise in order to enable individuals to foresee the circumstances in which their communication may be subjected to surveillance ("General Comment No. 16", 1988: para 8). In addition, the authorisation of mass surveillance must be provided in primary legislation. The use of delegated legislation does not meet the quality of law requirement. Any permissible interference with any human right is limited by the essence of the right, which must not be impaired. Thus, overcriminalization can only be prevented through a public process and a system of ongoing evaluation of agreed indicators related to measurable benefits of the application of the regulation. Overcriminalization would occur, when national legislation does not provide for a periodic public account and a cost-benefit review by a body representing society at large.

4.2.3 Implied Limitations Regarding Emergency Measures

The Special Rapporteur stressed that each counter-terrorism measure taken by a State that functions as an emergency power by modifying the existing protection of human rights under the ordinary law must be measured by the necessity and proportionality tests and requirements (A/HRC/37/52, 2018: para 43). In implementation of the proportionality requirement, the Special Rapporteur refers to the criteria of the HRC and other UN human rights bodies for a general standard, according to which the longer or more entrenched the emergency, the narrower the margin of deference that could be left to the State ("General Comment No. 29", 2001: para 6; "General Comment No. 35", 2014: para 65–66; Siracusa Principles, 1984: principle 9). Overcriminalization related to emergency powers could be categorised on the basis of three criteria proposed by the Special Rapporteur. First, emergency powers are least likely to persist when they are tailor-made to a specific and defined crisis. Second, emergency powers that are subject to robust domestic and international oversight are less likely to persist, because it will be revealed when States, security agencies, courts and other enforcers of modified legal rules overstepped the limits of permissible emergency regulation. Third, emergency powers are easier to end when they are not hidden in the ordinary law (A/HRC/37/52, 2018: para 55). In this regard, the Special Rapporteur points at a general risk of overcriminalization as the duration of emergencies increases. It becomes harder to seal off those parts of security, intelligence and policing systems that operate under counter-terrorism legislation from the ordinary criminal justice system that deals with ordinary crimes. Numerous examples can be cited, including the erosion of the right to silence and the use of special courts in some countries, which are initially for terrorist suspects only, but are then widened to accommodate other crimes and criminal gangs implicating broader sites of State security (A/HRC/37/52, 2018: para 59). For the same reason, the Special Rapporteur recommends care should be taken when expansive and powerful counterterrorism legislation or administrative practice are implemented to deal with particular parts of a territory, because it can seep across entire jurisdictions (A/HRC/37/52, 2018: para 60).

5 Conflict of International Obligations

According to the findings above, there are different obligations in international treaties and customary international law concerning the content and application of criminal law on particular acts of terrorism. A finding on overcriminalization will depend on the relationship between the different sources of international law in the respective situation, i.e. customary and treaty law on human rights, general and specific human rights obligations and international counter-terrorism treaties. International humanitarian law and refugee law may also provide additional standards, which were not included in the present review. The conflict of these contradicting obligations must be resolved.

In principle, international law does not know any hierarchy of its sources. This principle is contested by some with a view to the special status of human rights obligations. It is argued implicitly that human rights treaties, due to their 'normative' character, which distinguishes them from treaties which are merely an exchange of rights and obligations between States, occupy a superior position in international law, and that any treaties conflicting with them should therefore be set aside in situations of conflict. This argument relies either on the primacy rule of art. 103 of the UN Charter with regard to the purpose of the United Nations to achieve international co-operation in promoting and encouraging respect for human rights or a prevailing character of human rights as *ius cogens* according to art. 53 of the Vienna Convention on the Law of Treaties. The characterisation of basic human rights provisions as *jus cogens* norms could establish additional standards for criminalization as far as they would oblige States not only to respect, protect and fulfil the rights in question, but make them responsible for potential breaches which result from State action or inaction. In addition, legal acts adopted by States seeking to legitimise or authorise a violation of jus cogens, e.g. amnesties for acts of torture, should not be recognised or given effect to by any other State. Finally, States should have jurisdiction to prosecute and punish individuals responsible for jus cogens violations exercising extraterritorial jurisdiction (De Schutter, 2010: 59 et. seq.). However, given the lack of clarity, which human rights obligation belongs to *jus cogens* and lack of agreement on its consequences, these considerations remain outside the present review.

Thus, the conflict of international obligations has to be resolved on the basis of general principles and the interpretation of the provisions of the different treaties. International treaties should be interpreted according to articles 31–33 of the Vienna Convention on the Law of Treaties. In addition, specific rules apply for the interpretation of international human rights treaties.

6 Conclusion

The international obligations to criminalize certain acts of terrorism contribute to ensure effective protection of human rights against the transnational character of these acts (Alston & Goodman, 2013: 391). At the same time, counter-terrorism legislation and administrative practice that normalises the limitation of rights for certain groups has long-term costs, increasingly affirmed by practitioners and experts in the field of countering and preventing violent extremism (A/HRC/37/52, 2018: para 60). Counterterrorism legislation should be evaluated based on agreed standards and methodologies.

The different general and specific criteria developed and applied by the Special Rapporteur to national legislation and its implementation could be structured for a general test of overcriminalization applicable by different human rights actors. However, the issue of overcriminalization in the context of counterterrorism would pass the legality and legitimacy test unless the specific criteria applied by the Special Rapporteur, including the main arguments, could be brought within a more detailed framework of the proportionality test and, thus, provide a basis for review (Gerards, 2013: 466 et. seq.). Based on these qualitative criteria for criminal law, national judges can also play a role in the prevention of overcriminalization through mainstreaming international human rights evaluation in their interpretation of national law (Smith, 2013: 541).

Model legislation as provided on incitement to terrorism by the Special Rapporteur and a collection of the findings of the HRC, the CERD Committee and the CAT Committee related to the compliance of criminal law with international human rights obligations could be transferred into model provisions.

In the absence of an internationally accepted definition of terrorism there is a need to define the core elements that distinguish acts of terrorism from other criminal acts. In applying a human rights test to regulations, still, the State may be entitled to use violence against certain acts to safeguard the stability of its political order. If such legislation protects a regime that systematically violates human rights or allows overreach into non-violent politics and social life, the moral and political force of counterterrorism measures as special and exceptional will be undermined. In order for national legislation to pass the legality test, it should define clearly the concept of terrorism in their respective juridical system (Angli, 2013: 19; Meliá & Petzsche, 2013: 96).

The enactment of criminal legislation is a human rights concern, as such laws are rarely repealed. Overall, the limitation of human rights of each individual through criminal law has increased steadily and any future comprehensive review of the surveillance total in a particular country should include criteria balancing obligations deriving from international human rights law. In this regard, overcriminalization can also be caused by the cumulative or overlapping effect for an individual potentially falling within the area of application of the legislation. The Special Rapporteur proposed a mapping of all individual pieces of legislation and executive orders and understanding their cumulative effect on the total enjoyment of human rights (A/73/361, 2018: para 27; "Visit to Kazakhstan", 2020: para 21; A/HRC/37/52, 2018: para 37).

The procedural protections under the rule of law cannot compensate for the enactment of excessive substantive law (Husak, 2008: 61). At the same time, international human rights standards are considered to be largely powerless against the expansion of criminal law into endangerment law in the context of counterterrorism. Treaty bodies should systematically develop the international human rights obligations in this direction through interpretation in order to remain relevant for the development of criminal law, which has deep-rooted social and sociological causes in the so-called risk society. The 'hazard law' is precisely an expression of this future-oriented logic, which not only manages risks, but claims to be able to eliminate them politically. The definition of risk and threat determines the reach of criminal law. The application of a human rights test to the application of legislation in a particular case would also correct extensive discretionary power of the executive.

The public debate suggested by the Special Rapporteur for the passing of regulations of mass surveillance should be expanded to all counterterrorism legislation as a basis for a proportionality test. This debate should be based on an obligation of the government to articulate the rationale for a particular legislation that could be used for interpretation by the executive and the judiciary.

Bibliography

Alston, P., and Goodman, R. (2013) *International Human Rights*. New York: Oxford University Press.

Anglí, M. L. (2013) "What Does 'Terrorism' Mean?" In: Masferrer, A. and Walker, C. (eds.) *Counter-Terrorism, Human Rights and the Rule of Law: Crossing Legal Boundaries in Defence of the State*. Cheltenham: Edward Elgar Publishing.

Angst, D., and Lantschner, E. (2020) *Handkommentar Zum Icerd: Internationales Ubereinkommen Zur Beseitigung Jeder Form Von Rassendiskriminierung*. Germany: Nomos Verlagsgesellschaft Mbh & Co.

Bautista de Arellana v. Colombia, CCPR/C/55/D/563/1993 (1995). Available at: https://tbinternet.ohchr.org/_layouts/15/treatybodyexternal/Download.aspx?symbolno=CCPR%2FC%2F55%2FD%2F563%2F1993. Accessed on December 01, 2022.

Belyatsky v. Belarus, CCPR/C/90/D/1296/2004 (HRC 2007). Available at: https://undocs.org/Home/Mobile?FinalSymbol=CCPR%2FC%2F90%2FD%2F1296%2F2004&Language=E&DeviceType=Desktop&LangRequested=False. Accessed on December 01, 2022.

Böhm, M. L. (2011) *Der "Gefährder" und das "Gefährdungsrecht": eine rechtssoziologische Analyse am Beispiel der Urteile des Bundesverfassungsgerichts über die nachträgliche Sicherungsverwahrung und die akustische Wohnraumüberwachung*. Göttingen: Universitätsverlag Göttingen.

Convention on the Elimination of Racial Discrimination. (December 21, 1965) A/Res/2106 A (XX). United Nations General Assembly. Available at: https://www.ohchr.org/en/instruments-mechanisms/instruments/international-convention-elimination-all-forms-racial. Accessed on December 01, 2022.

Delgado Páez v. Colombia. CCPR/C/39/D/195/1985. (1990).

De Schutter, O. (2010) *International Human Rights Law: Cases, Materials, Commentary*. Cambridge: Cambridge University Press.

"General Comment No. 11 on Article 20". (1983) *United Nations Office of the High Commissioner of Human Rights*. Available at: https://tbinternet.ohchr.org/_layouts/15/treatybodyexternal/Download.aspx?symbolno=INT%2FCCPR%2FGEC%2F4720&Lang=en. Accessed on December 01, 2022.

"General Comment No. 16 on the Right to Privacy (Article 17)". (1988) *United Nations Office of the High Commissioner of Human Rights.* Available at: https://tbinternet.ohchr.org/_layouts/15/treatybodyexternal/Download.aspx?symbolno=INT%2FCCPR%2FGEC%2F6624&Lang=en. Accessed on December 01, 2022.

"General Comment No. 29 on States of Emergency (Article 4)". CCPR/C/21/Rev.1/Add.11 (2001). *International Covenant on Civil and Political Rights.* Available at: CCPR/C /21/Rev.1/Add.11 (undocs.org). Accessed on December 01, 2022.

"General Comment No. 31 on The Nature of the General Legal Obligation imposed on State Parties to the Covenant". CCPR/C/21/Rev.1/Add. 13. (2004) *United Nations Office of the High Commissioner of Human Rights.* Available at: https://www.ohchr.org/en/resources/educators/human-rights-education-training/c-general-comment-no-31-nature-general-legal-obligation-imposed-states-parties-covenant-2004. Accessed on December 01, 2022.

"General Comment No. 35 on Article 9". CCPR/C/GC/35. (2014) *United Nations Office of the High Commissioner of Human Rights.* Available at: https://undocs.org/Home/Mobile?FinalSymbol=CCPR%2FC%2FGC%2F35&Language=E&DeviceType=Desktop&LangRequested=False. Accessed on December 01, 2022.

"General Comment No. 36 on Article 6". CCPR/C/GC/36. (2019) *United Nations Office of the High Commissioner of Human Rights.* Available at: https://www.ohchr.org/en/calls-for-input/general-comment-no-36-article-6-right-life. Accessed on December 01, 2022.

"General Recommendation No. 31 on the Prevention of Racial discrimination in the Administration and Functioning of the Criminal Justice System". (2005) *United Nations Committee on the Elimination of Racial Discrimination.* Available at: https://www.refworld.org/legal/general/cerd/2005/en/64371. Accessed on December 01, 2022.

"General Recommendation No. 35 on Combating Racist Hate Speech". (CERD/C/GC/35) (2013) *United Nations Committee on the Elimination of Racial Discrimination.* Available at: https://undocs.org/Home/Mobile?FinalSymbol=CERD%2FC%2FGC%2F35&Language=E&DeviceType=Desktop&LangRequested=False. Accessed on December 01, 2022.

Gerards, J. (2013) "How to improve the necessity test of the European Court of Human Rights". *Icon-International Journal of Constitutional Law,* 11(2): 466–490.

"Human rights impact of counter-terrorism and countering (violent) extremism policies and practices on the rights of women, girls and the family". (2021) In: *Report of the Special Rapporteur on the Promotion and Protection of Human Rights and Fundamental Freedoms While Countering Terrorism, Fionnuala Ní Aoláin* (A/HRC/46/36). United Nations Human Rights Council. Available at: https://undocs.org/Home/Mobile?FinalSymbol=A%2FHRC%2F46%2F36&Language=E&DeviceType=Desktop&LangRequested=False. Accessed on December 01, 2022.

"Human rights impact of policies and practices aimed at preventing and countering violent extremism". (2020) In: *Report of the Special Rapporteur on the Promotion and Protection of Human Rights and Fundamental Freedoms While Countering Terrorism* (A/HRC/43/46). United Nations Human Rights Council. Available at: https://www.ohchr.org/en/documents/reports/ahrc4346-human-rights-impact-policies-and-practices-aimed-preventing-and. Accessed on December 01, 2022.

Husak, D. (2008) *Overcriminalization: The Limits of the Criminal Law*. New York: Oxford University Press.

"Impact of measures to address terrorism and violent extremism on civic space and the rights of civil society actors and human rights defenders". (2019) In *Report of the Special Rapporteur on the Promotion and Protection of Human Rights and Fundamental Freedoms While Countering Terrorism* (A/HRC/40/52). United Nations Human Rights Council. Available at: https://undocs.org/Home/Mobile?FinalSymbol=A%2FHRC%2F40%2F52&Language=E&DeviceType=Desktop&LangRequested=False. Accessed on December 01, 2022.

Interlocutory Decision on the Applicable Law: Terrorism, Conspiracy, Homicide, Perpetration, Cumulative Charging (STL-11-01/I). (2011) UN Special Tribunal for Lebanon (Appeals Chamber). Available at: https://www.refworld.org/jurisprudence/caselaw/stl/2011/en/77425. Accessed on December 01, 2022.

International Convention against the Taking of Hostages. (December 17, 1979) A/Res/34/146. United Nations General Assembly. Available at: https://undocs.org/Home/Mobile?FinalSymbol=A%2FRES%2F34%2F146&Language=E&DeviceType=Desktop&LangRequested=False. Accessed on December 01, 2022.

International Covenant on Civil and Political Rights. (December 16, 1966) A/Res/2200 A (XXI). Available at: https://undocs.org/Home/Mobile?FinalSymbol=A%2FRES%2F2200(XXI)&Language=E&DeviceType=Desktop&LangRequested=False. Accessed on December 01, 2022.

Joseph, S., and Castan, M. (2013) *The International Covenant on Civil and Political Rights: Cases, Materials, and Commentary* (3rd ed.). New York: Oxford University Press.

Krey, V., & Windgätter, O. (2012) "The Untenable Situation of German Criminal Law: Against Quantitative Overloading, Qualitative Overcharging, and the Overexpansion of Criminal Justice". *German Law Journal*, 13(6): 579–605.

Meliá, M., and Petzsche, A. (2013) "Terrorism as a Criminal Offence". In: Masferrer, A. and Walker C. (eds) *Counter-Terrorism, Human Rights and the Rule of Law. Crossing Legal Boundaries in Defence of the State*. Cheltenham: Edward Elgar Publishing.

Office for Democratic Institutions and Human Rights. (2007) *Countering Terrorism, Protecting Human Rights. A Manual*. Warsaw: Organisation for Security and Cooperation in Europe. Available at: https://www.osce.org/files/f/documents/d/6/29103.pdf. Accessed on December 01, 2022.

Parker, T. (2019) *Avoiding the Terrorist Trap: Why Respect for Human Rights is the Key to Defeating Terrorism*. London: Imperial College Press.

Report of the Special Rapporteur on the promotion and protection of human rights and fundamental freedoms while countering terrorism (A/69/397). (2014) United Nations General Assembly. Available at: https://undocs.org/Home/Mobile?FinalSymbol =A%2F69%2F397&Language=E&DeviceType=Desktop&LangRequested=False. Accessed on December 01, 2022.

Report of the Special Rapporteur on the promotion and protection of human rights and fundamental freedoms while countering terrorism (A/73/361). (2018) United Nations General Assembly. Available at: https://undocs.org/Home/Mobile?FinalSymbol =A%2F73%2F361&Language=E&DeviceType=Desktop&LangRequested=False. Accessed on December 01, 2022.

Report of the Special Rapporteur on the promotion and protection of human rights and fundamental freedoms while countering terrorism (A/HRC/31/65). (2016) United Nations Human Rights Council. Available at: https://undocs.org /Home/Mobile?FinalSymbol=A%2FHRC%2F31%2F65&Language=E&DeviceType =Desktop&LangRequested=False. Accessed on December 01, 2022.

Report of the special rapporteur on the promotion and protection of human rights and fundamental freedoms while countering terrorism on the human rights challenge of states of emergency in the context of countering terrorism (A/HRC/37/52). (2018) United Nations Human Rights Council. Available at: https://undocs.org /Home/Mobile?FinalSymbol=A%2FHRC%2F37%2F52&Language=E&DeviceType =Desktop&LangRequested=False. Accessed on December 01, 2022.

Resolution 1373. S/Res/1373. (September 28, 2001) United Nations Security Council. Available at: https://www.unodc.org/pdf/crime/terrorism/res_1373_english.pdf. Accessed on December 01, 2022.

Resolution 1624. S/Res/1624. (September 14, 2005) United Nations Security Council. Available at: https://undocs.org/Home/Mobile?FinalSymbol=S%2FRES%2F1624 (2005)&Language=E&DeviceType=Desktop&LangRequested=False. Accessed on December 01, 2022.

Resolution 2178. S/Res/2178. (September 24, 2014) United Nations Security Council. Available at: https://www.undocs.org/S/RES/2178%20(2014). Accessed on December 01, 2022.

Rome Statute of the International Criminal Court. (July 17, 1998) United Nations, Treaty Series, 2187(38544). Depositary: Secretary-General of the United Nations. Available at: http://treaties.un.org. Accessed on December 01, 2022.

Saul, B. (2012) "Civilising the Exception: Universally Defining Terrorism". In: Masferrer, A. (ed), *Post 9/11 and the State of Permanent Legal Emergency: Security and Human Rights in Countering Terrorism*. Dordrecht: Springer.

Schabas, W. A. (2004) *An Introduction to the International Criminal Court* (2nd ed.) Cambridge: Cambridge University Press.

Scheinin, M. (2020) "Security, Right to, International Protection". In: Wolfrum, R. (ed.), *The Max Planck Encyclopedia of Public International Law,* Oxford: Oxford University Press, 2008.

Siracusa Principles on the Limitation and Derogation Provisions in the International Covenant on Civil and Political Rights. E/CN.4/1985/4. (September 28, 1984) United Nations Economic and Social Council. Available at: https://undocs.org/Home/Mobile?FinalSymbol=E%2FCN.4%2F1985%2F4&Language=E&DeviceType=Desktop&LangRequested=False. Accessed on December 01, 2022.

Smith, S. F. (2013) "Overcoming Overcriminalization". *Journal of Criminal Law and Criminology*, 102(3).

Special Rapporteur on Counter-terrorism and Human Rights. A/HRC/RES/49/10. (April 12, 2022) United Nations Human Rights Council. Available at: https://undocs.org/Home/Mobile?FinalSymbol=A%2FHRC%2FRES%2F49%2F10&Language=E&DeviceType=Desktop&LangRequested=False. Accessed on December 01, 2022.

Suarez de Gueterro v. Colombia, CCPR/C/15/D/45/1979 (1982) Available at: https://tbinternet.ohchr.org/_layouts/15/treatybodyexternal/Download.aspx?symbolno=CCPR%2FC%2F15%2FD%2F45%2F1979. Accessed on December 01, 2022.

"Ten Areas of Best Practices in Countering Terrorism". (2010) In: *Report of the Special Rapporteur on the Promotion and Protection of Human Rights and Fundamental Freedoms While Countering Terrorism, Martin Scheinin* (A/HRC/16/51). United Nations Human Rights Council. Available at: https://undocs.org/Home/Mobile?FinalSymbol=a%2Fhrc%2F16%2F51&Language=E&DeviceType=Desktop&LangRequested=False. Accessed on December 01, 2022.

"The Right to Privacy in the Digital Age". (2014) In: *Report of the Office of the United Nations High Commissioner for Human Rights* (A/HRC/27/37). United Nations Human Rights Council. Available at: https://undocs.org/Home/Mobile?FinalSymbol=A%2FHRC%2F27%2F37&Language=E&DeviceType=Desktop&LangRequested=False. Accessed on December 01, 2022.

United Nations Global Counter-Terrorism Strategy. A/RES/60/288. (September 20, 2006) United Nations General Assembly. Available at: https://undocs.org/Home/Mobile?FinalSymbol=A%2FRES%2F60%2F288&Language=E&DeviceType=Desktop&LangRequested=False. Accessed on December 01, 2022.

United Nations Global Counter-Terrorism Strategy: Seventh Review. A/RES/75/291. (July 2, 2021) United Nations General Assembly. Available at: https://undocs.org/Home/Mobile?FinalSymbol=A%2FRES%2F75%2F291&Language=E&DeviceType=Desktop&LangRequested=False. Accessed on December 01, 2022.

"Visit to France". (2019) In: *Report of the Special Rapporteur on the Promotion and Protection of Human Rights and Fundamental Freedoms While Countering Terrorism*

(A/HRC/40/52/Add.4). United Nations Human Rights Council. Available at: https://www.ohchr.org/en/documents/country-reports/ahrc4052add4-report-special-rapporteur-promotion-and-protection-human. Accessed on December 01, 2022.

"Visit to Kazakhstan". (2020) In: *Report of the Special Rapporteur on the Promotion and Protection of Human Rights and Fundamental Freedoms While Countering Terrorism* (A/HRC/43/46/Add.1). United Nations Human Rights Council. Available at: https://undocs.org/Home/Mobile?FinalSymbol=A%2FHRC%2F43%2F46%2FAdd.1&Language=E&DeviceType=Desktop&LangRequested=False. Accessed on December 01, 2022.

Visit to Uzbekistan. (2022) In: *Report of the Special Rapporteur on the Promotion and Protection of Human Rights While Countering Terrorism* ((A/HRC/49/45/Add.1)). United Nations Human Rights Council. Available at: https://undocs.org/Home/Mobile?FinalSymbol=A%2FHRC%2F49%2F45%2FAdd.1&Language=E&DeviceType=Desktop&LangRequested=False. Accessed on December 01, 2022.

CHAPTER 5

Criminalization: Reflection on Theories

Chirag Balyan

1   Introduction

Criminalization stands as a cornerstone of modern legal systems, embodying the intricate interplay between societal norms, legal principles, and the administration of justice. As such, the theoretical exploration of criminalization represents a fundamental endeavor in understanding the underlying principles and objectives that guide the formulation and application of criminal laws. This chapter aims to provide a comprehensive examination of the theoretical foundations, critiques, and advancements in the field of criminalization.

Part I of this chapter delves into the inherent complexities surrounding the aims and functions of criminal law in establishing a normative theory. Despite its fundamental role in shaping societal behavior and maintaining order, the overarching objectives of criminalization often prove elusive, subject to interpretation and debate. Scholars have grappled with the inherent tension between the punitive and preventive functions of criminal law, questioning whether its aims truly align with principles of justice, deterrence, rehabilitation, or societal protection. By critically analyzing the perceived futility in defining the aims of criminal law, this section sets the stage for a deeper exploration of existing theoretical frameworks.

In Part II, the focus shifts towards an in-depth examination of prominent theories of criminalization proposed by leading legal scholars. Scholars such as Andrew Ashworth, Douglas Husak, Nicola Lacey, Antony Duff, Alan Norrie among others, have offered diverse perspectives on the nature and scope of criminalization. Through a comparative analysis of these theories, this section aims to elucidate the underlying assumptions, methodologies, and implications of different approaches to understanding the process of criminalization.

Building upon the foundation laid by existing theories, Part III undertakes a rigorous critique of these frameworks, interrogating their strengths, limitations, and potential areas for refinement. While each theory offers valuable insights into the complexities of criminalization, they are not without their shortcomings. Issues such as conceptual ambiguity, cultural bias, and practical applicability pose significant challenges to the development of a comprehensive theory of criminalization.

Finally, in Part IV, this chapter proposes a novel theory of criminalization based on Fuller's eight principles of legality. In addition to these foundational principles, the paper introduces six additional principles – fair and representative labeling of crimes, proportional and deserved punishment, necessity principle, presence of fault requirements, presumption of innocence, and burden of proof on the prosecution or complainant – to advance a composite theory of criminalization. Through the integration of these principles, this chapter seeks to offer a holistic framework that addresses the multifaceted nature of criminalization while providing valuable insights into the formulation and application of criminal laws in contemporary legal contexts.

However, I must clarify that I diverge from Fuller's proposition that laws failing to adhere to his principles of legality lack the force of law itself.

In essence, this chapter endeavors to contribute to the ongoing discourse surrounding criminalization by providing a comprehensive analysis of existing theories, critiques, and proposed advancements. By elucidating the complexities inherent in the process of criminalization, it aims to inform future research and policymaking endeavors in the field of criminal law and justice.

2   Futility of Aims and Functions of Criminal Law in Finding Normative Theory

What parameters should a legislature follow to decide whether a wrong should be labelled as a crime? The answer to this question has raised more disagreements than agreements.

One thing is definite, the criminal law should not be an automatic choice to deal with any kind of wrongs. It must be reserved for those serious wrongs which if they remain unpunished will shock the conscience of society and not just threaten the sense of security. The offence of culpable homicide, grievous hurt, rape, kidnapping etc. will fall under this category. Also, those property offences where in the course of commission, threat to bodily harm is real and imminent, can also be part of this category. The example of these would be robbery, dacoity, housebreaking, mischief by fire in a dwelling house. All civilized countries have a consensus that these offences must be dealt with only with criminal law.

However, there are a large number of criminal laws across the world which have been accused to be created through chaotic, whimsical, and unprincipled manner.

The unprincipled criminalization has made many to question the limits of criminal law. The inherent assumption in the above proposition is that there are indeed principles of criminalization and criminal law has its own boundaries. Both these assumptions are connected in the sense that when one starts writing about one the other one is naturally discussed.

But to know what these principles of criminalization are, one should be sure about what criminalization is (Duff, 2018: 52). The legal philosophers try to understand the meaning of criminalization with reference to the aims and functions of criminal law. There is no consensus on what the legitimate aims and functions of the criminal law are. These aims and functions depend upon the legal theory which a legal philosopher ascribes to.

Some theorists analyze the aims of criminal law with reference to aims of punishment. From this perspective, criminal law is a *sui generis* field of law which is characteristically motivated by punishment. For example, (Moore, 1997) gives primacy to the question of what to punish, then to the question of what to criminalize? The extension of viewing criminal law from the prism of punishment is to also highlight its retributive nature. The legitimacy of retribution is premised on finding moral blameworthiness and culpability of rational and autonomous individuals (Norrie, 2014). The consequence is insistence on *mens rea* requirement in the definition of crime. However, strict liability offences occupy the majority of the space in our penal codes. How does a normative theory of criminalization based on liberal ideals justify the punishment based on strict liability offences? In fact, Simester and von Hirsch argue that normatively strict liability offences are indeed defective (Simester and Hrisch, 2011: 7). But, Simons has presented an argument that in some scenarios strict liability may be justified even for culpability-based retributivists (Simons, 1996-97).

Therefore, attempts of philosophers to ascertain the spectrum of criminalization based on discordant views on aims and functions of criminal law is futile. Another challenge of this approach is that when an enquiry is to identify proper aims and functions of criminal law, legal philosophers essentially comment about what criminalization *ought* to be. This enquiry results into questioning whether criminalization *ought* to be used to inflict punishment in cases of – moral offences, dangerousness, inchoate offences, remote harms, regulatory offences, strict liability offences, preventive measures, etc. The *ought to be* approach implies that criminal law has some boundaries in which it must operate.

For Bentham, criminal law is justified if it furthers utilitarian ideals. Indian Penal Code was drafted by Macaulay based on Benthamite ideals (Chan, et al. 2011). According to Mill, the proper aim of criminal law is to prevent harm to others (Gray, 1991: 14). This is referred to as the harm principle. The modern account of harm principle is developed by Fienberg defining harm as "setback to interests" (Feinberg, 1984) (Feinberg, 1985) (Feinberg, 1989) (Fienberg, 1990). The alternate view to harm principle is legal moralism which keeps wrongdoing at the centre (Duff, 2018: 53–75). For example, Moore posits that the proper aim of the criminal law is to inflict deserved punishment for the wrongful conduct on the culpable wrongdoers (Moore, 1997).

The criminal law aims have also been characterized distinctively as to protect private interests or public wrongs (Duff, 2007: 140). Ripstein argues that the proper aim of criminal law is to prevent violation of equal freedom or of sovereignty (Ripstein, 2006: 216). Ashworth notes that criminal law has three core functions viz. declaratory, preventive, and regulatory (Ashworth, 2008).

But there is no consensus on a normative baseline to determine such boundaries. Further, the discussion of aims and functions of criminal law doesn't necessarily tell us about the intrinsic nature or distinctiveness of crime i.e., what makes wrong a crime? (Farmer, 2014: 81).

I am not arguing that there should not be any normative limits on criminal law. I am simply suggesting the difficulties in finding any boundaries of criminal law. Ashworth & Horder states that the boundaries of criminal law are large due to "exercise of political power at particular points in history" (Ashworth and Horder, 2013: 3). But what counts as large is not very clear.

The criminal law is a result of the socio-political milieu in which it operates. The criminal laws can be used to extend affirmative action protection by enacting laws which prohibits marginalization and prevents victimization of certain races, castes, gender, etc. The economy also plays an important role in shaping the boundaries of criminal law. The Indian government is taking constant efforts to remove criminal laws to enhance the ease of doing business and ease of living. Then there are international obligations which require the State to enact criminal laws on certain subjects. Even the implementation of criminal law doesn't happen in vacuum. The attitudes, beliefs, predispositions of police, prosecutors, and courts play a critical role in decisions such as – what to criminalize, whom to criminalize, extent of criminalization, or even not to criminalize at all. The intent of constitution makers as well as the legislature equally plays a significant part. This discretion can result in a continuum of over-criminalization, criminalization, and under-criminalization. None of these three phenomena are absolute, it varies according to State or non-State actors, subject, as well as the environment within which they operate. Having said that I will not stretch this argument, as Duff does, to suggest that principles of criminalization must reflect such realities. Duff argues that "[a] theory of criminalization must be grounded in an account of the role of criminal law as part of the institutional structure of a polity; and such an account must itself be grounded in an account of the nature and aims of a polity – in political theory."

3 Theories of Criminalization

Even if we confine our discussion to substantive criminal law, there is no single theory or set of principles which runs through any penal law (Hall and Glueck, 1958: 15). Hart, Jr. argues that the purpose of a master theory of criminalization is to "[decide] upon a course of action"; and such decisions do not occur in institutional vacuum (Hart Jr., 1958: 402).

The complexity of the criminalization process has dissuaded some legal philosophers from pursuing the master theory of criminalization. These scholars have moved from building a normative theory to understanding "the complex range of normative questions that bear on the various processes of criminalization" (Duff, et al. 2013).

The philosophers like Ashworth in their attempt to find such a normative theory have tried to find the core of criminal law (Ashworth, 2008), others have attempted to push the boundaries of criminal law to include a new range of conducts which are not traditionally considered to be part of the criminal law.

The casualty of this approach is that it undermines an individual as a rationale and an autonomous agent. These trends and practices of criminalization bring out the antinomies in the liberal theory of criminal law (Norrie, 2009).

While many philosophers wish that criminalization must be done by following normative standards, Husak (2008) and Baker (2016) identified normative standards from what the law is. In classifying wrongs as to how they should be dealt with – retributive justice or remedial justice; there are no prior established principles to make such a decision. However, this doesn't mean that no such principles exist. Huda argues that "general agreement of civilized countries, as shown by the result of the selection, strongly points to the existence of common principles leading to common results." (Huda, 1902: 3) Thus, by deductive reasoning some normative principles can be found from the penal laws.

Husak identified internal and external constraints on the criminal law and argued that internal constraints on the criminalization can be identified from the existing criminal laws. The four internal constraints which Husak identified from the criminal laws are: prohibited conduct must involve a nontrivial harm or evil; the conduct must be in some sense wrongful; punishment; punishment is justified only when and to the extent that it is deserved; and the onus of criminalization lies on those who initiate it. Baker insisted that moral constraints on the criminalization can be seen in the constitutional law framework (Baker, 2016). Baker argues that the right not to be criminalized is not just a fundamental human right rooted in morality but is also a constitutional right.

The approach of Husak and Baker in identifying what criminal law *ought to be* from what criminal law *is* has normative deficiencies. Husak recognizes in his works that criminalization can also be caused by excessive discretion vested with police, prosecutors, and courts (Husak, 2010: 624), but his own theory of constraints on criminalization fails to take this into account. As Gardener points out, an attempt to draw foundational principles from positive law is a non-starter. The criminal law is set in motion when a police officer with discretionary power decides to over-charge a trivial harm (Gardner, 2008). Baker's theory also suffers from the same vices. Moreover, constitutions by large don't have any explicit principle of right not to be criminalized. Latika has argued that in the absence of an explicit constitutional right not to be criminalized, unprincipled criminalization can be regulated by re-structuring the policy of criminalization along the principles of constitutional morality.

The use of constitutional morality to restructure policy of criminalization is difficult because judges decide constitutional morality on a case to case basis based on their beliefs and perceptions of what the constitution is or ought to be. Thus, constitutional morality like normativity has no consensus on its content and bounds. Constitutional morality can be used for decriminalization of certain offences or even striking down excessive powers of criminal justice system (CJS) functionaries, but how can legislature or CJS functionaries use it to restructure policy of criminalization is not convincing.

Another approach to determine the contours criminalization is through defining crime. This is both a problematic and a narrow approach. The approach is problematic because there is no agreed upon definition of crime. Therefore, how can one find out the scope of criminalization through the definition of crime? Even if we consider the positivist definition of crime i.e., crime is any wrong which is declared as such by the State, then also there are difficulties in gathering true scope of criminalization. The approach is narrow because it confines criminalization to substantive criminal law. In reality, criminalization could be a result of various actors of the criminal justice system. The actions of police, public prosecutors, and courts can also result in criminalization. Dubber argues that "an account of criminalization needs an account not of crime simpliciter, but of law in general, and of criminal law within it" (Dubber, 2010: 191).

4 Critique of Existing Theories of Criminalization

The current theories of criminalization have created a mass of confusion. Though these theories label themselves as normative, they seem to have abandoned that cause. The philosophers seem to be in contest to present a criminalization theory which conceptualizes a justificatory framework for the present state of criminal laws. I believe this is not a right starting point in creating criminalization principles. The present trend of criminal law is characterized by strict liability offences, reverse onus clauses, inchoate offences, possession offences, moral offences, offences based on paternalism, offences based on public opinion, disproportionate punishments, broad preventive powers, and wide discretion of CJS functionaries. What most of the theories of criminalization do is that they first identify the problem with each trend and then try to justify these trends by finding a broad theory which either justify all these trends or at least some of these trends. In essence they seek justification for everything that is wrong about criminal law today. Criminal laws, however bad they could be, as an instrument of social organization will always deliver some good. Does that mean they become justified? I suppose, no.

To my mind a respectable theory of criminalization should not aim to construct justificatory principles by attempting to accommodate even distortions of criminal law. The starting point for a normative theory should be to define legitimate boundaries of criminal law and then see whether existing trends are justified within those boundaries or not. The normative theory which is built by reverse engineering loses its essence with such an approach. The legitimacy of criminal law should not be judged by what benefit society might get out of it but by the measure of its own inherent quality.

The modern State uses criminal law for primarily three purposes. First, is exact revenge. The State uses the instrumentality of criminal law to take retribution so that people don't take law and order into their own hands. So, the maintenance of law and order is an incidental objective. The primary objective of the State is to tell society that one need not worry about criminal wrongdoings, we care for you, and we will use our machinery to take your revenge.

Second, is to deter people from committing wrongdoings. The State creates criminal law to warn people that if you commit criminal wrongs, then you must face the consequences viz. to deal with the might of the State and the criminal law. The mushroom growth of criminal law is because of the belief of the State that individuals may not commit proscribed wrongs if they know criminal law will be the consequence. Third, is to prevent crimes. Accordingly, the State based on prediction takes punitive measures against individuals who are deemed a risk to the society.

If we pragmatically question the necessity of using criminal law for these three purposes, I understand that no philosopher will doubt the appropriateness of achieving these purposes through criminal law. However, one can find a general consensus amongst philosophers that to some extent each of these purposes raises some questions of normative validity. The primary reason is that these measures are used by the State even when they are not desirable. This results in excessiveness of criminal law. The criminal law by its nature can be said to be exacting but it is not excessive, its purposes are necessary as well as legitimate. However, the manner in which the State employs the criminal law makes it excessive as well. Therefore, an appropriate theory of criminalization must check this excessiveness. Ashworth in this area has made some important contributions by invoking principles including the principle of – minimalist criminal law, criminal law as a means of last resort, principle of proportionality, and principle of necessity. But these principles by themselves are not adequate. My own account of normative theory of criminalization will speak for itself why I call Ashworth's account inadequate.

5   Proposing a Theory of Criminalization

In any legal system which is governed by the rule of law, criminal law must have some constraints. These constraints should guide the decision of the legislature as well as of those who implement criminal law on a day-to-day basis in society as well courts. The aim of such constraints must be to restrict State excessiveness. They should ensure that criminal law is not just any other tool to impose sanctions on individuals. Fuller's eight principles of legality can put effective checks on State excessiveness (Fuller, 1969: 209–10). These principles are, generality, promulgation, non-retroactive laws, clarity, no contradictions, possibility of compliance, constancy, and congruence between official action and declared rule. In fact, the advantage of rule of law approach in formulating principles of criminalization is that it treats individuals as end in themselves and thus, recognizes their capacity for autonomous decision-making. The rule of law approach much like criminalization principles aims to establish a constraining framework for the exercise of power. The rule of law approach ensures that power be it with legislature or police or courts to criminalize is not exercised on ad hoc or purely discretionary basis.

The aim of a normative theory of criminalization should be to inform lawmakers how criminal laws ought to be drafted. As far as substantive law is concerned it deals with issues including selection of wrongs as crime, definition of offence, nature of punishment, quantum of punishment, selection of defenses and their scope. Under procedural law, criminalization theory must attempt to limit the discretion of police, prosecutors, courts, and other institutions. The effort must be to develop objective criterions, and checks and balances which can ensure the decision making by CJS functionaries doesn't cause unnecessary criminalization.

Therefore, to construct a composite theory of criminalization, six other principles can be added to the list of Fuller's eight principles. These are, fair and representative labelling of crimes, proportional and deserved punishment, necessity principle, presence of fault requirements, presumption of innocence, & burden of proof on the prosecution or complainant.

Now I'll make a brief comment on how these fourteen principles can contribute to a normative theory of criminalization.

5.1 *Generality*

The criminal laws must be general in nature. These rules should not distinguish or differentiate between various subjects on the basis of caste, color, race, gender etc. Stated in this manner, the principle will pose difficulties to monetary bonds as a requirement of bail which has been proved to be more detrimental to poor and marginalized communities.

However, generality also doesn't mean affirmative protection to the vulnerable groups such as children, women, historically marginalized castes, races and religion can't be provided. The principle of generality must ensure equality amongst equals. It will be a check on arbitrary power of the State to use criminal law to target some communities or groups. So, from a viewpoint of substantive law, the principle of generality will challenge laws which criminalizes certain tribes. For example, the colonial law passed by the British India government in 1871 titled as the Criminal Tribe Act (CTA) was passed, labelling about 200 communities in several provinces as "criminal" communities under this Act. The colonial officers made significant efforts to identify several communities as born "criminals." It gave the police control over nomadic communities. Specifically, these communities had to register themselves at the nearest police station and obtain a license. They could not go out of their designated district without the permission of the police. If they changed their residence, information had to be supplied and permission requested. If a member of a community was not present for more than a year in their settlement without police permission, they had to suffer through three years of prison time (Singh, 2021). Even after independence these nomadic tribes were freed from one derogatory colonial identity but remained marked by another postcolonial identity. The behavior of the police did not change, and the Habitual Offender

Act, 1952 re-created the conditions that caused the marginalized and stigmatized nomadic communities.

5.2 *Promulgation*

This principle requires that laws must be known to the public. The public must have fair and reasonable notice about expected behavior. For criminal laws to be legitimate, the proper notice requirement must insist that laws must not only be promulgated but they must be widely circulated and advertised even in the local languages. Macaulay proposed that each member of the population should be furnished with a copy of the Code in their own native language (Macaulay, et al. 1838). The reasonable time must elapse between promulgation and application of law. The executive criminal laws are usually not consistent with this requirement. Though these laws satisfy promulgation requirements in technical sense, since these laws are drafted behind closed doors, the public is usually not aware how and when these laws are passed. The requirement of maxim that ignorance of law is not an excuse makes such executive laws more onerous. The Indian case of *State of Maharashtra v.* MH *George* (AIR 1965 SC 722) exemplifies this issue. Even criminal law researchers can't tell the precise extent of how many criminal laws are in operation on a given day, then how can we expect an ordinary person to be aware of these laws especially when they are promulgated in official gazettes. Most of such laws don't require mandatory advertisement and dissemination of such laws.

Therefore, I suggest that an additional requirement to promulgation should be mandatory public and stakeholder participation. The criminal law should not be created by the mere brute force of majority of the legislatures or just by the executive whims and fancies. The theory of criminalization must insist that lawmakers before enacting a criminal law must put the reasons before the society that why particular wrongs could not have been dealt with by any means other than the criminal law. As Edward Coke stated, "The law is unknown to him that knoweth not the reason thereof and the knowne certaintie of the law is the safetie of all" (Coke 1628). This must be followed by the mandatory public consultation and discussions on the repercussion of crime. In fact, requirement that such criminal laws should be cleared by supermajority is not a bad idea. Even a majoritarian government, on an average have a vote share of 40–45% (Ramani, 2019). Therefore, government with full majority in parliament also doesn't reflect the aspirations of even half of the population. The executive criminal law in this sense doesn't cater to aspiration of people at all. Therefore, as a matter of rule, executive should not have the power to create criminal laws.

In any case, the mere fact that crimes are public wrongs should not be enough to justify criminalization. Public discourse and participation must be the precursor to labeling of crimes. I don't mean to say that criminal law should reflect populist notions. I am just insisting that there should be mandatory public participation in criminal law making. Ultimately, the legislature must pass laws using the principled approaches, I have suggested in this paper. The participation of the public in the process of creation of criminal law ensures inclusivity and adds another layer of legitimacy. This added layer of legitimacy is important because authority of the legislature to pass a criminal law doesn't necessarily give it legitimacy.

The participative criminal law making also provides enough time to the public to adjust their beliefs, attitude, and actions in consonance with the new regime. It educates the people about crime in making. Criminal law serves an important purpose of education. It communicates to rationale agents that they should decide their actions and conduct considering the content of criminal law. The requirement of 'notice' of criminal law usually means that when criminal law is enacted it must be declared so to the public. The notice requirement is better fulfilled if there is participative criminal law making. The foremost criticism of existing principles of criminalization is that they don't consider that criminal law doesn't operate in vacuum, and it operates in historical, social, economic, political, constitutional, and religious context. The mandatory public participation and discourse on each aspect of criminal law will ensure that the environment in which criminal law exists and operates is also taken into consideration.

To sum up, criminal laws must be promulgated. Additionally, there must be mandatory advertisement in all the local languages. Further, laws must not be promulgated without compulsory public and stakeholders' consultation. The legislature must provide reason to the society that the wrong can't be effectively and efficiently addressed by any other means but criminal law. The executive as a matter of rule should not be allowed to create criminal law.

5.3   Non-retroactive Laws

The principle of non-retroactivity of criminal laws is a widely accepted principle across civilized nations. It is based on the principle of "Nullum crimen sine lege" which means there can't be a crime without a law. Similarly, the principle *"nullum poena sine lege"* means no punishment without law. The preventive detention or pre-trial detention imposes punishment without any substantive criminal law. Therefore, preventive powers of the State are difficult to justify as per this principle of legality. Duff argued for creating preventive crimes in order to overcome this difficulty.

I suggest that a slight deviation from the principle of non-retroactivity can be permitted by ensuring that preventive punishment is based on an objective criterion only when it is necessary and is used as a means of last resort.

5.4   Possibility of the Compliance

In a strict sense, the criminal law should be complied if it exists and is notified as well. Despite fulfilling formal validity requirements, some criminal laws could be so onerous that they should not be required to be complied. In a normative system, criminal laws requiring impossible must not exist and even if they exist their non-compliance should not attract punishment. Criminal laws which command impossible confer "lawless unlimited power" (Fuller, 1964) to the State and its agencies.

Fullers gives the example of state of affair offences, possession offences, as well as strict liability offences. A just law can't require a person of unsound mind to obey the law all the time. Similarly, a person who does an act under mistake of fact or by accident or inadvertence with no fault of her own should not be held liable as such men "can't pattern their actions after the law."

Further, a person should not be liable for violating the immigration laws if such person couldn't board the flight to leave the country for reasons beyond her control. Technically speaking, any single day of unauthorized stay in a foreign country violates the criminal law. However, there could be state of affairs such as pregnancy due to which airline authorities may not permit a lady to board the flight (Finau v Department of Labour, 1984). Fuller argues in this situation the law must not punish the pregnant lady as it was impossible for her to comply with this law.

With respect to *mens rea* requirement in the definition of crime, Fuller argues that its presence ensures that citizens can obey the law. Fuller notes that strict criminal liability of a person who might have acted innocently and with due care is "the most serious infringement of the principle that the law should not command the impossible."

5.5   Constancy

This principle as applied to criminal laws entails that criminal laws should remain relatively consistent, and when alterations occur, the resulting impact and rationale for the modifications must be ascertainable at any given moment. Frequent alterations render the legal framework unstable, causing individuals to lack confidence in understanding or predicting legal provisions. Consequently, the law becomes neither easily graspable nor practical to enforce.

5.6 Clarity

Lawmakers frequently draft criminal statutes with broad and ambiguous language. Their concern lies in the possibility that if they define the terms too narrowly and precisely, canny criminals might discover methods to circumvent the literal wording of the law. However, when criminal statutes are broad and lacking in precision, they grant significant discretionary power to criminal justice functionaries, enabling them to suppress activities they disapprove of. In the context of Indian Penal Code, 1860 there has existed confusion about use of words such as 'common intention', 'maliciously', sufficient in the ordinary course of nature to cause death' etc (Yeo and Wright, 2011: 5).

Given that criminal law serves as a direct manifestation of the interplay between a government and its populace, it is constitutionally prudent for this relationship to be explicitly delineated within a criminal code. Such codification, subject to thorough deliberation by a democratically elected legislature, solidifies the legal framework governing citizen-state interactions. (Law Commission for England and Wales, 1989).

Vague laws empower authorities to potentially prosecute individuals at their discretion, and citizens who are aware of this tend to avoid pushing boundaries or displeasing those in power. The principle of clarity serves as a safeguard against this form of potential abuse. In these circumstances, the principle of clarity imposes a substantial, rather than a weak, constraint on the substance of criminal laws. Even HLA Hart while commenting on the House of Lords decision in DPP v. Shaw pertinently observed, "The particular value which they sacrificed is the principle of legality which requires criminal offences to be as precisely defined as possible, so that it can be known beforehand what acts are criminal and what are not" (Hart, 1963: 12).

The canons of publicity, clarity and constancy constitute the principle of clear communication of criminal law.

5.7 Non-contradiction

The principle of non-contradiction holds paramount significance in legal systems, particularly within the domain of criminal law. This principle assumes heightened importance due to the profound implications it carries for individual liberty and dignity. It is imperative that all facets of criminal legislation demonstrate coherence and consistency, encompassing procedural protocols, prescribed penalties, and the substantive elements defining offenses.

Ensuring harmony among various provisions of criminal laws within a legal framework is essential to uphold the integrity of the justice system. For instance, it is untenable for one statute to mandate a certain punishment for a particular offense while another statute within the same legal system stipulates a different penalty for the same crime. Similarly, conflicting definitions of criminal acts across statutes can erode the credibility and efficacy of the legal framework.

In response to concerns regarding overcriminalization, efforts to streamline and rationalize administrative criminal laws have been proposed. Recommendations advocating for the revision or repeal of redundant statutes aim to prevent the imposition of disproportionate penalties on individuals. The Fuller principle of non-contradiction emerges as a pivotal tool in this endeavor, serving to maintain the coherence and integrity of criminal legislation.

By adhering to the principle of non-contradiction, lawmakers can navigate complexities within the legal framework and mitigate inconsistencies that may undermine the administration of justice. Upholding this principle fosters confidence in the legal system, promotes fairness, and safeguards individual rights. Therefore, embracing the Fuller principle of non-contradiction remains indispensable in the formulation and implementation of criminal laws, ensuring their effectiveness and adherence to fundamental principles of justice.

5.8 Congruence between Official Action and Declared Rule

Lon Fuller has explored the concept of the congruence between official action and declared rules within legal systems. Fuller argues that for a legal system to function effectively and maintain its integrity, there must be a consistency between the actions of authorities and the principles articulated in the law. This congruence ensures that individuals can rely on the predictability and fairness of legal processes. When there is a misalignment between official actions and stated rules, it undermines the legitimacy of the legal system and erodes public trust. Fuller emphasizes the importance of adherence to legal principles by those in positions of authority to uphold the inner morality of law and preserve the rule of law within society.

This concept is particularly relevant in understanding under-enforcement in criminal law and the exercise of prosecutorial and police discretion in criminal law. Under-enforcement occurs when there is a discrepancy between the legal standards established by statutes and the actual enforcement efforts by law enforcement agencies.

In criminal justice systems, prosecutors and police officers have considerable discretion in determining which cases to prioritize, investigate, and prosecute. This discretion can lead to variations in enforcement practices across jurisdictions and cases. When law enforcement agencies fail to pursue certain offenses or individuals consistently, despite legal mandates to do so, it creates a disjunction between official actions and stated rules.

Moreover, prosecutorial and police discretion can be influenced by various factors, including individual biases, resource availability, and public opinion. Consequently, there may be instances where certain offenses or individuals receive lenient treatment, while others face harsher consequences, leading to perceptions of unfairness and undermining public trust in the legal system.

Therefore, it is important to have greater congruence between official actions and declared rules to prevent over-criminalization and mass incarceration.

5.9 Fair and Representative Labelling of Crimes

There are two key functions of labelling crimes: differentiation and description. Thus, Ashworth and Horder (2013) have argued that this principle requires the law to respect and signal 'widely felt distinctions between kinds of offences and degrees of wrongdoing' and 'that offences are subdivided and labelled so as to fairly represent the nature and magnitude of the law breaking'.

The principle of fair labeling within the realm of criminal law has garnered substantial scholarly attention, underscoring the imperative of accurately categorizing offenses to reflect their severity and moral reprehensibility. This principle is directed towards averting stigmatization and bias in the criminal justice process, ultimately facilitating equitable outcomes and diminishing the likelihood of recidivism.

Fair labeling in criminal law encompasses not only the differentiation of various types of wrongdoing through distinct crime labels but also the precise representation of the magnitude of the offense. Adherence to fair labeling principles serves to enhance transparency, accountability, and the overall integrity of criminal laws within legal frameworks. Moreover, fair labeling serves as a mechanism to safeguard defendants' rights by ensuring that crime labels align with the nature and impact of the offenses committed.

Efforts aimed at achieving fair and equitable labeling of crimes intersect with broader discourses on social justice, equality, and the mitigation of systemic biases within law enforcement. Addressing issues of label imbalance and bias in crime classification is imperative to mitigate unfairness and discrimination within the criminal justice system. Additionally, fair labeling principles contribute to shaping global discourse on accountability and justice, thereby informing the development of international crimes and concepts in international criminal law.

5.10 Proportional and Deserved Punishment

For other bodily harms and property offences, the criminal law must be used with strict justification. That too, in such cases imprisonment must not be ordinarily used. I understand that one of the aims of criminal law is to also allow individuals to peacefully enjoy their property rights. Some constitutional philosophers can also argue that for meaningful enjoyment of life and liberty, rights in property must be vigorously defended. But I reckon that criminal law is an extreme measure to defend all kinds of property rights. In my opinion, liberty *for* property is not a suitable bargain. First reason is that the right to liberty is fundamental to human existence, whereas property rights largely depend upon the legal system. Second reason is that criminalizing all kinds of property offences are unevenly onerous on economically weaker sections and marginalized communities. To be clear, I am not against the proposition that for property offences there should not be any criminalization at all, I am suggesting that other non-punitive measures must be the first choice and if they are not appropriate then even in criminal law, deprivation of liberty must be the last option and not an automatic choice. The economic sanctions such as fine, confiscation could prove to be equally deterrent in such situations.

The most problematic aspect of criminal law is not the general concept of punishment. It is a specific form of sanctions which curtails life or liberty that requires strict justification. The deprivation of liberty through arrest or imprisonment or like measures is the most powerful weapon in the armory of the State. Therefore, it must be used as a means of last resort. Here I am avoiding mentioning the ultimate form of punishment viz. deprivation of life. There are serious debates as to whether, death penalty should be even an option in criminal law statutes. This is not a place to discuss it here.

A theory of criminalization must use imprisonment as a last resort. The alternatives to imprisonment must be used in the majority of offences. The other forms of punishment such as fine, community service, probation, restitution, exemplary and punitive compensation, confiscation of property, deprivation of corporal property or intellectual property, must be given preference.

As far as cyber offences or new age offences are concerned, the present CJS might be completely inefficient and non-productive. The internet offences must be combated with sophisticated technology and not crude institutions of criminal justice administration. There can be security by design or other technological tools to ensure online crimes don't take place. And even if they take place, the technology crimes must be detected, investigated, as well as adjudicated through technology. Considering the quantum of such online crimes, our existing CJS will crumble down under its weight or will become irrelevant. Long story short, the tools and techniques of conceptualizing and dealing with crime in the physical world should not be supplanted to the virtual world. Therefore, my principles of criminalization don't say anything about cyber offences. In fact, I haven't seen any major work on principles of criminalization which considers the impact of their theory on cyber offences and related new age offences.

5.11   Necessity Principle

The principle of necessity in criminal law advocates for the use of criminal sanctions only when absolutely essential, making it the last resort in law enforcement efforts. Rooted in the idea that criminalization should be reserved for the most serious offenses, it emphasizes exploring less coercive measures first, such as civil remedies, administrative actions, or restorative justice processes. Proportionality in criminal law further supports this notion, aligning punishment severity with offense seriousness.

International legal instruments, like the United Nations Basic Principles on the Use of Restorative Justice Programs in Criminal Matters, promote restorative justice as an alternative to prosecution. This approach aims to repair harm caused by crime and foster reconciliation between offenders, victims, and communities, reducing reliance on punitive measures.

Scholars emphasize addressing root causes of criminal behavior through social interventions, education, mental health support, and community development programs to prevent crime and reduce reliance on criminalization. By investing in crime prevention strategies and tackling underlying social inequalities, societies can lower crime rates and foster a more equitable legal system.

The necessity principle ensures judicious and proportionate use of criminal sanctions, maintaining a balance between social order and individual rights. Authorities must assess if criminalization is truly warranted, considering factors like offense severity and available alternatives. This approach prevents over-criminalization and fosters a nuanced understanding of when criminalization is justified, promoting human rights protection and social harmony in legal systems.

Accordingly, the legislature must state in their bill about the cost of creating a new crime on public exchequer. I believe this will make the public give a second thought on their philosophy of when criminal law must be used. When the public will start seeing how their hard-earned money is used on CJS, they may resist the idea of using CJS for trivial and less serious wrongs. This principle of criminalization also takes into consideration that criminal law operates in an economic system where the cost of every State endeavor to deal with wrongs ultimately falls on taxpayers.

The legislature must consider the impact of criminal law on ease of doing business and on ease of living (Press Information Bureau, Government of India, 2022). Prime Minister of India Narendra Modi addressing the Chief

Minister's Conference stating its government achievement of abolishing 1450 laws stressed the need of abolishment by the State as well "for the rights of the citizens of your state, for their ease of living."

The criminal law sanctions which are imposed for not adhering to regulatory compliances should not be enacted unless failure to observe such compliance will have grave impact on the health and safety of the public or it affects the national security. The failure to observe compliances of economic laws, banking laws, corporate law, taxation laws, environmental law, as a matter of rule, the punishment of imprisonment should not be prescribed. The payment of fine, punitive compensation, freezing of bank accounts, seizure of property, community service should be the preferred form of punishment.

5.12 *Presence of Fault Requirements*

The imprisonment must be provided only if the definition of offence requires proof of moral blameworthiness. Hart insisted that "there should be no criminal liability without fault" (Hart, 1958: 595) Hart in his later work while critiquing Barbara Wooton's (Wootton, 1897–1988) proposition that criminal strict liability shall replace fault requirement stated, "Among other things, we should lose the ability which the present system in some degree guarantees to us, to predict and plan the future course of our lives within the coercive framework of the law. For the system which makes liability to the law's sanctions dependent upon a voluntary act not only maximizes the power of the individual to determine by his choice his future fate; it also maximizes his power to identify in advance the space which will be left open to him free from the law's interference" (Hart, 1968: 181).

Again, instead of enacting laws as strict liability offences, an opportunity must be given to the defendant to negate the presumption of *mens rea* by introducing reverse onus clauses.

And even further, if such wrong prescribes imprisonment as a punishment then it must make sure that hierarchy of punishments must be provided by the legislature and the imprisonment must be last in such hierarchy. The judge entrusted to impose such imprisonment must be required to state that imprisonment is deserved. The judge must use imprisonment only when finding as to moral blameworthiness has been made. Further, the judge must be satisfied that if the offender is not imprisoned then the society's conscience will be shocked.

5.13 *Presumption of Innocence*

While traditionally, the operation of Presumption of Innocence (POI) begins after the criminal charge has been framed, there are four applications of POI.

Firstly, POI, at pre-trial stage can serve as an important safeguard to prevent arbitrary arrest, pre-trial detention, and preventive detention. Secondly, at the trial stage POI requires a prosecutor to establish guilt of an accused. Thirdly, POI in the post-trial context can play a role in post-verdict procedures and compensation for acquitted defendants.

Lastly, POI can also act as a constraint on the power of lawmaker to enact strict-liability offences. From this perspective, the concept of POI can also be arguably used to insist that the culpability of wrongdoer must be proved. As a necessary corollary, any criminal law which does not require a presence of guilty mind can be argued to violate principles of POI. POI in this sense ensures that legislatures shall not enact strict liability offences. However, such proposition has not found support in ECHR as well as domestic jurisprudence but an English court in the case of Lambert noted that severity of punishment can make reverse onus disproportionate. Therefore, POI may also be used insist that evidentiary burden must be put on accused only when it is just and fair to do so. What emerges from this is that while POI principle may not be tenable to prevent legislator from enacting strict liability offences, it can at least provide a safe-guard wherein severe punishment has been prescribed for a crime.

Such an expansive role of POI raises issues about how the state and individuals should treat citizens not yet involved in the criminal process on the basis of dangerousness and security. This includes debates on the legitimacy of treating individuals as guilty or likely to engage in wrongdoing without a criminal conviction. The modern criminal statutes however enact provisions which are inconsistent even with the classical POI formulation. There are provisions in India wherein Statute has expressly provided that presumption of guilt should be drawn. Sections 34 and 35 of the Narcotic Drugs and Psychotropic Substances Act, 1985, allows the Court to presume a culpable mental state of the accused and also to presume the commission of an offence under the Act. Another example is Section 29 and 30 of the Prevention of Children from Sexual Offences Act, 2012 which allows for the guilt of the accused to be presumed for certain offences if the accused is prosecuted for the same. The Criminal Financing Act, 2017 of the UK is yet another example of same.

I submit that POI in pre-trial, trial, as well as post-trial context should be given the most expansive meaning considering the power imbalance between the State and accused as well as potential of criminal law to change someone's life forever just by simple initiation of it.

5.14   Burden of Proof

In criminal law as a matter of principle the burden of proof always lies on prosecution (Woolmington v. DPP, 1935). It is the responsibility of the prosecution to establish the guilt of an accused. In offences which have both *actus rea* and *mens rea* requirement, the prosecutor must establish both beyond reasonable doubt. That is the prosecution must prove that the accused committed the act and committed it with requisite mental state. However, with the rise of strict liability offences, the burden of proof requirement has been diluted. The prosecution in such strict liability offences has to only establish act requirement. Therefore, it is important that such strict liability offences shall not be enacted and even when the public welfare or expediency necessitates the enactment of strict liability offences, it must provide an opportunity to the accused to disprove mens rea through reverse burden. In democratic countries like India, Canada, and the United States the legal burden of the prosecution to prove foundational facts is well grounded through the case law jurisprudence. The legislature shall not put the burden to prove a negative fact on the accused especially when such fact is not especially within the exclusive knowledge of an accused. The legislature shall provide for drawing of presumption of guilt only when evidence presented by the prosecution possesses probative value, indicating the accused likely committed the crime. Furthermore, the legislature while prescribing the burden of proof must keep in mind that the accused shall not have to suffer hardship or oppression to prove his innocence.

To sum up, the legislature shall as a rule always impose the burden of proof on prosecution. The prosecution must be required to prove both actus rea and mens rea. Even when in exceptional situations, strict liability offence is created, common law presumption of mens rea as a rule should apply. In any case in strict liability offences the defendant must have an occasion to disprove the mens rea.

6 Conclusion

The process of criminalization is multifaceted and inherently linked to broader societal values, norms, history, and power dynamics. While each theory offers valuable insights into different aspects of criminalization, there is no singular approach that provides a comprehensive understanding of the complexities involved.

In this paper I have attempted to lay down principles of criminalization which should be followed. I haven't been able to give detailed arguments in support of my principles. I intend to develop them in my future works. For now, I believe that the principles I stated will put a new life to the old debate of criminalization. I am an optimist. I believe that criminal law is yet not a lost cause.

Bibliography

Ashworth, A., and Horder, J. (2013) *Principles of Criminal Law*. New York: Oxford University Press.

Ashworth, A, and Zedner, L. (2008) "Defending the Criminal Law: Reflections on the Changing Character of Crime, Procedure, and Sanctions." *Criminal Law and Philosophy* 2 (1): 21–51.

Ashworth, A. (2008) "Conceptions of Overcriminalization." *Ohio State Journal of Criminal Law*, 5: 408–425.

Ashworth, A. (2000) "Is the Criminal Law a Lost Cause?" *Law Quarterly Review*, 116: 225.

Baker, D. J. (2016) *The Right Not to be Criminalized Demarcating Criminal Law's Authority*. London: Routledge.

Balyan, C. (2020) "Overcriminalization in India." In: Balyan, C., et al. (eds) *Revisiting Reforms in the Criminal Justice System in India*. Gurgaon: Thomson Reuters.

Bilionis, L. D. (1998) "Process, the Constitution, and Substantive Criminal Law." *Michigan Law Review*, 96: 1269.

Black, J. (2002) "Critical Reflections on Regulation." *Australian Journal of Legal Philosophy* 27: 1.

Carrington, K., et al. (2015) "Southern Criminology." *The British Journal of Criminology*, 57 (1): 1–20.

Chan, C. W., et al. (2011) *Codification, Macaulay and the Indian Penal Code: The Legacies and Modern Challenges of Criminal Law Reform*. London: Routledge.

Coke, E. (1628) *First Part of the Institutes of the Laws of England*. London: Stevens.

Dubber, M. D. (2010) "Criminal Law between Public and Private Law." In: Duff, A., et al. *The Boundaries of the Criminal Law*. Oxford: Oxford University Press.

Dubber, M. D. (2005) "The Possession Paradigm: The Special Part and the Police Power Model of the Criminal Process." In: Duff, A., and Green, S. (eds) *Defining Crimes: Essays on The Special Part of the Criminal Law*. New York: Oxford University Press.

Duff, R. A. (2007) *Answering for Crime*. Oxford: Hart Publishing.

Duff, R. A., et al. (2014) *Criminalization: The Political Morality of the Criminal Law*. Oxford: Oxford University Press.

Duff, R. A., et al. (2013) *The Constitution of the Criminal Law*. New York: Oxford University Press.

Duff, R. A. (2018) *The Realm of Criminal Law*. New York: Oxford University Press.

Farmer, L. (2024) "Criminalization and Decriminalization." In: Gless, S., et al. (eds) *Elgar Encyclopedia of Crime and Criminal Justice Vol. 1*. Elgar Online: Edward Elgar Publishing. Available at: https://doi.org/10.4337/9781789902990.criminalization. decriminalization Accessed on March 01, 2024.

Farmer, L. (2014) "Criminal Law as an Institution: Rethinking Theoretical Approaches to Criminalization." In: Duff, R. A., et al. *Criminalization: The Political Morality of the Criminal Law*. New York: Oxford University Press.

Fienberg, J. (1990) *The Moral Limits of the Criminal Law 4: Harmless Wrongdoing*. New York: Oxford University Press.

Feinberg, J. (1984) *The Moral Limits of the Criminal Law 1: Harm to Others*. New York: Oxford University Press.

Feinberg, J. (1989) *The Moral Limits of the Criminal Law 3: Harm to Self.* New York: Oxford University Press.

Feinberg, J. (1985) *The Moral Limits of the Criminal Law 2: Offense to Others*. New York: Oxford University Press.

Finau v Department of Labour, 2 NZLR 396. (1984) Court of Appeal, Wellington, New Zealand.

Fletcher, G. (2007) *The Grammar of Criminal Law*. New York: Oxford University Press.

Fuller, L. L. (1969) *The Morality of Law*. London: Yale University Press.

Gardner, J. (2008) *Overcriminalization: The Limits of the Criminal Law*. Notre Dame Philosophical Reviews. Available at: https://ndpr.nd.edu/reviews/overcriminalization-the-limits-of-the-criminal-law/. Accessed on January 01, 2020.

Gray, J. (1991) *J.S. Mill On Liberty*. London: Routledge.

Hall, L., and Glueck, S. (1958) *Cases on the Criminal Law and its Enforcement*. St. Paul: West Publishing.

Hart, H. L. A. (1963) *Law, Liberty, and Morality*. Stanford: Stanford University Press.

Hart, H. L. A. (1958) "Positivism and the Separation of Law and Morals." *Harvard Law Review,* 71: 593.

Hart, H. L. A. (1968) *Punishment And Responsibility: Essays in The Philosophy of Law*. New York: Oxford University Press.

Hart Jr., H. M. (1958) "The Aims Of The Criminal Law." *Law And Contemporary Problems,* 23: 401–441.

Huda, S. S. (1902) *The Principles of the Law of Crimes in British India*. Calcutta: Butterworth.

Husak, D. (2010) "Overcriminalization". In: Patterson, D. (ed) *A Companion to Philosophy of Law and Legal Theory (2nd ed.)*. Singapore: Blackwell Publishing Ltd.

Husak, D. (2008) *Overcriminalization: The Limits of the Criminal Law*. New York: Oxford University Press.

Husak, D. (2004) "The Criminal Law as Last Resort." *Oxford Journal of Legal Studies,* 24(2): 207–235.

Law Commission for England and Wales. (1989) *Criminal Law: A Criminal Code for England and Wales (Vol. 1)*. London: HMSO.

Lacely, N., and Hanna, P. (2015) "To Blame or to Forgive? Reconciling Punishment and Forgiveness in Criminal Justice." Oxford Journal of Legal Studies, 35 (4): 665–696.

Levenson, Laurie L. (1993) "Good Faith Defenses: Reshaping Strict Liability Crimes". *Cornell Law Review*, 78: 401.

Luna, W. (2000) "Principled Enforcement of Penal Codes." *Buffalo Criminal Law Review*, 5: 515.

Macaulay, T. B., et al. (1838) *A Penal Code Prepared by the Indian Law Commissioners*. London: Pelham Richardson.

MacCormick, N. (2007) *Institutions of Law: An Essay in Legal Theory*. Oxford: Oxford University Press.

McSherry, B., et al. (2009) *Regulating Deviance The Redirection of Criminalisation and the Futures of Criminal Law*. Oxford: Hart Publishing.

Moore, M. S. (1997) *Placing Blame*. New York: Oxford University Press.

Nathulal v. State of Madhya Pradesh (India), AIR 1966 SC 43 (1965) Supreme Court, India.

Norrie, A. (2009) "Citizenship, Authoritarianism and the Changing Shape of the Criminal Law." In: Mcsherry, B., et al. (eds) *Regulating Deviance: The Redirection Of Criminalisation and The Futures of Criminal Law*. Oxford: Hart Publishing.

Norrie, A. (2014) *Crime, Reason and History*. New York: Cambridge University Press.

Norrie, A. (2005) *Law and the Beautiful Soul*. London: GlassHouse Press.

Packer, H. L. (1968) *The Limits Of The Criminal Sanction*. Stanford: Stanford University Press.

Prime Minister's Office. (2022) "English rendering of PM's address at Joint Conference of Chief Ministers and Chief Justices of High Courts". *Press Information Bureau*. Available at: https://www.pib.gov.in/PressReleseDetail.aspx?PRID=1821534. Accessed on January 01, 2022.

Ramani, S. (May 23, 2019) "Analysis: Highest-ever national vote share for the BJP". *The Hindu*. Available at: https://www.thehindu.com/elections/lok-sabha-2019/analysis-highest-ever-national-vote-share-for-the-bjp/article27218550.ece. Accessed on August 09, 2021.

Ramsay, P. (2006) "The Responsible Subject as Citizen: Criminal Law, Democracy and the Authoritarian State." *Modern Law Review*, 69 (1): 29.

Ripstein, A. (2006) "Beyond the Harm Principle." *Philosophy and Public Affairs*, 34: 215.

Simester, A. P., and Hrisch, A. (2011) *Crimes, Harms, and Wrongs: On the Principles of Criminalisation*. Oxford: Hart Publishing.

Simons, K. W. (1996–97) "When is Strict Criminal Liability Just." *Journal of Criminal Law & Criminology*, 87: 1075.

Singh, R. S. (2021) "Criminalisation and Political Mobilisation of Nomadic Tribes in Uttar Pradesh." *Economic and Political Weekly*, 56 (36): 1–11.

Stuntz, W. J. (2001) "The Pathological Politics of Criminal Law." *Michigan Law Review*, 100 (3): 505–600.

Tadros, V. (2010) "Criminalisation and Regulation." In: R.A. Duff. et al. (eds) *The Boundaries of the Criminal Law*, New York: Oxford University Press.

Tadros, V. (2011) *The Ends of Harm: The Moral Foundations of Criminal Law*. New York: Oxford University Press.

United States v. Kantor, 858 F.2d 534 (1988) 9th Circuit Court, United States of America.

Woolmington v. DPP, 1935 AC 462 (1935) House of Lords, United Kingdom.

Wootton, B. (1981) *Crime and the Criminal Law: Reflections of a Magistrate and Social Scientist*. London: Stevens.

Yeo, S., and Barry W. (2011) *Codification, Macaulay and the Indian Penal Code: The Legacies and Modern Challenges of Criminal Law Reform*. London: Routledge.

CHAPTER 6

Criminalization and the Presumption of Innocence

Sébastien Lafrance

1   Introduction

The State via its legislative body defines crimes and the scope of their meaning. Tomlin (2013: 63) aptly notes that there are "ongoing debates about the appropriate limits of … criminal law [and] there is a great deal of reasonable disagreement and uncertainty concerning the proper principles of criminalisation." Some contend that there are too many crimes covered by criminal law, whereas others believe that there are not enough. The author explores the foundations as well as the different meanings given to the concept of criminalisation, more specifically in light of the presumption of innocence, which also has, in turn, different understandings. The analysis adopts both a theoretical and practical approach. While this is not an exercise in comparative law, practical examples are used, mainly from the Canadian and Indian jurisdictions, to illustrate the application and interactions between the presumption of innocence and criminalisation. (Lafrance, 2020a; Gilles, 2012).

2   Criminalization

Justice Rand of the Supreme Court of Canada summarily defines a crime as "an act which the law … forbids" (*Margarine Reference*, 1949: 49–50). With respect to criminalisation, Bedi in Ch. 8 of this book defines it objectively as "the action of the State of categorising certain acts as criminal in nature." Interestingly, "[t]he terms *criminalization* and overcriminalization are ambiguous, and commentators have distinguished various meanings they may have" (Husak, 2010: 621; Chalmers and Leverick, 2014: 54).

What is meant by under-criminalization is easier to identify. It is "a countertrend to [the] increased criminalisation" (Rossow and Strang, 2009: 164). It corresponds to situations where criminal law "fails to subject conduct to punishment that satisfies the positive conditions in a normative theory of criminalization" (Husak, 2010: 622). Similarly, decriminalization would take away the criminal characteristics of a specific conduct that was previously criminalized. For example, possession of cannabis was *de*criminalised, under certain legal conditions, in some countries of the world (Canada, Italy, Portugal and Spain, to name a few) (Gautam, 2022a). Nonetheless, some still consider that this previously criminalized conduct is now *under* criminalised because it should have remained a criminal offence. In fact, being decriminalised does not prevent a conduct from suffering from a certain stigma in a society when, for example, it is still perceived by some of its citizens as 'immoral' in several countries, like homosexual behaviour (Lacey, 2009: 947; Mahapatra, 2023) or psychedelic consumption (Gautam, 2022b: 402).

The term 'overcriminalization' was coined by Kadish (1962; 1967). He criticises using criminal law to enforce moral beliefs (Ashworth, 2008: 407) in addition to using it in order to punish conducts that go beyond the target of the legislation (Luna, 2012: 785). The parliamentary and senatorial, when applicable, considerations given to the possible enactment of criminal offences by the legislature would correspond to the initial steps of criminalisation. Judicial decisions would, in turn, confirm or modify the scope of application of criminal offences (Chalmers and Leverick, 2014: 55). One could argue that courts may act as a safeguard against "criminal legislation [that] is (unjustifiably) used as means to attain aims other than those the criminal law is supposed to pursue" (Jalušič, 2020: 77; Duff, 2010). Viewed from that angle, courts monitor the decisions of the legislature in the criminalization of conduct. Courts would not create crimes. In that respect, the presumption of innocence might justify the court's role by conferring them "the power to scrutinise the legislator's criminalization choices" (Picinali, 2014: 245). However, being a 'safety net' would not give courts the role of involving themselves in "the moral criminalizing decisions that are the appropriate domain of a representative legislature" (Tomlin, 2013: 54–55). From that perspective, courts would be "ill-placed to make decisions about the proper scope of the *substantive* criminal law" (Tadros, 2007: 194), contrary to the legislature that has "the power to *make* something morally prohibited" (Lippke, 2016: 56). Nevertheless, this did not prevent the Supreme Court of Canada in the *Mabior* decision rendered in 2012, for example, from "criminalis[ing] HIV nondisclosure through treating all cases where there is a realistic possibility of transmission as aggravated sexual assault regardless of whether transmission of the virus takes place" (Grant, 2013).

There must be "some standards as to the *proper* level of criminalization" (Moore, 2014: 183). Tadros, (2016: 11) notes that "[a] common answer is that criminalization should be subject to a wrongness constraint: that is, that conduct may be criminalized only if it is wrongful." This principle would be unanimously endorsed by criminal law theorists (Cornford, 2017). Husak goes a step further in terms of defining a principled approach. He established what he calls 'internal constraints' to avoid overcriminalization: (1) nontrivial harms or evils should not be criminalized; (2) crimes must involve an element of 'wrongfulness'; (3) punishment can be imposed only when it is deserved; (4) the burden of proof should be placed on those who *advocate* the imposition of criminal sanctions (Husak, 2008). Let us note that the latter principle relates to the initial steps of criminalisation, namely at the legislative steps, before a conduct is, in fact, criminalized by way of its inclusion in the legislation.

3   Defining (Over)Criminalization

The concept of "overcriminalization is often discussed in terms of what it *does*, rather than what it *is*" (Haugh, 2015: 1200). Therefore, before initiating a discussion about what (over)criminalization does, and then before examining its interactions with the presumption of innocence, it is first appropriate to determine what it means, mostly because definitions help to delineate the contours of a concept (Cumyn, 2018).

The most popular, and succinct, definition of overcriminalization (Haugh, 2015; 1997–1998) is offered by Husak (2008, 4), which is that there is "too much punishment, too many crimes". Similarly, Larkin (2014: 745) defines it briefly, but he adds an element of morality to it: "the overuse and misuse of the criminal law to punish conduct traditionally deemed morally blameless." Haugh (2015; 1997–1998; Luna, 2005: 718) aptly notes, "While these definitions benefit from brevity, they also fail to do justice to the broad array of issues that overcriminalization encompasses." In addition, according to Pierce (2015–2016: 51), overcriminalization is triggered "when the government prosecutes an individual for a single act (or course of conduct) under a criminal statute whose main purpose has nothing to do with the defendant's conduct, yet which contains broadly worded provisions with words that, read literally, encompass it." A fictitious law that would criminalize the act of eating ice cream in order to fight against obesity that would be rampant in the population of certain countries might illustrate this last definition. The main purpose of this fictitious law may have nothing to do with the main issue that is meant to be punished. Think of an athletic Olympian who is prosecuted for eating an ice cream cone on the street with his friends. Nevertheless, that law would apply to that accused in that context. This may be similar to cases where provisions are considered as too broad, i.e. when "the means are too sweeping in relation to the objective" (R v. Heywood, 1994).

3.1 *Overcriminalization as a Many-Tentacled Creature*

A scary description of overcriminalization is given by Jones (2014: 933): "Think of it as a gargantuan, many-tentacled creature that has rapidly grown and risen from the depths of our criminal jurisprudence." With this description, we are one step away from the horror depicted in Goya's painting of *Saturn Devouring His Son*, which symbolises the autocratic Spanish State or Napoleon, two representations of a strong and invasive State. Criminalization "could swallow up almost every theoretically interesting question about criminal law, criminal responsibility, criminal justice and punishment" (Lacey, 2009: 942). In short, criminalisation, because it is multifaceted, may be seen as all-encompassing and pervasive, and then, distinguishing it from *over*criminalization becomes a difficult task. Husak contends that criminalization would be justified "only if it made a direct contribution to furthering a substantial State interest in relation to a non-trivial harm or wrong, and where this interest moreover could not effectively be advanced *by less intrusive means*" (Lacey, 2009: 940). China's social credit system would constitute a good example of what would *not* comply with Husak's proposition, being an invasive technology used by a State to monitor social activities, which criminal law might eventually cover (Nguyen, Lafrance and Vu, 2023; Nguyen, Lafrance, Ngoc and Nguyen, 2020). This technological tool could then contribute, at least indirectly, to the rise of overcriminalization by bringing to the fore a bigger quantity of crimes.

3.2 *Organic Limitation to Criminalization*

Haley (2019: 11) points out, "We do not ... label as crimes all conduct that we deem to be sufficiently wrongful or undesirable to require legal proscription". As such, the author submits that there might be an organic limitation to criminalisation. For instance, lying could fit in this proposition because lying will more than likely never be criminalized *in and of itself*, except for perjury. No one would dare saying that lying is acceptable in any shape or form, it is wrongful – with the exception perhaps of white lies. However, lying, as a crime *itself* (which excludes acts that may involve dishonesty as an element of the crime, such as for fraud or misrepresentation offences, for example), would not be sufficiently wrong to criminalize it at large, unless we accept to live in an Orwellian society where "Big Brother" checks, and more importantly judges, our every move (Orwell, 1949). Another cynical but practical example would stem from what Machiavelli writes, "when anyone and everyone can tell you the truth, you lose respect" (Machiavelli, 1532: 93), but does it mean that lying should be criminalized for that reason? We must answer by the negative.

3.3 Ambiguous Criminal Provisions

Criminalization has become since the past century, for those who share that view, a universal tendency (Haley, 2019: 1), and there would be now a "remarkable range of human activities ... subject to the threat of criminal sanctions" (Luna, 2012: 785), implying that it would be too much. From that perspective, criminalization is seen with a dim view, and has been described, when it goes beyond the parameters of what should be criminalized, as a "serious problem" (Luna, 2012: 787). The tenants of this view argue, as we have seen above, that there is 'too much' criminal law (Husak, 2008; 3; Husak, 2010: 621), meaning that the legislature criminalises too many behaviours. In addition, not only the legislature, but also judges have been criticised for creating 'too much criminal law' because, for example, they "have been all too willing to construe ambiguous ... criminal statutes *expansively*" (Smith, 2012: 544), then broadening the scope of application of what is covered by criminal law. This would be the case of Vietnam, for example, where when there is a contradiction between two laws, the law that is *less favourable* to the accused applies (Thi, 2012: 201).

However, the contention that there is too much criminal law based on the example of the interpretation given by the courts to ambiguous criminal provisions may not hold true everywhere. In Canada, for example, "if a penal provision is ambiguous, the interpretation *more favourable* to the accused is adopted" (R v. Hasselwander, 1993: paras 29–30), which would rather *narrow down* the application of criminal law as a punitive instrument that the State can use. This rule of lenity also applies in Europe, at least with Article 22 of Directive (EU) 2016/343 of the European Parliament and of the Council of 9 March 2016 ('Directive (EU) 2016/343') that reads, "The burden of proof for establishing the guilt of suspects and accused persons is on the prosecution, and *any doubt should benefit the suspect or accused person.*" The same also goes in India (Marwah, 2021).

Even though the courts' interpretation of ambiguous criminal provisions may not fully support the view that judges criminalize 'too much', it might still be possible to contend, as discussed above, that judges may not be best placed to decide issues that determine where the boundaries of criminal liability should lie (Prendergast, 2011: 297). In fact, according to this approach, "[t]he adjudicative activity of the courts is an integral part of criminalisation. Especially when statutory definitions are vague, it is the dialogue between legislator and courts that is responsible for identifying the elements of the crime" (Picinali, 2014: 253). Thus, despite the fact that the legislative body is subordinate to what the highest court of the land says, the fact remains that "[w]here a judicial decision is open to legislative reversal, modification, or avoidance, then it is *meaningful* to regard the relationship between the Court and the competent legislative body as a dialogue" (Hogg and Bushell, 1997: 79). Therefore, both the courts and the legislature could be prone to criminalize 'too much', but such dialogue could also contribute to prevent overcriminalization. The 'dialogue' that exists between the courts and the legislature then becomes useful when examining the application of 'internal constraints' that may be implemented. In turn, this may raise questions regarding what has been described as judicial activism made by the courts when they allegedly interfere with the will of the legislature (Bedi and Lafrance, 2020a: 53).

3.4 Tough-on-Crime Approach

Contrary to the view that there are "too many crimes", an opposite approach argues that a tough-on-crime approach, i.e. to increase the sanctions against people defined as criminals (Stobbe, 2018: 57), is called for because of the increase of criminal conducts in our modern society. From that standpoint, criminalization is understood as a positive thing, as it aims at the protection of citizens' lives and safety. It is true that while it brought along many undeniable benefits, the advances of the technology, for instance, also gave rise to criminal conducts that would not have existed in the past. There are always two sides to a medal: on one hand, the technical and technological evolution of the society makes people's lives easier and more comfortable, but, on the other hand, it also has the unwarranted effect of expanding criminality. For example, "[t]he widespread availability of computers and the Internet has resulted in new ways" (R v. Sharpe, 2001: para 166) for offenders to commit crimes. This "reflects a growing trend towards the criminalization" (Sharpe, 2001: para 179) of certain conducts. The growth of criminalization then becomes inevitable, and should not be seen, according to this approach, with a negative eye. Criminalization would then simply apply to new social phenomena, among other things.

Nevertheless, a tough-on-crime approach also has its downsides. For instance, Indonesia criminalized, in December 2022, sex outside of marriage (Karmini, 2022). Far from being a new phenomenon, this may rather reflect, as generally pointed out by Moore (2014: 56), the will of "official actors ... to clamp down on behaviour formerly tolerated." This is an example where "behavior once tolerated becomes increasing to social condemnation" (Haley, 2019: 7). The values of a society change, they are not static, just like "a living tree capable of growth and expansion within its natural limits" (Hunter v. Southam Inc, 1984: 156), but this does not mean that society's values always move forward, at least from a human rights perspective. Besides, "[c]riminalization of permissible preexisting behavior [may] invite dissention and political conflict" (Haley, 2019: 10), unless there is an 'overlapping consensus' about its criminalization (Tomlin, 2013: 63).

3.5 Cultural Relativism, Multiculturalism and Criminalization

Even though cultural relativism, which is the claim that ethical practices differ among cultures, could eventually support the contention that Indonesia evolved legitimately in that direction, it should be kept in mind that the concept of 'Asian values' or 'Asian exception', that is opposed to the notion of universality of human rights, has been clearly rejected by the United Nations (Hon. Kirby: 1995). In contrast, the former Prime Minister of Canada, Pierre Elliot Trudeau, commented fifty years ago about the *Criminal Law Amendment Act, 1968–1969*, commonly called the Omnibus Bill, saying that "there's no place for the State in bedrooms of the nation".

This is not to say that multiculturalism should not be celebrated (Lafrance, 2020b). On the contrary, criminalization of a conduct may serve, even though it is not its main purpose, as an eye-opener for some. Something like humour can also be used sometimes in law for that purpose (C. J. C. McLachlin, 2015), including eventually for something that looks like a joke at first glance. In 2020, there was a buzz online regarding what was deemed to be a spelling mistake on the label of a sandwich, whose alleged mistake was to display Roast Beef and *Criminalized* Onion (Stoneman, 2020), instead of *caramelized* onions. While this may only be funny for someone who does not think about this issue further, the fact remains that it is forbidden to eat some foods in certain cultures, including in India. As Pániker (2010: 483) notes, "Many strict Hindus do not eat ... onion[s] ... since they grow in 'impure' soil", then it is immoral for them to consume it. Therefore, nothing, in the abstract, would prevent a legislature from eventually criminalizing its consumption because of the possible harm it may cause, the harm being to go against the religious beliefs of a certain community. A harm does not need to be physical, think, for example, of the legal concepts of *solatium doloris* or *pretium doloris*. However, Husak (2008), whose "concept of overcriminalization is a useful point of reference" (Lacey, 2009: 942), established, as part of the 'internal constraints' on state punitive power, that the prohibited conduct must involve a non-trivial harm or evil. While criminalizing onions may be trivial for some, it would not be so for others because of their religious beliefs, as we have seen. A moral issue for one may not be a moral issue for the other.

3.6 The Fictitious Criminalization of Onions

The fictitious criminalization of onions may also raise another issue. Tomlin (2013: 63) remarked that "epistemic minimalist will advocate only criminalizing conduct where there is an 'overlapping consensus' on the criminalization of the conduct." Such a consensus is unlikely to be problematic to achieve for offences like murder, rape, and theft since "[n]early all societies – even from the earliest times – have condemned violent acts against persons and property" (Haley, 2019: 9). Nevertheless, in a multicultural society, such as India or Canada, an 'overlapping consensus' may often be hard to reach, given the differences of views and beliefs about so many things. This is especially true in situations as Bedi has argued in chapter 8 of this book that "criminalisation has become a method for legislators/government to show to their people that they are serious about a particular problem *plaguing* the society." Thus, how could something as specific as onions be eventually criminalized? May onions plague our society, any society, as a serious issue, even for the countries where a portion of its population is forbidden to eat certain foods? Is it an absolute requirement for something to plague a society to justify its criminalisation? Think of the criminalization of the culture of oysters in Canada, pursuant to section 323 of the Criminal Code, to remain in the food theme. All these questions remain unanswered.

3.7   *Preventing Crimes as Criminalization*

Criminalization of a conduct not only means to punish a specific conduct, but it may also seek to prevent the commission of a criminal offence. For example, this is what the deterrence principle of punishment, included in the criminal law of most common law jurisdictions, aims to achieve. Therefore, based on the previous example of 'criminalized onions', the label displaying that they are criminal could serve that purpose, even though it is not recognised as a criminal offence by the legislation, namely the criminal or penal code, for instance. This label could still be identified as being an act of criminalization since the latter "might even occur without any kind of official action at all, where actors take steps to comply with the criminal law of their own volition" (Chalmers and Leverick, 2014: 55). Here, it is true that not buying this sandwich made of criminalized onions would not be act in compliance with the criminal law, but it could still be an extension of criminal law, at least by proxy. In addition, if some customers took this label seriously, it could then depict the propensity of the State to over-criminalize anything and everything, or at least exemplifies it, to a certain extent.

4   (In)Existence of Crimes in Canada and India

Husak's catchy and all-encompassing definition mentioned above may be problematic because it may also include crimes that are not criminally enforced as being part of overcriminalization, even though he writes later himself that criminalization also depends on "the existing practices of criminal justice officials" (Husak, 2010: 623). In that context, one must remain cautious regarding the alleged outstanding number of crimes that would exist in both India and Canada, for example, since there may be, on occasion, a distorted perception about that (Barbe, 2009: 14). Some crimes may have been struck down by courts, then they could not be enforced legitimately, but they may remain on the books. In Canada, such was the case until 2018 for the following offences (when they were repealed): Challenging someone to a duel (section 71); Advertising a reward for the return of stolen property (section 143); Possessing, printing, distributing or publishing crime comics (paragraph 163(1)(b)); Publishing blasphemous libel (section 296); Fraudulently pretending to practise witchcraft (section 365); and issuing trading stamps (section 427).

Other types of crimes may also be considered in force, but they are unlikely to be enforced as much as other crimes because of their nature, the resources required to enforce them, etc. For instance, as previously mentioned, Canada's Criminal Code has a section devoted to oysters (section 323). In addition, you may be fined in the city of Toronto for swearing in public since "[w]hile in a park, no person shall ... use profane or abusive language" (Toronto Municipal Code: para 608-3). Outdated laws are also unlikely to be enforced. For example, there is a bylaw in the city of Toronto, in Canada, that prohibits dragging a dead horse down Yonge Street on Sundays. Nowadays it would be fair to say that nobody would even think of possibly committing this offence, either on Sunday or on any other day of the week. India is not exempt either of such archaic legislation, for example paragraph 2(1) of the Indian Aircraft Act, 1934 that categorises balloons and kites as aircrafts.

No offences mentioned above, to just name a few, should be cited as evidence of overcriminalization (Husak, 2010: 623). Their sole existence on paper may not be determinative to conclude that there is an excessive criminalization because the latter also depends, as said, on "the existing practices of criminal justice officials" (Husak, 2010: 623), namely judges and prosecutors.

4.1   *Presumption of Innocence*

The principle of the presumption of innocence provides that each person should be presumed innocent until his or her guilt is proven. It is considered as a cardinal principle in criminal law and "a fundamental tenet of the common law" (Theophilopoulos, 2001: footnote 26) because, as Tadros and Tierney (2004: 402) recall, "this principle ... is generally seen as better for the guilty to go free than the innocent be convicted."

One may wonder how the power of the State to criminalize conduct can be limited. Husak (2011: 99) emphasises the need for "principles to limit the circumstances under which the State is allowed to inflict punitive sanctions." The presumption of innocence may serve as a normative constraint on criminalization (Lacey, 2009: 949) as well as a protection against wrongful criminalization (Tadros, 2007; Tomlin, 2013), hence its relevance in our study. In short, this principle "acts as a check on the limitless power of the State" (Bedi, 2021: 367; Ashworth, 2006: 249–250).

4.1.1 Basic Principles

The Supreme Court of Canada defined the presumption of innocence in the seminal decision *R. v. Oakes*:

> The presumption of innocence protects the fundamental liberty and human dignity of any and every person accused by the state of criminal conduct. ... the presumption of innocence is crucial. It ensures that, until the state proves an accused's guilt beyond all reasonable doubt, he or she is innocent. This is essential in a society committed to fairness and social justice. The presumption of innocence ... reflects our belief that individuals are decent and law-abiding members of the community until proven otherwise.

This definition is not only relevant for Canadian criminal law, but it also has been relied upon by several other common law jurisdictions, for example in South Africa (S v. Zuma, 1995: para 22) and in Turks and Caicos Islands (Young v. Regina, 2014: para 7), to just name a few.

The presumption of innocence is not a new principle. It goes back to Roman Law where it appears, in Latin, in the Digest of Justinian in the 6th century as *ei incumbit probatio qui dicit, non qui negat*, which literally translates to 'proof lies on him who asserts, not on him who denies'. More recently, this principle first appeared in the United States' jurisprudence in the *Coffin* decision of the United States Supreme Court rendered in 1895. In common law jurisdictions, the presumption of innocence has enjoyed long-standing recognition as shown in the leading case, *Woolmington v. Director of Public Prosecutions*, where Viscount Sankey wrote (1935: 481–482), "Throughout the web of the English Criminal Law one golden thread is always to be seen, that it is the duty of the prosecution to prove the prisoner's guilt". This means practically that all the elements of the offence charged against the accused have to be proven by the prosecution. If there is a reasonable doubt raised about only one of these elements, for instance, the accused must be acquitted.

What may come as a surprise is that there is no mention of the presumption of innocence per se in *Woolmington*. Nevertheless, Ferguson (2016: 134) noted, "Although Woolmington is often treated as being a resounding endorsement of the presumption [of innocence], it actually focused more on the burden of proof, and the two have often been treated as synonymous." This connection between the burden of proof and the presumption of innocence is also echoed, for example, in the seminal decision of the Supreme Court of Canada in *Lifchus* (1997: para 13) where it stated, "the onus resting upon the Crown to prove the guilt of the accused beyond a reasonable doubt is inextricably linked to the presumption of innocence." Interestingly, Huynh Tan Le and Bedi (2022: 362) state that the "[p]resumption of innocence is not only the golden rule", as described in *Woolmington*, "but also a significant human right protection", thus expanding the scope of application of this principle. The Canadian jurisprudence shows this dual dimension of the presumption of innocence.

In Canada, the presumption of innocence finds different forms throughout the criminal process: "[t]he Canadian Courts have drawn a distinction between the content of the presumption of innocence in its broader application as a *substantive* principle of fundamental justice and its *operation at trial*" (Schwikkard, 1999: 80). It is provided by paragraph 11(d) of the *Canadian Charter of Rights and Freedoms* (hereinafter '*Charter*'), which was enacted in 1982 and is enshrined in the Canadian constitution, and this paragraph applies at the trial stage (R v. Pearson, 1992: 683). In addition, this presumption is *inferentially* protected by section 7 of the *Charter* via the right to life, liberty and security of the person (because the presumption of innocence is also a principle of fundamental justice) (R v. Oakes, 1986). The presumption of innocence also finds roots in paragraph 11(e) of the *Charter* (R v. Zora, 2020; R v. Antic, 2017), whose application is focused on bail hearings (Lafrance, 2021: 297; Gautam and Lafrance, 2020: 130). Further, the extent of the application of the presumption of innocence does not stop here. For instance, LeBel J. and Fish J. of the Supreme Court of Canada wrote (dissenting but not on this point) in the *Sinclair* decision that "[t]he right to silence, the right against self-incrimination, and the presumption of innocence are *interrelated* principles" (2010: para 159). Thus, the presumption of innocence is not limited in Canada to the trial stage when a court must decide at the end of the judicial process whether an accused is guilty of a criminal offence. This open-ended application of the presumption of innocence is not unique to Canada. The same goes, for example, in South Africa (Schwikkard, 1998: 403).

The different meanings and applications given to the presumption of innocence (Huynh Tan Le and Bedi, 2022: 360) led some to challenge the existence of a univocal meaning scope given to the presumption of innocence (Weigend, 2013). This is undeniably true when observing that several common law jurisdictions countries (Canada, New Zealand, United States, etc.) as well as non-common law jurisdictions (France, Italy, etc.) gave it a constitutional protection as opposed to other jurisdictions that have not given it such a status (Pattabhi and Bharti, 2016: 57). Some of these latter countries, like India, would rather give it a human right status, without giving it the status of a fundamental right (Bedi, 2021: 368; *Noor Aga*; *Gurbaksh Singh Sibbia*).

The wide acceptance of the presumption of innocence around the planet undoubtedly shows its objective importance (Huynh Tan Le and Bedi, 2022: 361). It is provided by most human rights treaties, namely paragraph 11(1) of the Universal Declaration of Human Rights; paragraph 14(2) of the International Covenant on Civil and Political Rights; paragraph 6(2) of the European Convention of Human Rights; paragraph 48(1) of the European Union Charter, etc. The presumption of innocence is "formulated in a broadly similar way" in all these legal instruments (van Kempen, 2014). Conversely, it is stated that "there exists diversity and discrepancy in providing and applying this principle in various jurisdictions" (Huynh Tan Le and Bedi, 2022: 362, 364–365).

These two latter approaches may seem to be conflicting, but there are different ways of reconciling them. First, one possible way to reconcile these two different views about the scope of the presumption of innocence could consist in pointing out that the former focuses on the *formulation* of this principle while the latter addresses its *application*. Second, another way to reconcile these views would be to note that the former speaks to *international* standards regarding this principle as opposed to the latter that emphasises the differences that exist about this principle between *national* jurisdictions. Third, a further way to explain these two alleged different understandings of the presumption of innocence could also be based on the contention that the former could simply include the latter, like Russian dolls (matryoshka), removing the possible contradictions between these two approaches. This means that being 'broadly formulated' would not preclude the possibility that there could be underlying differences between them at the time of its application.

4.1.2   Reverse Burden of Proof

A discussion is worth having regarding the reverse burden of proof in criminal law, especially in the context of the study of the presumption of innocence and criminalization because "[t]he most fertile ground for debate over the presumption of innocence in recent times has concerned offences in which the burden of proof is placed on the defence" (Tadros and Tierney, 2004: 416; Allen, 2021: 117). A reverse burden of proof corresponds to "a statutory provision requiring that the accused be responsible for providing evidence on some relevant point, either to raise a doubt about whether the point is true or to show on balance of probabilities that it is not true" (Coughlan, 2020: 617).

Generally speaking, at least in Canada, "the burden of proof rests on the prosecution throughout the *trial* [, which] never shifts to the accused" (R v. Lifchus, 1997: para 36). The rationale to justify this principle is based on the argument that "every reverse burden is *prima facie* a breach of the presumption of innocence because it introduces the possibility that the accused can be *convicted* despite reasonable doubt as to their guilt" (Allen, 2021: 115). This rule could suffer, in the abstract, from some exceptions, even in Canada, if we look at the criminal judicial proceedings in its entirety. For instance, at the bail stage, when the nature of a charge laid against the accused gives application to section 515(6) of the Criminal Code, this would automatically shift the burden on him or her. However, at the bail stage, an accused would not be *convicted* of an offence so early during the criminal judicial process, but he or she could be eventually *detained* not *convicted* (Schwikkard, 1998: 402), *pending trial*. This would confirm, if understood properly, the rule mentioned above, and then the reverse burden of proof would not be an exception to that rule after all. Besides, the presumption of innocence would only apply, according to Picinali (2014: 253), when a criminal offence is, in fact, created by the legislature, contrary to what some other authors argue (Tomlin, 2013), i.e. "[w]ithout criminalisation there would be no criminal offence to charge and, therefore, no presumption to enforce."

In Europe, Article 22 of the Directive (EU) 2016/343 – which Directive pertains, inter alia, to the interpretation of Article 6 of the European Convention for the Protection of Human Rights and Fundamental Freedoms ('ECHR') reads, "[t]he presumption of innocence would be *infringed* if the burden of proof were shifted from the prosecution to the defence". Conversely, Picinali (2014: 248) argues that the decision of the European Court of Human Rights in *Salabiaku v. France*, interpreting paragraph 6(2) of the ECHR, "suggests [that this latter paragraph] prescribes *no blanket ban* on such evidentiary device. In particular, the presumption [of innocence] is not violated as long as the Contracting State uses a reverse burden 'within reasonable limits'". Article 22 of the Directive (EU) 2016/343, which seems to make a blanket statement against the legality of any shift of the burden of proof from the prosecution to the defence, seems to be in contradiction with the latter interpretation of paragraph 6(2) of the ECHR that would rather allow it, at least 'within reasonable limits' (Salabiaku v. France, 1988: para 28). As a side note, that reference to 'reasonable limits' might resemble, if not echo, the legal rationale of the oft-cited *Oakes* test established in 1986 by the Supreme Court of Canada. Summarily, this test provides that a restriction on a right or freedom, including the presumption of innocence, will be justified, via the application of Section 1 of the *Charter*, only if it is reasonable and demonstrably justified in a free and democratic society.

A reverse burden of proof, either allegedly justified via the above-mentioned 'reasonable limits' or upheld as a necessary exception to the presumption of innocence as it is the case in India (Bedi, 2021: 379) or else, would have a State, according to Picinali (2014: 249), "criminalize [a] behaviour in the complete absence of the element of which the burden has been reversed". Therefore, if this element were a constituent of the crime, the reverse burden would then breach the presumption of innocence. For example, section 114A of the Indian Evidence Act, 1872, presumes the absence of consent in certain prosecution for rape displacing the presumption of innocence with that of guilt, at least with respect to the issue of consent. The Supreme Court of India had stated in 1979 in the landmark case *Tuka Ram v. State of Maharashtra*, commonly known at the *Mathura* case, that "[t]he onus is always on the prosecution to prove affirmatively each ingredient of the offence it seeks to establish and such onus never shifts." This wording is quite similar to the one used by the Supreme Court of Canada in its *Lifchus* decision, previously cited, rendered twenty-eight years later, but the similarity between the two decisions stops here. The public outcry and protests that were caused by the acquittal of the accused in the Mathura case led to the addition of section 114A to the Indian Evidence Act. Cherukuri (2021: 1) observes, "[m]ore often than not, public moral outrage and a call to reform laws only emerge after sexual assaults against women". This is exactly what seems to have happened following the Mathura case in India.

Sundby (1989: 462) describes one of the approaches regarding the reconciliation of the competing interests raised by the presumption of innocence, namely the substantivist school of thought, as one that "believes that just because a fact is included within a crime's definition ... does not mean that the fact is 'necessary' to constitute the crime charged" (1989: 475). Along the same lines, there would be a breach of the presumption of innocence where "the legislature ... removes some of the conditions of liability from the definition of an offence" (Tadros, 2014: 459; Ferguson, 2016: 142). Discussing the expansivist views, Picinali (2014: 247) remarks, "if A, B, and C are considered relevant [conditions] to punishment, the lawmaker cannot define guilt as depending on A and B only, so as to place the burden of proving C on the defendant." This could be the effect of section 114A of the Indian Evidence Act, discussed above, that removes the obligation for the prosecution to prove the lack of consent in certain prosecution for rape. This approach "has implications for criminalisation" (Picinali, 2014: 245) because "[w]hen assessing whether the presumption of innocence has been breached through considering whether conduct without the element subject to the reverse burden could legitimately be made a crime, courts weigh reasons for criminalizing" (Picinali, 2014: 255).

According to the substantivist approach, "[t]he presumption [of innocence] is violated when a person is convicted of conduct that should not be subject to punishment, *whether or not a reverse burden is involved*" (Picinali, 2014: 245). Referring again to the example of sexual assault (rape) discussed above, it is undeniable that such an offence should be subject to punishment. Nevertheless, consent, which is the subject of the reverse burden of proof provided by Article 114A of the Indian Evidence Act, is pivotal, or 'necessary' (Sundby 1989: 475), to the nature of this offence (R v, Chase, 1987; R v. Ewanchuk, 1999), otherwise it may simply turn into a consensual sexual activity, then removing the necessity to punish such conduct.

However, the substantivist approach does not challenge that, it rather argues that "a reverse burden on a particular fact is compatible with the presumption [of innocence] only if the prohibited behaviour, considered *without (the negative of) that fact*, would be deserving of punishment". Therefore, what this approach seems to contend is that, in fact, having a reverse onus or not does not make a difference at the end of the day as to whether a conduct should be criminalized or not, then the reverse burden of proof would be compatible with the presumption of innocence if the conduct should in principle be criminalized.

Going back to our initial discussion of criminalization, more specifically as to "the proper level of criminalization" (Moore, 2014: 183), it is expected that nobody in their right mind would challenge that a sexual assault (rape) is wrongful, then meeting the above-mentioned 'wrongness constraint' (Cornford, 2017: 615) that justifies its criminalisation. That being said, as Tomlin (2013: 56) notes, "murder is properly criminalisable even if [a] legislature does not recognise it as so, and ... eating bread should not be criminalized, regardless of what [a] legislature thinks." The latter adds a morality element to criminalisation. Murder, as rape, is, in and of itself, wrong whereas eating bread could hardly be considered as such.

Pursuant to another approach, the purpose theory, "a reverse burden is incompatible with the presumption of innocence if the occurrence of the particular fact that the defendant is required to prove would make the conduct fall outside the lawmaker's target" (Picinali, 2014: 247). Requesting the accused to prove consent with respect to a sexual assault (rape) would do just that since if consent were proven, there would be no such thing as a sexual assault. Therefore, based on this approach, the presumption of innocence would be breached in that context, contrary to the substantivist approach. The same conclusion, but not via the same reasoning, would be reached by the tenants of the proceduralist approach, which focuses on the constituents of the crime definition as defined by the lawmaker, who contends that "only reverse burdens regarding the negative of an element of the crime conflict with the presumption of innocence" (Picinali, 2014: 246).

Determining whether a reverse burden breaches the presumption of innocence should also be based, according to Picinali (2014: 244–245), on an understanding of the nature of that presumption, i.e. whether it is substantive or procedural. This is, in turn, a key consideration in the various approaches regarding the possible interactions between the presumption of innocence and criminalisation, which are examined in the last section of this chapter.

4.1.3   Procedural or Substantive Right?

While the principle of the presumption of innocence itself is not controversial (Roach, 2006: 249), its scope of application has been hotly debated. Even though some argue, "protecting innocence is too important … to be cabined to the discrete categories of substantive, procedural or evidential law" (Roach, 2006: 301), the fact remains that these categories, among others, have caught the attention of several scholars, and they remain key when it comes to criminalisation. This relates to the following questions, encapsulated by Picinali (2014: 244), as to "how do courts interpret the presumption? – and a normative question – how should courts interpret it?"

The presumption of innocence can mainly receive two meanings, a 'procedural' or a 'substantive' one. Its procedural side "concerns only the proof of facts at trial" (Lippke, 2016: 20), then limiting its applications to criminal proceedings. In that sense, it would not have "implications for the content of [the] substantive elements [of a crime] themselves" (Tadros and Tierney, 2004: 407). This understanding of the presumption of innocence is the one that finds "the most favour with common lawyers" (Allen, 2021: 119; Moore, 2014: 183), including with the courts. Its substantive meaning rather relates to the innocence in the sense of moral innocence (Prendergast, 2011: 304), meaning, for some, that "the presumption of innocence restrains … what can be marked out as criminal in the first place" (Duff, 2005; Lippke, 2016: 60). It should protect citizens against acts that are deemed criminal by law when they should not be considered so (Tadros, 2007: 197).

The Supreme Court of Canada states in *Pearson* (1992) that "[s]ections 11(*d*) and 11(*e*) define the *procedural* content of the presumption of innocence at the bail and trial stages of the criminal process and constitute both the extent and the *limit* of that presumption at those stages." This so-called limit might be seen as a roadblock to any possible recognition by the Court of a substantive dimension to the presumption of innocence. However, in *J.J.*, in a more recent decision of the Court rendered in 2022, the dissenting reasons of Rowe J. may have left the door open for the Court to eventually recognise such a substantive dimension. Rowe J. writes that section 11(d) of the *Charter*, which had been identified by the Court's jurisprudence as a procedural protection, provides for "interlocking *substantial* and procedural protections" (*J. J.*, 2022: para 335). He also writes later that "[i]n addition to its *substantive* content, s. 11(d) provides for certain *procedural* guarantees" (2022: para 339). It must be noted that a dissenting opinion is not without weight and may pave the way of the future: "The 'great dissents' of the nineteenth and twentieth centuries in the United States provide additional and persuasive evidence of the potential contribution of dissenting opinions to the law's evolution" (Hon. L'Heureux-Dubé, 2000: 506). Let us recall that although the Court already gave a substantive dimension to the presumption of innocence in the past as a fundamental principle of justice under section 7 of the *Charter* (R v. Oakes, 1986: 119; R v. Lyons, 1987: 361; R v. Noble, 1997: 107), this was not under its section 11(d). Therefore, could these dissenting reasons of Rowe J. in *J. J.* eventually constitute the basis of an argument, in one way or another, for the highest court of the land to justify itself in marking a certain conduct as criminal? Could it rather be done via section 7 of the *Charter*? This remains to be seen, especially because doing so could be considered as a breach of the sacrosanct principles provided by Montesquieu's doctrine of the separation of power, and because such a bold move by the Court might be identified by some as a form of 'judicial activism' (Bedi and Lafrance, 2020).

4.1.4   Interactions between the Presumption of Innocence and Criminalization

Now that we have examined, on one hand, the underlying foundations and some of the issues related to criminalization and, on the other hand, the dual dimension given to the presumption of innocence, let us briefly discuss some of the interactions that may exist between the two in light of a principled approach, more specifically the thesis advanced by Tomlin. Summarily, the first part of his thesis is that "incorrect decisions about criminalisation, convictions, and sentencing are ultimately all instances of unjust punishment – in each case someone is given punishment they should not be given." (Tomlin, 2013: 53; Lippke, 2016: 66). Therefore, expressed in plain terms, a wrongful conviction, which is an incorrect decision about conviction, would be, according to him, the equivalent of a wrongful criminalisation, mostly because "unjust criminalisation and wrongful conviction are ultimately mistakes of the same type: giving people punishment they should not receive" (Tomlin, 2013: 45, 52–53). A wrongful conviction breaches the presumption of innocence (Van Sliedgret, 2009: 265), so would a wrongful criminalisation.

A clear connection between criminalization and the presumption of innocence in Tomlin's theory is that the latter should not apply to the wrongness of punishing people, but it should also apply when deciding about criminalizing a specific conduct (Tomlin, 2013: 44–45). Consequently, the second part of his thesis is that there can be criminalization of a conduct when we are sure beyond a reasonable doubt that the suggested criminalization is morally grounded (Tomlin, 2013: 53), both at the legislative and judicial stage. This proposition stands out because the legislature does not proceed usually with this in mind when assessing the possible adoption of new legislations or provisions regarding criminal law. This thesis only works under the umbrella of a *substantive* approach for the presumption of innocence because it must be *morally* grounded (Tomlin, 2013: 52); it does not only concern the proof of facts at trial as the procedural approach sees it. Unlike Husak, his thesis does not contend necessarily that there are too many crimes enacted by the legislature because, for instance, the legislature can also wrongly fail to criminalize conducts when it should (Tomlin, 2013: 59), think of foods containing arsenic, which is not banned in the United States! (Cahn, 2023), but criminalization must be principled.

5 Conclusion

Criminalization may be seen either with a positive eye or with a dim view. As a hotly debated issue, some argue that it is rampant, that it should be fought against, others contend that there should be more. Both the legislature and the courts may over-criminalize. The presumption of innocence has two main dimensions, i.e. procedural and substantive. When understood as substantive, it may serve as a constraint on criminalization as well as a protection against wrongful criminalization to avoid overcriminalization. Therefore, the seed has been planted, mostly by the doctrine but also by the jurisprudence, for further developments regarding the interactions between criminalization and the presumption of innocence. It will be interesting to see eventually in which direction(s) it goes.

Disclaimer: *The views, opinions and conclusions expressed herein are personal to this author and should not be construed as those of any of the employers of this author.*

Bibliography

Allen, J. (2021) "Rethinking the Relationship between Reverse Burdens and the Presumption of Innocence". *The International Journal of Evidence and Proof*, 25(2): 115–134.

Ashworth, A. (2006) "Four Threats to the Presumption of Innocence". *International Journal of Evidence and Proof*, 10(4): 241–279.

Ashworth, A. (2008) "Conceptions of Overcriminalization". *Ohio St. J. Crim. L.*, 5: 407–425.

Barbe, E. (2009) "La pénalisation à l'étranger". *Pouvoir*, 1(128): 13–25.

Bedi, S. (2021) "Presumption of Innocence and Reverse Onus Clauses: The State of Criminal and Constitutional Jurisprudence in India". In: Biddulph, S., et al. (eds), *The Presumption of Innocence*. Vietnam: Hong Duc Publishing House.

Bedi, S., & Lafrance, S. (2020) "The Justice in Judicial Activism: Jurisprudence of Rights and Freedoms in India and Canada". In: Khurshid, S., et al. *The Supreme Court and the Constitution: An Indian Discourse*. New Delhi: Wolters Kluwer.

Cahn, L. (January 10, 2023) "18 Things You Think Are Illegal but Aren't". *Reader's Digest*. Available at: https://www.rd.com/list/things-you-think-are-illegal-but-arent/. Accessed on January 01, 2024.

Canadian Charter of Rights and Freedoms, Part 1 of the *Constitution Act, 1982*, being Schedule B to the *Canada Act 1982* (UK), 1982, c 11.

Chalmers, J., & Leverick, F. (2014) "Quantifying Criminalization". In: Duff, R. A., et al. (ed.), *Criminalization: The Political Morality of the Criminal Law*. Oxford: Oxford University Press.

Cherukuri, S. (2021) "Sexual Violence against Women, the Laws, the Punishment, and Negotiating the Duplicity". *Law*, 10(27): 1–13.

Coffin v. United States, 156 U.S. 432, 453 (1895) Supreme Court, United States of America.

Cornford, A. (2017) "Rethinking the Wrongness Constraint on Criminalisation". *Law and Philosophy*, 36: 615–649.

Coughlan, S. (2020) *Criminal Procedure (4th ed.)*. Toronto: Irwin Law Inc.

Criminal Code of Canada, RSCc C-46 (1985).

Criminal Law Amendment Act (Can.), c. 38 (1968–1969).

Cumyn, M. (January 15, 2018) "Pourquoi définir les concepts juridiques?". *Chaire de rédaction juridique Louis-Philippe-Pigeon*. Université Laval. Available at: https://www.redactionjuridique.chaire.ulaval.ca/actualites/pourquoi-definir-les-concepts-juridiques. Accessed on March 08, 2020.

Directive (EU) 2016/343. (2016) European Parliament and of the Council. On the strengthening of certain aspects of the presumption of innocence and of the right to be present at the trial in criminal proceedings.

Duff, R. A. (2005) "Strict Liability, Legal Presumptions, and the Presumptions of Innocence". In: Simester, A. (ed) *Appraising Strict Liability*. Oxford: Oxford University Press.

Duff, R. A. (2010) "Perversions and Subversions of Criminal Law". In: Duff, R. A., et al. (eds) *The Boundaries of the Criminal Law*. Oxford: Oxford University Press.

Ferguson, P. R. (2016) "The Presumption of Innocence and Its Role in the Criminal Process". *Criminal Law Forum*, 27: 131–158.

Gautam, K. (2022a) *Cannabis Indica: Perception vs Potential*. Gurugram: Oakbridge.

Gautam, K. (2022b) "Book Review: Cannabinoids and the Brain". *Jindal Global Law Review*, 13(2): 401–408.

Gautam, K., and Lafrance, S. (2020) "A Comparative Survey of The Law of Bail in India and Canada". In: Khurshid, S., et al. (eds) *Taking Bail Seriously*. Gurugram: LexisNexis India.

Gilles, I. (2012) *Lessons from India's Constitutional Culture: What Canada Can Learn*. Master in Law Thesis, McGill University. Available at: https://escholarship.mcgill.ca/concern/theses/kh04dt01g?locale=en. Accessed on December 01, 2022.

Grant, I. (2013) "The Over-Criminalization of Persons with HIV". *University of Toronto Law Journal*, 63(3): 475–484.

Gurbaksh Singh Sibbia v. State of Punjab, INSC 70 (1980) Supreme Court, India.

Haley, J. (2019) "Rethinking Criminalization: Aims, Attributes, and Alternative Approaches". *Willamette Journal of International Law and Dispute Resolution*, 26(1–2): 1–41.

Haugh, T. (2015) "Overcriminalization's New Harm Paradigm". *Vanderbilt Law Review*, 68(5): 1191–1242.

Hogg, P. W., & Bushell, A. A. (1997) "The Charter Dialogue between Courts and Legislatures (Or Perhaps the Charter of Rights Isn't Such a Bad Thing after All)". *Osgoode Hall Law Journal*, 35(1): 75–124.

Hunter v. Southam Inc., 2 SCR 145 (1984) Supreme Court, Canada.

Husak, D. (2008) *Overcriminalization: The Limits of the Criminal Law*. New York: Oxford University Press.

Husak, D. (2010) "Overcriminalization". In: Patterson, D. (ed) *A Companion to Philosophy of Law and Legal Theory (2nd ed.)*. Singapore: Blackwell Publishing Ltd.

Husak, D. (2011) "Reservations about Overcriminalization". *New Criminal Law Review*, 14(1): 97–107.

Huynh Tan Le, D., and Bedi, S. (2022) "Presumption of Innocence: Comparing Vietnamese Law with Established International Jurisprudence". *Criminal Law Forum*, 33: 359–308.

Jalušič, V. (2020) "Less Than Criminals: Crimmigration "Law" and the Creation of the Dual State". In: Šalamon, K. (ed) *Causes and Consequences of Migrant Criminalization*. Switzerland: Springer Nature.

Jones, G. (2014) "Over-Criminalization and the Need for Crime Paradigm". *Rutgers Law Review*, 66(4): 931–[iv].

Kadish, S. H. (1962) "Legal Norm and Discretion in the Police and Sentencing Processes". *Harvard Law Review*, 75(5): 904–931.

Kadish, S. H. (1967) "The Crisis of Overcriminalization". *The Annals of the American Academy of Political and Social Science, 374*(1): 157–170.

Karmini, N. (December 6, 2022) *Indonesia's Parliament votes to ban sex outside of marriage*. Billings Gazette. Available at: https://billingsgazette.com/news/national/govt-and-politics/adultery-a-punishable-offense-in-indonesias-new-penal-code/article_562f43e1-5143-5fc6-a9ae-338953683b03.html. Accessed on August 07, 2023.

Kirby, M. (1995) "A Challenge for the Future – The United Nations Strengths and Weaknesses". *United Nations Association of Australia*. Available at: http://www.lawfoundation.net.au/ljf/app/&id=A37A4B55F0370365CA2571A8001C51FD. Accessed on December 01, 2022.

Lacey, N. (2009) "Historicising Criminalisation: Conceptual and Empirical Issues". *Modern Law Review, 72*(6): 936–960.

Lafrance, S. (July 08, 2020) *Should Canadian Law Matter to Indian Jurists? Advocating for More Substantial Legal Discussion between the 'Long Lost Siblings'*. The Contemporary Law Forum Available at: https://tclf.in/2020/07/08/should-canadian-law-matter-to-indian-jurists-advocating-for-more-substantial-legal-discussion-between-the-long-lost-siblings/. Accessed on January 01, 2021.

Lafrance, S. (July 07, 2020) *The Beauty of Differences: Multiculturalism through the Eyes of a Humanist*. Socio Legal Literary. Available at: https://sociolegalliterary.in/the-beauty-of-differences-multiculturalism-through-the-eyes-of-a-humanist/. Accessed on February 01, 2021.

Lafrance, S. (2021) "The Presumption of Innocence in Canada: A Comparative Perspective with Vietnam". In: Biddulph, S., et al. (eds) *The Presumption of Innocence*. Vietnam: Hong Duc Publishing House.

Larkin, Jr., & Paul, J. (2014) "Regulation, Prohibition, and Overcriminalization: The Proper and Improper Uses of the Criminal Law". *Hofstra Law Review*, 42: 745.

L'Heureux-Dubé, C. (2000) "The Dissenting Opinion: Voice of the Future?". *Osgoode Hall Law Journal, 38*(3): 495–517.

Lippke, R. L. (2015) "The Presumption of Innocence in the Trial Setting". *Ratio Juris, 28*(2): 159–179.

Lippke, R. L. (2016) *Taming the Presumption of Innocence*. New York: Oxford University Press.

Luna, E. (2005) "The Overcriminalization Phenomenon". *American University Law Review, 54*(3): 703–746.

Luna, E. (2012) "Prosecutorial Decriminalization". *J. Crim. L. & Criminology*, 102: 785–820.

Machiavelli, N. (2014) *The Prince*. Great Britain: Penguin.

Mahapatra, D. (January 20, 2023) "Supreme Court rejects RAW objections, sends Kirpal's name for high court judge again". *Times of India*. Available at: https://timesofindia.indiatimes.com/india/supreme-court-rejects-raw-objections-sends-kirpals-name-for-high-court-judge-again/articleshow/97150393.cms. Accessed on January 06, 2024.

Marwah, P. (September 1, 2021) *Interpretation of Statutes: Strict Construction of Penal Statute*. Indian Legal Wing. Available at: https://www.indianlegalwing.com/post/interpretation-of-statutes-strict-construction-of-penal-statutes. Accessed on May 06, 2024.

McLachlin, B. (August 14, 2015) *The Legal Profession in the 21st Century – Remarks of the Right Honourable Beverley McLachlin P.C., Chief Justice of Canada*. Supreme Court of Canada. Available at: https://www.scc-cs c.ca/judges-juges/spe-dis/bm-2015-08-14-eng.aspx. Accessed on December 01, 2022.

Moore, M. S. (2014) "Liberty's Constraints on What Should be Made Criminal". In: Duff, R. A., et al. (eds), *Criminalization: The Political Morality of the Criminal Law*. New York: Oxford University Press.

Nguyen, V. Q., et al. (2020) "Legal and Social Challenges Posed by the Social Credit System in China". *International Journal of Innovation, Creativity and Change*, 14(5): 413–428.

Nguyen, V. Q., et al. (2023) "China's Social Credit System: A Challenge to Human Rights". *The Law, State and Telecommunications Review*, 15(2): 98–116.

Noor Aga v. State of Punjab, 16 SCC 417 (2008) Supreme Court, India.

Orwell, G. (1949) *Nineteen Eighty-Four*. London: Secker & Warburg.

Pániker, A. (2010) *Jainism – History, Society, Philosophy and Practice*. Delhi: Motilal Banarsidass Publishers (translated from Spanish).

Pattabhi, R., et al. (2016) "Reverse Burdens: A Threat to Presumption of Innocence". *NPA Criminal Law Review*, 3(1): 47–74.

Picinali, F. (2014) "Innocence and Burdens of Proof in English Criminal Law". *Law, Probability and Risk*, 13(3–4): 243–258.

Pierce, M. (2015–2016) "The Court and Overcriminalization". *Stanford Law Review Online*, 68: 50–60.

Prendergast, D. (2011) "The Constitutionality of Strict Liability Offences". *Dublin University Law Journal*, 33: 285–318.

Reference Re Validity of Section 5(a) of the Dairy Industry Act, SCR 1 (1949) ('Margarine Reference'), Supreme Court, Canada.

Roach, K. (2006) "The Protection of Innocence Under Section 7 of the Charter". *S.C.L.R.*, 34(2d): 249–303.

Rossow, I. and Strang, J. (2009) *Drug Policy and the Public Good* (1st ed.). Oxford: Oxford University Press.

R. v. Antic, 1 SCR 509 (2017) Supreme Court, Canada.

R. v. Chase, 2 SCR 293 (1987) Supreme Court, Canada.

R. v. Ewanchuk, 1 SCR 330 (1999) Supreme Court, Canada.

R. v. Hasselwander, 2 SCR 398 (1993) Supreme Court, Canada.

R. v. Heywood, 3 SCR 761 (1994) Supreme Court, Canada.

R. v. J.J., SCC 28 (2022) Supreme Court, Canada.

R. v. Lifchus, 3 SCR 320 (1997) Supreme Court, Canada.
R. v. Lyons, 2 SCR 309 (1987) Supreme Court, Canada.
R. v. Mabior, 2 SCR 584 (2012) Supreme Court, Canada.
R. v. Noble, 1 SCR 874 (1997) Supreme Court, Canada.
R. v. Oakes, 1 SCR 103 (1986) Supreme Court, Canada.
R. v. Pearson, 3 SCR 665 (1992) Supreme Court, Canada.
R. v. Sharpe, 1 SCR 45 (2001) Supreme Court, Canada.
R. v. Sinclair, 2 SCR 310 (2010) Supreme Court, Canada.
R. v. Zora, SCC 14 (2020) Supreme Court, Canada.
Salabiaku v. France. 13 EHRR 379 (EHRR 1978) European Court of Human Rights.
Schwikkard, P. J. (1998) "The Presumption of Innocence: What Is It?". *South African Journal of Criminal Justice*, 11(3): 396–408.
Schwikkard, P. J. (1999) *Presumption of Innocence*. Kenwyn: Juta & Co. Ltd.
Smith, S. F. (2012) "Overcoming Overcriminalization". *Journal of Criminal Law and Criminology*, 102(3): 537–592.
Stobbe, M. J. (2018) *Was Stephen Harper Really Tough on Crime? A Systems and Symbolic Action Analysis*. Ph.D. thesis, Department of Sociology, University of Saskatchewan.
Stoneman, T. (September 20, 2020) "A 'Criminalized Onion' is a Rapscallion. *Hoagie's Law*". Available at: https://stonemanlegal.com/blog/2020/09/hoagies-law/.
Sundby, S. E. (1989) "The Reasonable Doubt Rule and the Meaning of Innocence". *Hastings L.J.*, 40: 457–510.
S v Zuma, ZACC 1 (1995) Constitutional Court, South Africa.
Tadros, V. (2007) "Rethinking the Presumption of Innocence". *Criminal Law and Philosophy*, 1: 193–213.
Tadros, V. (2014) "The Ideal of the Presumption of Innocence". *Criminal Law and Philosophy*, 8: 449–467.
Tadros, V. (2016) *Wrongs and Crimes*. Oxford: Oxford University Press.
Tadros, V., & Tierney, S. (2004) "The Presumption of Innocence and the Human Rights Act". *Modern Law Review*, 67(3): 402–434.
Theophilopoulos, C. (2001) *The Right to Silence and the Privilege Against Self-Incrimination: A Critical Examination of a Doctrine in Search of Cogent Reasons*. Ph.D. thesis, Faculty of Law, University of South Africa.
Thi, T. L. P. (2012) *La détention provisoire – étude de droit comparé – droit français et droit vietnamien* [Pretrial Detention – Comparative Law Study – French Law and Vietnamese Law]. Ph.D. thesis, Faculty of Law and Political Science, Université Montesquieu – Bordeaux IV.
Tomlin, P. (2013) "Extending the Golden Thread? Criminalisation and the Presumption of Innocence". *The Journal of Philosophy*, 21(1): 44–66.
Tuka Ram v. State of Maharashtra, SCR (1) 810 (1979). Supreme Court, India.

Kempen, P. H. (2014) "Introduction – Criminal Law and Human Rights". In: Kempen, P. H. (ed) *Criminal Law and Human Rights: The International Library of Essays on Criminal Law*. England/USA: Ashgate.

Van Sliedgret, E. (2009) "A Contemporary Reflection on the Presumption of Innocence". *Revue internationale de droit pénal*, 80(1): 247–267.

Weigend, T. (2013) "There is Only One Presumption of Innocence". *Netherlands Journal of Legal Philosophy*, 42(3): 193–204.

Woolmington v. Director of Public Prosecutions, A.C. 462 (UKHL 1935) House of Lords, United Kingdom.

Young v. Regina, TCACA 2 (TCACA 2014) Court of Appeal, Turks and Caicos Islands.

CHAPTER 7

Democratic Erosion by Parochial Measures: A Study of Rising Criminalization of Free Speech in India

Yogesh Pratap Singh

1   Introduction

There is a growing tendency to outlaw peaceful expression and arrest critics at both the national and state level in India. There is a noticeable increase in the number of cases filed under various preventive detention laws nationwide since 2014. Many people involved in nothing more than sharp criticism of the government were arrested, held in pre-trial detention, and forced to defend themselves in cumbersome criminal proceedings. Fear of prosecution forced others to engage in self-censorship. The assault on democratic ethos is so incremental that the Supreme Court had to issue notice to government on the sustained use of Section 66A of the Information Technology Act, 2000 despite the fact that this provision was declared unconstitutional in the year 2015 by the apex court in *Shreya Singhal case* (*Shreya Singhal v. Union of India*, 2015). The court termed it as "a shocking state of affairs" and sought a response from the Central Government. The illiberal propensity strikes at the very core of liberal democratic constitutionalism. The Human Rights Watch made an appeal to the government of India to drop all pending charges and investigations against those who are facing prosecution for the exercise of their right to freedom of expression. It also requested government to stop the abuse of the legal process and amend or repeal relevant laws to bring them in tune with international human rights standards (Bajoria and Lakhdhir, 2016). However, despite appeal from Human Rights Watch and apex court's remark, the government of India has submitted a proposal for the "criminalisation of offensive messages" during ongoing negotiations to draft a new legally-binding UN treaty on tackling cybercrime which is an exact duplication of the language of the Section 66A of the IT Act. This chapter primarily intends to explore the declining democratic trend in Indian liberal democracy by examining the specific preventive detention measures taken or contemplated by the government of India to restrict the freedom of speech and measures directed at curbing dissent to governmental policies.

2 Free Speech: Philosophical Justifications

There are three distinct justifications in the realm of philosophy which rationalises the importance of free speech. The first typology stems from a pledge to holding those in power accountable to the people i.e. *accountability justification*. Second typology stems from the idea of individualism i.e. *liberty justification*. And third typology asserts a pledge to discover truth i.e. *truth justification*.

The accountability justification argues that power holders in the society are essentially self-interested. As power is the ability to affect another exercise, power holders are essentially committed to retaining and possibly increasing their hold on the power. Therefore, to hold power-holders accountable to people, freedom of speech is deployed as one of the most effective means. The accountability argument challenges the authority of power holders and attempts to public scrutiny of governmental actions and point out faults in governance with its political, epistemological and moral dimensions as advanced in the writings of Thomas Paine and Jeremy Bentham.

Thomas Paine contended that all governments should be always held accountable to people at large. He further argued that for a democratic society decorated with certain inalienable natural rights people in power must be held accountable by a free and unrestricted press (Paine, 1791: 141, 142). On the other hand, Jeremy Bentham's argument was slightly different from Paine on moral and epistemological grounds where he viewed democracy in terms of its tendency to maximise utility of inalienable rights i.e. greatest happiness for the greatest number. Though Bentham too argued that freedom of speech is necessary for holding power holders accountable in the same ways as Thomas Paine.

The liberty justification upholds freedom of speech as an indispensable manifestation of the 'natural rights' of free men. As reflected by Barendt that 'people will not be able to develop intellectually and spiritually, unless they are free to formulate their beliefs and political attitudes through public discussion, and in response to the criticisms of others.' (Barendt, 1985: 14) In the realm of philosophy this perspective was developed in terms of positive and negative liberty. Positive liberty is characterised as '*freedom to*'; asserted as the freedom to express oneself as directed by one's own rational energies and usually expressed as freedom to speak, communicate, convey, and express. Berlin while explaining positive liberty observed:

> The 'positive' sense of the word 'liberty' derives from the wish on the part of the individual to be his own master. I wish my life and decisions to depend on myself, not on external forces of other men's acts of will. I wish to be a subject not an object; to be moved by reasons, by conscious

purposes, which are my own, not by causes which affect me, as it were from outside.

BERLIN, 1969: 131

The conception of negative liberty or "freedom from" emanates from the notation of individuality and its protection from external forces including freedom from censorship. John Stuart Mill in his essay 'On Liberty' underlines the concept of negative liberty as an *a-priori* restraint and argues that unless men and women are protected from interference, humanity, with its propensity to diversify and experiment, will not develop and flourish (Mill, 1859/1977: 229). He writes:

> that the sole end for which mankind are warranted, individually or collectively, in interfering with the liberty of action of any of their number, is self-protection. That the only purpose for which power can be rightfully exercised over any member of a civilised community, against his will, is to prevent harm to others.
>
> MILL, 1859/1977: 223

Mill in this essay also attempts to justify freedom of speech from another perspective which asserts the search for truth as a key manifestation of the expression of individuality. *The truth argument* therefore centred around the argument that unconstrained search for the truth is a necessary component of a rational human agent. Mill writes:

> If all mankind, minus one, were of one opinion, and only one person was of the contrary opinion, mankind would no more be justified in silencing that one person, than he, if he had the power, would be justified in silencing mankind.
>
> MILL, 1859/1977: 229

John Stuart Mill in his abovementioned statement highlights the phenomenon called 'dissent', *i.e. to differ in opinion or feelings, or 'to disagree' which is the hallmark of the inquisitive spirit of mankind.* If the opinion is true, then by suppressing it humanity is deprived of the truth and will not progress. If the opinion is false then humanity again loses, because if the opinion is false it will be shown to be so, but its expression is useful, for it forces us to restate the reasons for our beliefs (Hoffman & Graham, 2007: 43). Therefore humankind benefits when a person is permitted to express his views freely, even if he is alone in professing that opinion (Singh & Nayak, 2020). However, the truth argument is based on certain suppositions: *first* that a belief in existence of truth that can be acknowledged by the human intellect or senses; *second*, a belief in the ability of human being to attain truth or at least an approximation of the truth and *third*, that truth is valuable to mankind and worth pursuing as an end in itself. Frederick Schauer encapsulates the essence of truth argument very succinctly:

> Throughout the ages many diverse arguments have been employed to attempt to justify a principle of freedom of speech. Of all these, the predominant and most persevering has been the argument that free speech is particularly valuable because it leads to the discovery of truth. Open discussion, free exchange of ideas, freedom of enquiry, and freedom to criticise, so the argument goes, are necessary conditions for the effective functioning of the process of searching for the truth. Without this freedom we are said to be destined to stumble blindly between truth and falsehood.
> SCHAUER, 1981: 15

The history of science and of spirituality are also series of disagreements and dissents with prevailing state of affairs or notions. However, the disagreements are barely perceived as they are generally treated to be a continuity of normal (Singh, 2016). The truth of the moment of Albert Einstein was the dissent with the then existing notions of time, space and energy. The dissent of $E = mc^2$ soon became the consent. Copernicus dissented to challenge the long-held notion that the Earth was the centre of the Solar system (Singh, 2014). This reluctant radical dissenter set in motion a chain of events that eventually produced the greatest revolution in thinking that Western civilization has seen. His ideas were realised only after 100 years when Kepler, Galileo, and Newton[1] fabricated on the heliocentric Universe of Copernicus and produced the revolution that swept away completely the ideas of Aristotle and replaced them with the modern view of astronomy and natural science (Singh, 2014).

Similarly, spiritual dissents later became consents. Such moments have an inbuilt truth potential because of dissent. Religious dissent goes back at least as far as ancient Egypt. Records indicate that a pharaoh named Akhenaten tried to establish a monotheistic state religion centred on the worship of the Sun God Ra (Singh, 2014). But the priests of the other ancient gods opposed him and eventually conquered his dynasty. In ancient Greece, the eminent

---

1 All scientists are in fact dissenters who thought differently from the mainstream thought or knowledge.

philosopher Socrates voiced doubts about the existence of the gods of Greek mythology, and this was one of the charges against him that led to his execution. A brief survey of the history of spirituality shows the magnitude of dissent both at inter-religion and intra-religion levels (Singh, 2014):

Buddhism developed as a dissent against several vices existing in Sanatan Hinduism like caste system, rituals, spirits or the devil to alleviate human sufferings (Wright, 2020). An overwhelming portion of Dalit community led by the architect of the Indian Constitution Dr. B.R. Ambedkar adopted Buddhism in India which preserved dissent as part of its Bible (Singh, 2014). Dissent arose in Buddhism within the lifetime of Buddha, its founder when Maha-Kassapa lamented the decay of the religion.[2]

Like Buddhism, Jainism too grew on the ancient land of India as a dissent that emphasised on non-violence, ahimsa, and respect for all living beings. Jainism promotes a simple and ascetic lifestyle and has had a significant impact on Indian culture and philosophy. The religion emphasises self-discipline and spiritual growth through meditation, contemplation, and good conduct. Later disagreement in Jainism gave birth to two major branches: *Digambara* and *Svetambara* (Jainism | Encyclopedia.com, n.d.).

Christianity emerged in the Roman Empire as a religion of dissent, eventually becoming the dominant religion of the empire. The central tenet of Christianity was the belief in the death and resurrection of Jesus, who is seen as the son of God and saviour of humanity. Today, Christianity is one of the largest religions, with followers in every corner of the globe. However, dissent and disagreement have been a part of Christianity since its inception. Early Christians disagreed over theological and organisational issues, leading to the formation of different denominations. Throughout history, Christian thinkers and leaders have expressed dissent on issues such as religious authority, social justice, and political power. Today, Christianity remains diverse, with various denominations holding differing views on various theological, moral, and social issues. The spirit of dissent and disagreement has also inspired positive change and growth within the religion (Stromberg, 1954).

---

2 Maha-Kassapa complained the number of rules was few, but the number of monks who became properly trained was many; now, by contrast, there are many rules, but few of the monks are becoming accomplished in the training. This was the dissent from the top: one of the foremost monks, who eventually took over the leadership of the religion, is complaining that the rules don't work. Complaint against the (prolix) monastic code from one of its foremost proponents is significant. The fact that the canon preserves dissent of this kind is even more significant.

Islam emerged in the 7th century in the Arabian Peninsula as a dissenting religion against the polytheistic beliefs and practices of the time. Islam spread rapidly, reaching as far as Spain in the west and India in the east. During its early centuries, Islam faced opposition and dissent from both within and outside the religion, leading to the formation of various sects. The two divisions within the tradition are the Sunni and Shia, each of which claims different means of maintaining religious authority. Today, Islam is the second largest religion in the world and continues to face dissent and disagreement on a variety of issues, including theological interpretation, political power and cultural identity.

India's triumph over the British Empire is largely a testimony of the people's power of dissent set in motion by the Mahatma and explained in his defence at the great Ahmedabad trial. There he contended (Iyer, 1992: 187):

> affection cannot be manufactured or regulated by law. If one has no affection for a person so system, one should be free to give the fullest expression to his disaffection, so long as he does not contemplate, promote or incite to violence. But I hold it to be a virtue to be disaffected towards a Government which in its totality has done more harm to India than any previous system. India is less manly under the British rule than she ever was before. Holding such a belief, I consider it to be sin to have affection for the system.
> GANDHI, 1924

> I am endeavouring to show to my countrymen that violent non-co-operation only multiplies evil and that as evil can only be sustained by violence, withdrawal of support of evil requires complete abstention from violence. Non-violence implies voluntary submission to the penalty for non-co-operation with evil. I am here, therefore, to invite and submit cheerfully to the highest penalty that can be inflicted upon me for what in law is a deliberate crime and what appears to me to be the highest duty of a citizen. The only course open to you, the Judge, is either to resign your post and thus dissociate yourself from evil, if you feel that the law you are called upon to administer is an evil and that in reality I am innocent; or to inflict on me the severest penalty if you believe that the system and the law you are assisting to administer are good for the people of this country and that my activity is therefore injurious to the public weal.
> GANDHI, 1924

He had no illusion about courts and robes not fears of that little threat of little men 'drest in a little brief authority' to use contempt power from the Legislative House or Judicial Branch.

> it does not require much reflection to see that it is through courts that a Government establishes its authority and it is through schools that it manufactures clerks and other employees. They are both healthy institutions when the Government in charge of them is on the whole just. They are death-traps when the Government is unjust.
> GANDHI, 1924

During the days when millions of Indians were slayed a single Gandhi was a stronger one-man boundary force than the Indian army on other borders, as Lord Mountbatten had said. Why? Because the dynamic dissent, with soul's infinite strength, that Gandhi expressed against communal lawlessness and, earlier, against British satanic law, proved the proposition that there is a boundless power for human justice in each one of us which can subdue the violent 'lawlessness' of the law and of life by the non-violent use of soul force (Iyer, 1992: 188). Gandhiji in wider perspective explained the duty to dissent:

> we must refuse to wait for the wrong to be righted till the wrong doer has been roused to a sense of his iniquity. We must not for fear for ourselves or others having so suffer remain participatory in it. But we must combat the wrong by ceasing to assist the wrong-doer directly or indirectly.
>
> If a father does an injustice, it is duty of his children to leave the parental roof. If the headmaster of a school conducts his institution on an immoral basis, the pupils must leave the school. If the chairman of a corporation is corrupt, the members thereof must wash their hands clean of this corruption by withdrawing from it; even so if a government does a grave injustice the subject must withdraw co-operation wholly or partially, sufficiently to wean the ruler from his wickedness. In each case conceived by me there is an element of suffering whether mental or physical. Without such suffering it is not possible to attain freedom.
> GANDHI, 1927

A brief reference of history was essential for understanding the human experience and our understanding of the importance of free speech and the phenomenon of dissent. It provides context and perspective on current events and helps us make informed decisions. History helps us understand the origins and evolution of cultures, institutions, and political systems, as well as their impact on the world today. Additionally, history allows us to understand how societies have responded to challenges and conflicts, and how they have overcome adversity. Studying history also helps to promote critical thinking, cultural empathy, and an appreciation for diversity. In this chapter the author undertakes to show how much Indian soil is prepared to nourish one of the most fundamental and cherished ideals of humanity i.e. freedom of speech and dissent by examining the execution of various laws which have the tendency to outlaw dissent and criticisms.

3 Constitutional Vision and Judicial Engrafting of Free Speech

Freedom of speech and expression was documented as an important fundamental right under the Indian Constitution under Article 19(1) (a). It is essential for the functioning of democracy, as it allows individuals to express their opinions and ideas freely and openly, which can lead to the exchange of diverse perspectives and the formation of informed opinions. It also promotes accountability, transparency and ensures that the government is held accountable for its actions. The right to freedom of speech and expression is therefore crucial for protecting individual liberty and promoting democratic values in India (Tripathi, 1958). However, this right is subject to reasonable restrictions under Article 19(2) for reasons such as defamation, contempt of court, the security of the state, public order, decency, and morality.

The Indian Supreme Court played a vital role in interpreting and upholding this right over the years. Two early cases decided by the Supreme Court i.e. *Romesh Thapar v. State of Madras* (1950) and *Brij Bhushan v. State of Delhi* (1950) set the tone for generous interpretation of Article 19 (1) (a) of the Constitution. In the decades that followed, the Supreme Court gradually expanded the scope of the right to freedom of speech and expression. In several landmark cases, the court struck down laws and regulations that were seen as unjustified restrictions on free speech. In *Sakal Papers v. Union of India* (1962), the Supreme Court struck down a law entitled 'The Newspaper (Price and Page) Act, 1956' which empowered the government not only to regulate the price of newspapers but also the size and space of advertisement on the ground that it was an unjustified restriction on freedom of press which is an integral part of Article 19 (1) (a). This progressive judicial trend was followed in *Bennett Coleman and Co. v. Union of India* (1973) and *Express Newspapers (Bombay) (P) Ltd. v. Union of India* (1986) where apex court observed the importance of press very aptly and held that it is implicit in the freedom of speech and expression.

In later years also, the Supreme Court continued to play a vital role in protecting the right to freedom of speech and expression. It upheld the right of individuals to express their opinions on political and social issues, even if those opinions were controversial or unpopular. *Kedar Nath Singh v. The State of Bihar* (1962), *Prabha Dutt v. Union of India* (1982), *S. Rangarajan v. P. Jagjivan Ram* (1989), *Tata Press Limited v. Mahanagar Telephone Nagar Limited* (1995), *R. Rajgopal v. State of Tamil Nadu* (1995) were some of the landmark judgements delivered by the Supreme Court which expanded the horizons of freedom of speech and expression.

In *Shreya Singhal v. Union of India* (2015), the Supreme Court declared that Section 66A of the Information Technology Act, 2000 which criminalized online speech was unconstitutional because it was an unjustified restriction on the right to freedom of speech and expression. Section 66A was vague and incapable of precise definition and hence declared against the basic tenets of criminal law. Justice Nariman employed the famous American doctrine of chilling effect that has grown from an emotive argument into a major substantive component of first amendment adjudication of the United States. The court accepted the contention of the petitioner and declared that section 66A produced a chilling effect and forced people to abridge their speech and expression of any form of dissent, howsoever innocent. Justice Nariman narrates few examples: A certain section of a particular community may be grossly offended or annoyed by communications over the internet by liberal views:

> such as the emancipation of women or the abolition of the caste system or whether certain members of a non-proselytizing religion should be allowed to bring persons within their fold who are otherwise outside the fold. Each one of these things may be grossly offensive, annoying, inconvenient, insulting or injurious to large sections of the particular communities and would fall within the net cast by section 66A.
> *Shreya Singhal v. Union of India*, 2015

Therefore, section 66A was declared indefensible because it had no instant nexus with any of the constitutionally permitted grounds on which state may impose reasonable restrictions on the freedom of speech and expression (*Shreya Singhal v. Union of India*, 2015). The court also explained the conditions under which restrictions may be imposed. For instance, if free speech is to be restricted on the specific ground of public order, the law placing such a constraint has to satisfy the test of clear and present danger, another test *"that has been used by American Court for almost a century to determine the speech, the government may restrain"* (*Shreya Singhal v. Union of India*, 2015).

Seeing the trend of opinions delivered by the Supreme Court since *Romesh Thaper (Romesh Thapar v. State of Madras*, 1950), and *Brij Bhusan (Brij Bhushan v. State of Delhi*, 1950) it would not be an overstatement to say that the Supreme Court which was hostile initially to many fundamental rights including Article 21 and 14 of the Constitution, construed Article 19(1)(a) very big-heartedly as an endearing fundamental right since inception (Singh, 2015). Though, one can get some decisions which gave a narrow view of the article 19(1)(a), but should be given little weight. One such decision was *M.S.M. Sharma v. Srikrishna Sinha* (1959) where free speech was made subservient to archaic legislative privileges. In spite of some of these aberrations we are confident for the affluent future of free speech in the country. However, the Supreme Court should not act like a parent who favours one child over another (Singh, 2015).

4 Growing Criminalization of Free Speech

In the year 2016 Human Rights Watch (HRW) released a report entitled "Stifling Dissent: The Criminalization of Peaceful Expression in India" which outlined that government machinery are employing old and new legislations to confine NGOs, block internet sites and target marginalised groups and religious minorities (Bajoria and Lakhdhir, 2016). These remarks are pertinent because it came when we see a *prima facie* surge in cases filed against dissenting voices especially on social media. The HRW also raised serious objections to colonial provision of Indian Penal Code criminalizing defamation and recommended that it must be repealed in the light of the observations made by the United Nations Human Rights Committee (Bajoria and Lakhdir, 2016). But, the Supreme Court of India which so far has been protective of freedom of expression had recently upheld the constitutional validity of section 497 of IPC which criminalises defamation observing that they do not clash with the right to free speech. Sedition, criminal defamation, Unlawful Activities (Prevention) Act are consistently being used to suppress criticisms of government.

4.1 *Misuse of Sedition Law*
Section 124A of the IPC popularly named as law of sedition has a deep colonial root. It was part of the draft proposal of Lord Macaulay which was presented in 1837, however, the provision was dropped from the final draft of IPC when passed in 1860. This was later incorporated by way of an amendment in 1870. Section 124A was based on English Treason Felony Act 1848 which empowered the state to deal with dissenters, mutinous activities, and rebellions. This provision was used to suppress the freedom fighters including Mahatma Gandhi, Bal

Gangadhar Tilak etc. Section 124A has been used as a tool of political repression by successive Indian governments to intimidate and persecute activists, journalists, human rights defenders, students, filmmakers, singers, actors, and writers.

The apex court on multiple occasions had dealt with the interpretation and misuse of sedition law and have laid down the conditions where a speech could be considered seditious. In *Kedarnath v. the State of Bihar* (1962), the Supreme Court limited the use of this provision to "activities involving incitement to violence or intention or tendency to create public disorder or cause disturbance of public peace." (*Kedar Nath v. State of Bihar*, 1962) In *Indra Das v. State of Assam* (2011) and *Arup Bhuyan v. State of Assam* (2011), the Supreme Court unequivocally stated that only speech that amounts to "incitement to imminent lawless action" can be criminalized. Later in *Balwant Singh v. State of Punjab* (1994), the Supreme Court clearly stated that "every expression of criticism is not sedition, and the real intent of the speech is to be taken into consideration before beaming it as a seditious act." Unfortunately, in spite of guidance provided by the apex court for limited use of this provision, its misuse to curb dissenting voices is rampant especially in the current political regime.

Since the National Crime Records Bureau (NCRB) started collecting data in 2014, 399 sedition charges have been filed throughout the country. In 2014, Jharkhand had the most incidences (18), followed closely by Bihar (16). In 2015, Bihar had nine cases, followed by West Bengal (4). On the other end of the spectrum was Uttar Pradesh, which had six instances while Haryana had twelve in 2016. It was Assam, (19), Haryana (13) and Himachal Pradesh (8) that had the highest incidences in 2017. There were a total of 18 instances of sedition in 2018 in Jharkhand, followed by 17 cases in Assam, 12 cases in J&K, and 9 in Kerala.

There were 93 cases in 2019 and in addition, the conviction rate for 2019 is the lowest it has ever been, at 3.3%. According to the NCRB, just one trial out of 30 completed that year ended in a conviction. During 2019, when the most incidents of sedition were recorded, Karnataka (22), Assam (17), J&K (11) and Uttar Pradesh (10), were the states with the highest, followed by Nagaland (8).

Conversely, 73 cases in 2020 were registered. For accusations made under Section 124A of the Indian Penal Code (IPC), which is now being litigated in the Supreme Court, the conviction rate has fluctuated between 3% and 33% throughout the years. In 2020, the number of cases still pending in court have risen to 95%. The number of charge sheets filed by the police has decreased. 322 cases were filed between 2016 and 2020, although only 144 of those cases resulted in charges being filed. While 23 were found to be untrue or the product of a drafting mistake, 58 were closed owing to a lack of evidence. The percentage of cases that are still unsolved has gone from 72% in 2016 to 82% in

2020. There have been a number of recent incidents in the states of Assam, Uttar Pradesh, and Kashmir.

A healthy democracy enables its citizens to express their displeasure and disapproval of government actions. A comprehensive examination of all restrictions on free speech and expression must be conducted before any restrictions are imposed (Tiwary, 2022). The recent redirection of the Supreme Court to put on hold the primitive sedition law is prima facie evidence of its abuse by governmental authorities. The three-judge bench of the Supreme Court headed by the then Chief Justice of India N. V. Ramana and Justices A. S. Bopanna and Hrishikesh Roy in *s. g. Vombatkere v. Union of India* observed that in the interest of justice, it "hopes and expects states and Centre will refrain from registering any fresh FIR, continue with investigation or take any coercive measure by invoking section 124A of IPC, while the law is under consideration." (Scroll, 2021) In response to court's observation the Union government has filed an affidavit informing the apex court that it had decided to re-examine section 124A of the IPC, in wake of the criticism against the law's "application and abuse." During a critical time when a perception amongst citizenry was created that crucial judgements in the Supreme Court are decided in the favour of the government, this direction of the Supreme Court has come as a ray of hope for constitutional democracy. (*Scroll*, 2021).

4.2 *Excessive Use of Unlawful Prevention Activities Act*

On the recommendations of the Committee on National Integration and Regionalization appointed by the National Integration Council, the Constitution (Sixteenth Amendment) Act, 1963 was enacted. Pursuant to this, the Parliament enacted the Unlawful Activities (Prevention) Act, 1967 to provide effective prevention of certain unlawful activities of individuals, associations, terrorist activities, and matters connected therewith. The UAPA was amended in the years 2004, 2008, 2013 by the governments to make it more severe.

In 2016, 922 cases, in 2017, 901 cases and in 2018, 1,182 cases were registered under UAPA.[3] 92% of these cases were registered from five states (Uttar Pradesh, Jammu & Kashmir, Assam, Jharkhand and Manipur) (Dantewadia & Padmanabhan, 2020). Its rampant misuse can be illustrated by example that the police invoked this draconian law to book several people for using social media via a VPN. UAPA faced severe criticism because it was used to curb dissent (Dantewadia & Padmanabhan, 2020).

---

3 *See* NCRB Data.

UAPA was once again amended in the year 2019 to provide it more teeth and now it strongly resembles its predecessors TADA[4] and POTA,[5] in fact, severer than them. Both TADA and POTA had sunset clauses for three and two years respectively, but UAPA has taken the shape of anti-terrorism law without any sunset clause. The problems in the law are manifold such as wide definition of terrorism, presumption of guilt, period of police remand, denial of bail and breach of privacy and liberty.

The amendment increases the period of police remand from 15 days to 30 days, thereby giving rise to apprehensions of custodial torture and ill treatment. The time period of judicial remand is increased to a blanket 90 days, regardless of the gravity of the offence.[6] More consequentially, the proviso to sub-clause (b) enhances the time limit of judicial custody to a maximum of 180 days. Which means that for about six months the accused remains in custody without even a charge sheet being filed. The UAPA excludes section 438, CrPC 1973[7] from applying to terrorist acts [Unlawful Activities Prevention Act, 1967: § 43D(2)]. Clause (e) stipulates that no person shall be released on bail or on his own bond unless the Public Prosecutor is heard. Clause (f) operates independently from cl (e), and states that if the court is satisfied that the case diary or the investigating officer's report under section 173, Cr.PC 1973 sustain a reasonable belief that the accusations against the person are *prima facie* true, then bail shall not be granted. These provisions make securing bail almost impossible; in fact, they transform bail into a narrow exception rather than the norm. Clause (e) makes no stipulations as to what the public prosecutor needs to establish; the stipulations of cl (f) reduce to little more than the court's subjective satisfaction that a reasonable *prima facie* case exists.

These amplified powers of investigation endorsed searches, seizures and arrests based on "personal knowledge" of the police officials with any prior approval of either Director General of Police or validation from a superior judicial authority. This was against the right to privacy (*K.S. Puttaswamy v. Union of India*, 2017)[8]

---

4   The Terrorist and Disruptive Activities (Prevention) Act, 1987 (hereinafter referred to as 'TADA) was an Indian anti-terrorism law which was in force between 1985 and 1995 (modified in 1987) under the background of the Punjab insurgency.
5   The Prevention of Terrorism Act 2002 (Act No. 15 of 2002 hereinafter referred to as 'POTA') was an Act to make provisions for the prevention of, and for dealing with, terrorist activities.
6   *Id.* Section 43D (2).
7   Direction for grant of bail to person apprehending arrest.
8   A Nine-judge bench of Supreme Court held that privacy is an attribute of human dignity.

and liberty of individuals guaranteed by national and international standards.[9]

Data on arrests, trials, charge-sheets, and more from the National Crime Records Bureau has been analysed by Fact Checker for seven years (2014–2020). On average 985 cases have been registered under UAPA during 2014–2020 which reveals that there is a rise of 14.38% every year (Doshi & FactChecker.in, 2021). There has been an average of 40.58% cases up for investigation in the seven years which were sent for trial and only 4.5% of them are completed (Doshi & FactChecker.in, 2021). The cases pending investigation were 1,857 in 2014, which rose by 37% (highest one-year jump) to 2,549 in 2015 and now, according to the latest data, the number was 4,021 in 2020. The highest number of cases i.e. 1226 were registered in the year 2019 followed by 1,182 cases in 2018. There is a slight decline in 2020 when 796 cases were registered. Note: Each case can have more than one accused.

4.2.1 State-Wise Detention under UAPA

From the period 2014 and 2020, 10,552 people were arrested and 253 were convicted under the UAPA. More than 1,500 individuals were arrested each year and 36 people were convicted on average. Those convicted may have been convicted of crimes that were reported in the current year or cases that were ongoing in the past.

There were 61.3 percent of arrests under the UAPA in Manipur in 2015 but by 2019, that number has reduced to 19.81 percent. Assam was home to 11.34 percent of all UAPA arrests in the nation but it was reduced to 5.75 percent by 2020. On the other hand, in Jammu and Kashmir growth was from 0.8% in 2015 to 11.6% in 2019.

Bihar, Jharkhand, and Uttar Pradesh are other states that account for the most UAPA arrests i.e. 7,050 between 2015 and 2019. This includes 30.6 percent in Manipur, 19.8 percent in Uttar Pradesh, 14.22 percent in Assam, 8.04 percent in Bihar, and 7.31 percent in Jharkhand. Over the last six years, these six states have accounted for more than 87% of all arrests made in the UAPA.

4.2.2 Rising Pendency under UAPA

Between 2014 and 2020, an average of 4,250 UAPA cases are awaiting investigation each year, with an average of 3,579 cases (or around 85 percent) still

---

9 It is contrary to the provisions of the International Convention on Civil and Political Rights (ICCPR), which guarantees against any arbitrary and unlawful interference with a person's privacy.

awaiting inquiry at the end of each year. Between 2014 and 2020, an average of 1,834 cases were sent to trial each year, with 95.4% of those cases, or an average of 1,748 cases still awaiting a trial at the end of the year. Approximately 43.02 percent of outstanding cases have been on hold for one to three years, 17.2 percent have been on hold for three to five years, and 9.31 percent have been on hold for more than five years, according to statistics from 2017.

In the light of the crime statistics, we can see how long UAPA cases have been on hold because of an ongoing investigation. There were 4,101 cases still awaiting investigation by the end of 2020, however 44.33 percent of them had been awaiting inquiry for more than three years and 34.01 percent had been awaiting investigation for one year to three years. More than one-third of the instances pending inquiry in the previous four years are between the ages of one and three years old. According to statistics submitted in the Rajya Sabha by the Union Home Ministry, just 2.2% of cases filed under the Unlawful Activities (Prevention) Act between 2016 and 2019 resulted in court convictions (Doshi & FactChecker.in, 2021).

The Supreme Court has also criticised this legislation on several occasions. Justices Deepak Gupta and D.Y. Chandrachud have observed that the UAPA should not exist in its present form, and that it should not be used as a tool to silence dissent (Doshi & FactChecker.in, 2021). Justice Aftab Alam former judge, Supreme Court of India expressed that UAPA has failed us on both accounts, national security, and constitutional freedoms (Sinha, 2021). Justice M.B. Lokur, former judge, SC is of the view that accountability on officials must be fixed in cases where those charged with UAPA, sedition or NSA are found innocent. He said that long periods of incarceration or denial of bail to accused in such cases, particularly on medical grounds, is nothing but a "soft torture." (Sinha, 2021) Justice Krishna Iyer very aptly observed:

> Preventive sections privative of freedom, if incautiously proved by indolent judicial processes, may do deeper injury. They will have the effect of detention of one who has not been held guilty of a crime and carry with it the judicial imprimatur, to boot. To call a man dangerous is itself dangerous; to call a man desperate is to affix a desperate adjective to stigmatise a person as hazardous to the community is itself a judicial hazard unless compulsive testimony carrying credence is abundantly available.
> *Prabha Dutt v. Union of India*, 1982

4.2.3 Continuance of Ill-Conceived National Security Act

Even after the bitter experience of emergency and subsequent defeat in polls Indira Gandhi soon returned to power and enacted a new preventive detention law i.e. the National Security Act (NSA), 1980 which continues till present. The NSA empowers the central and state governments to exploit preventive detention (Paine, 1791: 141, 142) in certain cases (National Security Act, 1980: § 3). The central and state governments, as well as district magistrates and police commissioners [National Security Act, 1980: § 3(3)],[10] are authorised to detain any person in order to prevent him from acting in any manner prejudicial to state interest including public order and national security [National Security Act, 1980: § 3(1)(a)]. Any detention under NSA is required to be referred to the Advisory Board within 3 weeks of detention and (National Security Act, 1980: § 10) the board has to give its report within 7 weeks of detention (National Security Act, 1980: § 11). The Advisory Board consists of Judges of the High Court or persons qualified to be appointed as the judge of High Court. However, person detained does not have the right to be legally represented [National Security Act, 1980: § 9(2)].

In *Maneka Gandhi*, the Supreme Court muscularly echoed that Articles 14, 19 and 21 will offer a composite test for any legislation or executive action rather than examining it in silos. It also enthusiastically supplanted *"procedure established by law"* in Article 21, with *"Due Process"* despite the extensive debates in the Constituent Assembly pointing to the contrary (Singh, 2021). Yet, the attitude of the Supreme Court with respect to preventive detention law has not changed. In this context the SC examined the constitutional validity of the National Security Act in *A. K. Roy v. Union of India* (1982). The court not only entirely upheld the validity of the NSA but also failed to ask the government to implement the amendments made in Article 22(4) to (7) by 44th Constitutional Amendment Act 1978 providing additional safeguards to detenu under preventive detention law (Singh, 2021).

The design and application of NSA raised many baffling jurisprudential questions and as a result of this, it produced a very complex series of case laws construing virtually each and every phrase of the NSA.[11] The NSA was too far from the standards of international human rights. Broad sweeping powers in the hands of the executive and secret board proceedings predictably have led to misuse of NSA. The successive governments at the Centre have also been guilty of abuse of preventive detention laws by invoking them against the

---

10   The authority to issue detention order may be delegated by the executive to local district magistrates or commissioners of police for specified time period which may go up to three months at a time.
11   A person detained under NSA must be communicated the grounds of detention within 5 days which may be extended to 10 days in exceptional circumstances. The maximum permissible period of detention under NSA is 12 months.

dissenting voices. The governments in several states of India especially UP did make excessive use of the National Security Act, 1980 during the pandemic (Khan, 2022).

NCRB data suggests an up rise: 697 NSA detainees in 2018 against 501 in 2017. By August 2020, the Yogi Adityanath Government in Uttar Pradesh has invoked this law against 139 people. Out of these 76 cases for cow slaughter, 13 linked to anti-Citizenship Amendment Act protests in the state, six to crimes against women and children and 37 to heinous crimes (Mathur, 2021). The High Court of judicature at Allahabad while quashing several orders under NSA across 32 districts in UP and cancelling preventive detentions of 94 people, painted a very bad picture on the failure of systemic safeguards and constitutional protections for citizens. It was also found during proceedings that the district magistrates had passed the detention orders in a mechanical manner solely on the basis of police reports and without application of reasonable mind and denial of due process to the detenu (Mathur, 2021).

4.3 Cases Registered under Void Provision of IT Act

The apex court in the *Shreya Singhal case* (*Shreya Singhal v. Union of India*, 2015) held section 66A of IT Act unconstitutional on account of its "vague" and "arbitrary" nature. A research conducted by Abhinav Sekhri and Apar Gupta for Internet Freedom Foundation (IFF) found in 2018 that section 66A is still being used to prosecute individuals all around the nation and based on this information PUCL approached the court to execute the court's ruling.[12] Around 200 cases were pending before the court when this provision was declared unconstitutional in 2015 and now reports demonstrate that even after March 2015, 1,307 cases were registered under the law (Mathur, 2021). The bench headed by Justice Nariman observed that "this is shocking." The Attorney General of India informed the bench that the "statute books" still carry Section 66A of the IT Act, which was struck down as unconstitutional. … If your lordships see the IT Act book, there is only a small asterisk and a footnote that says that provision is deleted by order of Supreme court. No one reads the footnote" (Mathur, 2021).

A three-judge bench headed by the then Chief Justice of India U. U. Lalit issued an order on 12 October 2022 in the PUCL petition seeking a direction to the Centre and courts across the country to ensure cases are not registered

---

12 The petition filed by PUCL mentioned that 381 cases were registered in Maharashtra, 295 in Jharkhand and 245 in UP since the 2015 Supreme Court judgment. 73 FIRs were lodged in Chhattisgarh after 2015, of which seven resulted in acquittal, one was withdrawn and 20 were closed. Proceedings have been initiated to delete the section in 30 cases, while in 15 they are likely to be dropped.

under the outlawed provision. The bench observed that "such criminal proceedings, in our view, are directly in the teeth of the directions issued by this court in *Shreya Singhal v.* Union of India." (Sinha, 2022) The bench further directed that those cases where the alleged violation has "been projected" and citizens were facing prosecution for the alleged violation of the law, the "reference and reliance upon the said section" from all these crimes or criminal proceedings shall stand deleted (Sinha, 2022). Apex court directed state police chiefs as well as home secretaries and competent officers in Union Territories to instruct the entire police force not to register any complaint or crime with reference to any violation under Section 66A. However, the bench clarified that this direction shall apply only with respect to charges under scrapped Section 66A. But if the act in question has other charges and offences under other provisions then it will continue.

4.4 *Criminal Defamation Law Upheld*

In addition to above-mentioned excessively used preventive detention device, various governments have also misused the criminal defamation (Indian Penal Code, 1860: § 499, 500) law to stifle free speech. Journalists, especially commenting on the governmental policies were arrested for their social media conversations (Nayak, 2016). The provision was misused by the government of Tamil Nadu to silence journalists from calling out mal-governance in the state in the wake of the Chennai floods (Nayak, 2016).

The use of colonial criminal defamation law in India has been criticised for curbing free speech and silencing dissent. The law has been used by powerful individuals and organisations to intimidate and silence those who raise uncomfortable questions or express dissenting opinions. This has raised concerns that the law could be abused to stifle free speech and intimidate journalists, activists, and ordinary citizens. Critics argue that the law is outdated and inconsistent with international standards on freedom of expression. In recent years, there have been calls to reform the law or repeal it altogether, with many arguing that the law is no longer necessary in a democratic society and that civil remedies are sufficient to protect individual reputations. However, the Supreme Court has upheld the constitutionality of the law for the sake of protection of reputation, but its use remains a contentious issue in India (*Devidas Ramachandra Tuljapurkar v. State of Maharashtra,* 2015). The court held that the law serves as a reasonable restriction on the freedom of speech and expression guaranteed under the Indian Constitution, in order to protect the reputation of individuals. The court emphasised that the right to reputation is also a fundamental right and can be restricted in the interest of public order. The decision was controversial, with many arguing that the law was prone to abuse and could be used to silence dissent and stifle free speech. However, the court maintained that the law was necessary to balance the rights of individuals and the freedom of speech, and that it would not be misused in practice.

5 Conclusion

In 2021, the World Press Freedom Index (WPFI)[13] ranked India at 142 (out of 180) and marked it as 'one of the world's most dangerous countries for journalists trying to do their job properly' (Reporters Without Borders, 2021). One of the primary reasons cited for the same, in addition to continuing factors, was the rise of nationalism and religious right-wing sentiments tightening the noose around media. Gag orders, invoking sedition charges, concerted hate campaigns, threats and violence have increased for those who fail to swim with the tide of intolerance. Misuse of preventive detention laws and criminal defamation law to stifle free speech has become a despicable evil which negates the essence of libertarian philosophy. Considering the political climate of partition, these colonial devices may have been justified on the ground that democracy needed protection at both ends. While it needs to be protected against uncontrolled executive power, equally it requires protection against any internal forces trying to sabotage democratic constitution. It appeared realistic that time to make preventive detention constitutionally permitted but keeping all through preventive detention as a routine practice raises serious doubts. The Constitution provided certain restrictions on exercise of this power and also provided safeguards which were further fortified in 1978 but failed to be implement which again raises serious doubts on the intention and *modus operendi* of the executive.

The courts have also been suspicious of declaring detention orders invalid on account of vagueness of the grounds communicated to the detenu (*Dr. Ram Krishan Bharadwaj v. The State of Delhi*, 1953). Due to this inconsistent jurisprudence, the courts have accepted a very broad interpretation of activities

---

13   The WPFI is an annual ranking scale published by a Paris-based NGO, Reporters without Borders (French: *Reporters sans frontiers*) (RSF) since 2002. This index is not an assessment of the quality of journalism in a country, but rather purely evaluates the level of freedom enjoyed by the media. Although RSF is an NGO, and not a statutory body, nevertheless over a period of several years they have received recognition at international level for their work and studies conducted, and have also attained a consulting status for bodies like United Nations (UN), United Nations Educational, Scientific and Cultural Organization (UNESCO), Council of Europe, etc.

which are prejudicial to the public order. For instance, courts have upheld detention orders on grounds that detenu had committed robbery (*Gora v. State of West Bengal*, 1975), association with a notorious gang of dacoits (*Rajendra Kumar v. Superintendent, District Jail Agra*, 1985), brandished and fired a weapon in a public place (*Kali Charan Mal v. State of West Bengal*, 1975), hurled stones at the car of his political opponents (*Somaresh Chandra Bose v. Dist. Magistrate, Burdwan*, 1972), set fire to a school building, threatened violence to coerce a contractor to provide him employment (*Yogendra Singh v. State of Bihar*, 1984; *Madhu v. Police Commissioner, Thana*, 1985) and fired at police officers (*Kanu Biswas v. State of West Bengal*, 1972). Invocation of preventive detention laws against writers, journalists, cartoonists, activists for trivial and minor issues like cow slaughter, criticising policies of the government or voices of dissent cannot be justified on any ground. Frank La Rue, a former UN Special Rapporteur on freedom of expression has rightly stated:

> "freedom of expression is not only a fundamental right but also an 'enabler' of other rights, "including economic, social and cultural rights, such as the right to education and the right to take part in cultural life and to enjoy the benefits of scientific progress and its applications, as well as civil and political rights, such as the rights to freedom of association and assembly. ... [A]rbitrary use of criminal law to sanction legitimate expression constitutes one of the gravest forms of restriction to the right, as it not only creates a 'chilling effect,' but also leads to other human rights violations."

6 The Future Recourse

a. Many countries such as Ireland, Australia, Canada, Ghana, Nigeria, and Uganda have either diluted or have completely done away with sedition laws. The United Kingdom, which is the basis of Indian law, sedition has been abolished by the Coroners and Justice Act, 2009. The apex court in India has put this law on hold and the government of India has given affidavit in the apex court in *S.G. Vombatkere v. Union of India* that it will seriously reconsider the continuance of sedition law in its present form but it's high time that the Supreme Court must ensure that section 124 A is given a rapid burial.

b. There seems to be too much secrecy in the operation of the preventive detention and proceedings of the advisory board. The public has an interest in knowing generally about the operation of law, grounds of detention, factual allegations against him, probable prejudicial acts sought to be prevented by means of detention; how do the advisory boards view the allegations, the grounds, the apprehensions, and the representations; in what kind of cases do these boards seek more information from the appropriate government; in what circumstances, if at all, do advisory boards report that there is no sufficient cause of detention. This requires lifting the blanket provision of secrecy from the proceedings and reports of the advisory boards and by arranging for adequate publicity of all but specified cases, or, at least, of specified cases (Singh, 2021).

c. The possibility of providing legal assistance also needs attention. The appearance of a lawyer need not necessarily make the proceeding judicial process, but it may help the detenu understand the ground communicated to him and may help him in preparing his defence. It may perhaps help to obviate the difficulties created by the vagueness of the grounds communicated to the detenu which is so normally predominant.

d. The current legal regime for preventive detention also needs severe surgery. The rising number of cases and abysmally low conviction rate under the current UAPA strikingly displays that it is not meant for conviction. The purpose of this law is only to detain people without any accountability on the part of the administration. The detention eventually might result in acquittal but who shall be responsible for the substantial time of one's life detained in jail. Considering the hard constitutional reality, following amendments may be made to the existing regime to avoid excessive use of police power (Singh, 2021).

   (i) The definition of terrorism needs to be revised and made more specific. The inclusive terms present in the definition need to be removed. An exhaustive and restrictive definition of terrorism will restrict the discretion of authorities.

   (ii) Section 43E should be amended so that the reversal of presumption of innocence is restricted to only exceptional situations. Specifically, mere possession should not be made a ground for reversal, so as to minimise the possibility of evidence being planted. Also, inclusive terms such as 'other substances of a similar nature' should be removed from the provision.

   (iii) The provision enhancing police remand should be removed. If at all extending judicial remand to 180 days is necessary, surely it is justified only in the most exceptional cases, and not as a matter of routine. Hence the requirement for extending judicial remand beyond 90 days should be made more stringent.

(iv) Bail should be made the rule and not the exception. Denial of bail must be made valid only on specific grounds, such as the possibility of tampering with evidence, or influencing witnesses, or committing further crimes etc. Specific grounds for refusing bail should be incorporated into the statute.

(v) Finally, there must be a provision for initiating mandatory legal action against errant officers who allegedly invoke the stringent provisions of NSA or UAPA wrongfully. Government must also be vicariously held responsible if detention is proven wrong.

e. Sections 499 and 500 of the Indian Penal Code which criminalize defamation compel citizens and the media to perceive self-restraint and self-censorship and therefore undermine the public interest. Therefore, time has come to abolish criminal defamation, and the government and the Supreme Court must take this issue on priority.

f. Besides above-mentioned points, it is also required that the Government of India must notify Section 3 of the Forty-fourth Amendment Act, 1978 which was conceived to provide some additional safeguards to detenu after the bitter experience of emergency.

Bibliography

A. K Roy v. Union of India, AIR 710 (1982) Supreme Court, India.

Arup Bhuyan v. State of Assam, 3 SCC 377 (2011) Supreme Court, India.

Bajoria, J. and Lakhdir, L. (2016) *Stifling Dissent*. Human Rights Watch. Available at: https://www.hrw.org/report/2016/05/25/stifling-dissent/criminalization-peaceful-expression-india. Accessed on May 01, 2019.

Balwant Singh v. State of Punjab, 2 SCR 9 (1994) Supreme Court, India.

Barendt, E. (1985) *Freedom of Speech*. Oxford: Clarendon Press.

Bennett Coleman & Co. v. Union of India, AIR 106 (1973) Supreme Court, India.

Berlin, I. (1969) *Four Essays on Liberty*. New York: Oxford University Press.

Brij Bhushan v. State of Delhi, Supp SCR 245 (1950) Supreme Court, India.

Dantewadia, P., and Padmanabhan, V. (2020, February 25) "Sedition cases in India: What data says". *Mint*. Available at: https://www.livemint.com/news/india/sedition-cases-in-india-what-data-says-11582557299440.html

Devidas Ramachandra Tuljapurkar v. State Of Maharashtra, 1 SCC 6 (2015) Supreme Court, India.

Doshi, G. D. (November 15, 2021) *In seven years, 10,552 Indians have been arrested under UAPA – but only 253 convicted.* Scroll.In. Available at: https://scroll. in/article /1010530/in-seven-years-10552-indians-have-been-arrested-under-uapa-and-253 -convicted. Accessed on January 01, 2022.

Dr. Ram Krishan Bharadwaj *v.* The State of Delhi, AIR 318 (1953) Supreme Court, India.

Express Newspapers (Bombay) (P.) (Ltd.) v. Union of India, AIR 515 (1986) Supreme Court, India.

Gandhi, M. K. (194) *Young India 1919–1922.* Madras: S. Ganesan.

Gandhi, M. K. (1927) *Young India 1924–26.* Madras: S. Ganesan.

Gandhi, M. K. (1962) *The Law and The Lawyers.* Ahmedabad: Navajivan Publishing House.

Gora v. State of West Bengal, AIR 473 (1975) Supreme Court, India.

Hoffman, J., & Graham, P. (2007) *Introduction to Political Theory.* New York: Routledge.

Indian Penal Code, No. 45 of 1860 (1860).

Indra Das v. State of Assam, 4 SCR 289 (2011) Supreme Court, India.

Iyer, V. R. K. (1992) *Justice at Crossroads.* New Delhi: Deep & Deep Publications.

(2018) *Jainism.* Encyclopedia.com. Available at: http://www.encyclopedia.com /topic /Jainism.aspx. Accessed on January 01, 2022.

Kali Charan Mal v. State of West Bengal, AIR 999 (1975) Supreme Court, India.

Kanu Biswas v. State of West Bengal, AIR 1656 (1972) Supreme Court, India.

Kaunain Sheriff, M. (April 7, 2021) "94 out of 120 orders quashed: Allahabad High Court calls out abuse of NSA in Uttar Pradesh". *The Indian Express.* Available at: https: //indianexpress.com/article/express-exclusive/national-security-act-uttar-prad esh-police-detentions-cow-slaughter-ban-7260425/. Accessed on May 01, 2022.

Kedar Nath Singh v. State of Bihar, AIR 955 (1962) Supreme Court, India.

Khan, A. A. (May 23, 2022) *Use and Abuse of NSA during Covid.* Manupatra. Available at: https://articles.manupatra.com/article-details/Use-and-Abuse-of- NSA-during -Covid. Accessed on January 01, 2022.

K. S. Puttaswamy v. Union of India, 10 SCC 1 (2017) Supreme Court, India.

Madhu v. Police Commissioner, Thana, Cr. L. J. 341, 344 (1985) Bombay High Court, India.

Mathur, A. (July 5, 2021) *Supreme Court 'shocked' over scrapped Section 66A law's use in FIRs, issues notice to Centre.* India Today. Available at: https://www.indiatoday .in/law/story/section-66a-of-it-act-still-in-use-supreme-court-notice-to-centre -1824015-2021-07-05. Accessed on May 01, 2022.

Mill, J. S. (1977) On Liberty. In: Robson, A.P. and Robson, J. M. (eds) *Collected Works: Vol. XVIII.* Toronto: University of Toronto Press. (Original work published 1859).

M. S. M. Sharma v. Srikrishna Sharma, AIR 395 (SCI 1959) Supreme Court, India.

National Security Act, No. 65 of 1980 (1980) Supreme Court, India.

Nayak, N. (May 22, 2016) *Criminal defamation survives: a blot on free speech.* Mint. Available at: https://www.livemint.com/Opinion/Zx8Qs6oDFFqJ7bjYB0aGjO /Criminal-defamation-survives-a-blot-on-free-speech.html. Accessed on May 01, 2022.

Paine, T. (1791) *The Rights of Man*. Oxford: Oxford University Press.

Prabha Dutt v. Union of India, AIR 6 (SCI 1982) Supreme Court, India.

Prevention of Terrorism Act, No. 15 of 2002 (2002).

Rajendra Kumar v. Superintendent, District Jail Agra, Cr. L.J. 999, 1004 (1985) Allahabad High Court, India.

Reporters Without Borders (2021) *Modi tightens his grip on the media*. Available at: https://rsf.org/en/india. Accessed on May 01, 2022.

R. Rajgopal v. State of Tamil Nadu, AIR 264 (SCI 1995) Supreme Court, India.

Romesh Thapar v. State of Punjab, AIR 124 (SCI 1950) Supreme Court, India.

Sakal Papers v. Union of India, AIR 305 (SCI 1962) Supreme Court, India.

Schauer, F. (1981) *Free Speech: A Philosophical Enquiry*. Cambridge: Cambridge University Press.

Sedition law is colonial, says Supreme Court as it agrees to examine its constitutional validity (July 15, 2021) Scroll.In. Available at: https://scroll.in/latest/1000267/sedition-law-is-colonial-says-supreme-court-as-it-agrees-to-examine-its-constitutional-validity. Accessed on January 01, 2022.

Shreya Singhal v. Union of India, AIR 1523 (SCI 2015) Supreme Court, India.

Singh, Y. P. (November 27, 2014) "Demise of Dissent". *The Statesman*. Available at: http://119.82.71.49/thestatesman/epapermain.aspx?pgno=16&eddate=2014-11-27&edcode=820009. Accessed on January 01, 2021.

Singh, Y. P. (April 30, 2015) "At Least Free Speech is Safe". *The Statesman*. Available at: http://epaper.thestatesman.com/489976/The-Statesman-Kolkata/30th-April-2015#page/16/2. Accessed on January 01, 2021.

Singh, Y. P. (September 16, 2016) "Needed in Judiciary, Cautious Dissent". *The Tribune*. Available at: http://epaper.tribuneindia.com/938036/Delhi-Edition/NCR_16_September_2016#page/9/2. Accessed on January 01, 2021.

Singh, Y. P., and Nayak, A. (January 24, 2020) "Quandary of divergent opinion". *Deccan Herald*. Available at: https://www.deccanherald.com/opinion/comment/quandary-of-divergent-opinion-797665.html. Accessed on January 01, 2021.

Singh, Y. P. (2021) "Anatomy of Preventive Detention Laws in India: A Historical and Critical Perspective". In: Dubey, D. and Bedi, S. (eds) *Arrest and Detention in India: Law, Procedure and Practice*. Thousand Oaks: Sage Publishing House.

Sinha, B. (July 25, 2021) *'Failed' law, 'misused to stifle dissent': Ex-SC judges speak out against UAPA, sedition, NSA*. ThePrint. Available at: https://theprint.in/judiciary/failed-law-misused-to-stifle-dissent-ex-sc-judges-speak-out-against-uapa-sedition-nsa/702572/. Accessed on October 01, 2021.

Sinha, B. (October 12, 2022) *Don't try anyone under invalid Sec 66A of IT Act, SC raps Centre, states; scraps ongoing cases*. ThePrint. Available at: https://theprint.in/judiciary/dont-try-anyone-under-invalid-sec-66a-of-it-act-sc-raps-centre-states-scraps-ongoing-cases/1164801/. Accessed on January 01, 2023.

Somaresh Chandra Bose v. Dist. Magistrate, Burdwan, 2 SCC 476 (SCI 1972) Supreme Court, India.

S. Rangarajan v. P. Jagjivan Ram, 2 SCR 204 (SCI 1989) Supreme Court, India.

Stromberg, R. N. (1954) *Religious Liberalism in Eighteenth-century England.* Oxford: Oxford University Press.

Tata Press Limited v. Mahanagar Telephone Nigam Limited, 5 SCC 139 (1995) Supreme Court, India.

Terrorist & Disruptive Activities Prevention Act, No. 28 of 1987 (1987).

Tiwary, D. (May 31, 2022) "399 sedition cases since 2014, pendency high". *The Indian Express.* Available at: https://indianexpress.com/article/explained/sedition-cases-pendency-explained-7912311/. Accessed on May 01, 2023.

Tripathi, P. K. (1958) "Free Speech in the Indian Constitution: Background and Prospect". *Yale Law Journal, 67*(3): 384.

Unlawful Activities (Prevention) Act, No. 37 of 1967 (1967).

Wright, L. (2020) *Depth Study – Belief Systems – Buddhism.* AceHSC. Available at: https://www.acehsc.net/resource/depth-study-belief-systems-buddhism-lynne-wright/. Accessed on May 01, 2023.

Yogendra Singh v. State of Bihar, B.B.C.J. 727 (1984) Patna High Court, India.

CHAPTER 8

The Jurisprudence of Constitutional Morality and the Pathologies of Criminalization

Shruti Bedi

1   Introduction

Criminal law has received the sustained attention of scholars over decades on the issue of overcriminalization. The distinguished legal theorist Prof. Andrews Ashworth in his book *Positive Obligations in Criminal Law* posits the question, "Is the criminal law a lost cause?" (2013: 1–30). The lack of a principled approach in categorizing new offences, leads to an affirmative response. India has not remained immune from the plague of 'overcriminalization'. Prof. Bajpai "roughly estimates" that "12,000 to 1.5 lakh" laws maybe criminalizing actions (2019). He further states that "more than 350 statutes in India prescribe punishment of varying nature." Numerous civil laws relating to "family, allowances, land, consumers, housing environment, marriage, maintenance etc." also stipulate criminal sanctions (Bajpai, 2019). The decriminalization of a few offences under the newly minted Bhartiya Nayay Sanhita, 2023 is simply an innocuous effort. Unprincipled criminalization results in creation of new offences on unscientific grounds as well as pervasive arbitrariness in the criminal justice system. Indeed, as Husak says, "the most pressing problem with the criminal law today is that we have too much of it" (2008: 3).

Sanford Kadish also criticises the "overuse" of criminal law specially to enforce "morals" like the criminalization of homosexual behaviour, prostitution, abortion, gambling, and narcotics; "to provide social services; and to avoid legal restraints on law enforcement" (1967: 157). Criminal law is not the only technique available to the State for regulating the conduct and activities of the citizens. In effect criminal sanction is one of the harshest tools to regulate such conduct. At the rate, new categories of crime and punishment have been introduced in the Indian criminal justice system, the apprehension pertains to the absence of consonance of such legislative activity with the fundamental principles of criminal law like presumption of innocence, equality, proportionality etc (Bharadway, 2020).

Any policy of the State on criminalization must conform to constitutional morality. The constitutional principles of constitutional morality must define any conduct being criminalized. This principled approach may ultimately lead to the decriminalizing of certain actions like passive begging, homosexuality, adultery, and the non-criminalizing of marital rape. Justice (Dr.) D.Y. Chandrachud (currently, Chief Justice of India) vehemently reflects that "it is not the "common morality" of the State at any time in history, but rather constitutional morality, which must guide the law" (*Joseph Shine v. Union of India*, 2019: para 143).

The chapter traces the Indian legislature's penchant for criminalization of conduct. The cause for alarm is highlighted through instances of the state's exercise of legislative power. It goes on to delve into various schools of thought on criminalisation. In the scrutiny of the traditional principles on criminalization, the harm principle has been studied in detail from the aspect of its relevance to criminalization. Considering the questionable application of these principles, the author explores the possibility of constitutional morality as being the guiding force for the policy on criminalisation. Also analysed is the Indian judiciary's effort to de-criminalize certain offenses like adultery and homosexuality by holding them unconstitutional and violative of basic constitutional norms. The author relies on the importance of constitutional morality as the soul of the Indian Constitution to formulate the policy of criminalization. Democracy flourishes when precedence is given to justice over the desires of the majority.

2   Pathologies of Criminalization

"Crimes are wrongful commissions punishable by law" (Bhateja, 2019). Criminalization is the action of the state of categorising certain acts as criminal in nature. When such process oversteps the limits of reason, it is termed as over-criminalisation. Voluminous criminal codes are inherently inimical to liberty and freedom. Pathologies of criminalization take various forms. Criminal sanction is being overused to criminalize conduct that previously would not have been subject to punishment. Sanctions which are criminal in nature directly impact the rights of people and consequently such sanctions must be customised with greatest caution. Criminalization also occurs on account of heightened penalties for acts considered as minor violations of public order. The increasing spate of criminalization leads to a sense of persecution amongst the people (Arzt, 1981). Further the enforcement and prosecution of such offences imposes an additional load on the over-burdened criminal justice system. Jail authorities in India must grapple with over-crowded prisons and lack of access to basic necessities of "clean drinking water, nutritious food, hygienic lavatories etc. The suffering of an accused does not end after serving the sentence. Former prisoners face difficulties in resuming their lives and finding gainful employment" (Bhateja, 2019).

There exist numerous civil laws that stipulate criminal sanctions like matters pertaining to "family, allowances, land, consumers, housing environment, marriage, maintenance etc." (Bajpai, 2019). Some of these laws have outlived their purpose. Enforcement of some laws has become problematic due to the usual public resistance to certain laws like traffic and environment regulations. Some laws are misused like the anti-terror laws. In a politically charged climate, governments are under pressure to create new offences in the fight against terrorism. Recently, the Unlawful Activities Prevention Act, 1967 has been amended to classify individuals as terrorists without any prior judicial process to validate the action of the government (The Unlawful Activities (Prevention) Amendment Act, 2019).

Governmental errors occur when innocent people are unjustly arrested and imprisoned. Arrests carried out under the Dowry Prohibition Act, 1961; sedition laws; and the Narcotics and Psychotropic Substances Act, 1985 contribute to a large share of excessive arrests (Singhal, 2021). Wrong convictions leave long lasting scars not only on the "prisoner but also his family – children, spouse, parents and siblings" (Lynch, 2017). The fact that 77.1% of the prison population is of under-trials (Chawla, 2022) portrays the futility of criminalisation. As a result, by reducing criminal codes, the mistaken arrests and convictions of innocents are also reduced.

2.1   *Criminalization of Triple* Talaq

The Supreme Court in 2017 set aside the practice of instantaneous *Triple Talaq* by declaring it unconstitutional in *Shayara Bano v. Union of India* (2017). Therefore, even if a Muslim man now utters *talaq*, it will not lead to a divorce. The marriage will continue. Unfortunately, the Muslim Women (Protection of Rights on Marriage) Act, 2019 enacted subsequent to the judgment, prescribes a jail term of up to three years for the pronouncement of *talaq* (Section 4). Therefore, the woman who is still married can now file a case against her husband under this provision which make the utterance of *talaq* by the husband a cognisable offence. However, in reality, hardly any woman will file a case against her husband while she is still married to him.

2.2   *Criminalizing Corporate Social Responsibility*

As a part of the mandatory corporate social responsibility (CSR) requirements, a company with a net worth of at least Rs 500 crore, a turnover of Rs 1,000 crore or a net profit of Rs 5 crore is obligated to spend 2% of its average profit over the previous three years on CSR. Over the years, a voluntary act was converted into a legal obligation. However, under The Companies (Amendment), 2019 non-compliance with the CSR requirements was criminalized. A company not fulfilling the CSR obligations, is punished with fine between fifty thousand rupees and twenty-five lakh rupees and every officer of such company who is in default is punishable with imprisonment up to three years or with fine between fifty thousand rupees and five lakh rupees, or with both (section 135(7)). Criminalization of such conduct which was traditionally dealt with under the civil law, may not be the right approach.

At a time when India has been struggling with imposition of criminal sanctions under the goods and services tax (GST), the 48th GST Council meeting held on 17th December 2022 has recommended the decriminalization of certain offences under section 132 of the Central Goods and Services Tax (CGST) Act, 2017 (Statesman, 2022). Initially investors used to be discouraged due to the criminal sanctions especially in small, trivial, and petty matters (Bajpai & Karuna, 2022). Decriminalization will encourage people to engage more in business activity and investment.

Unfortunately, criminalization has become a method for legislators/government to show to their people that they are serious about a particular problem plaguing the society. In fact, criminalization is to be employed only as a means of last resort, i.e., when everything else fails. It is the "ultima ratio" of legislative endeavour – "an uttermost means in uttermost cases" (Kishore, 2019).

3 Schools of Criminalization

Under the jurisprudential analysis of criminalizing criminal behaviour in society, morals, and legal codes play an important role. Morality is defined as a "set of rules or principles that guide the process of making decisions and behaviour in society" (IvyPanda, 2022). Included within this understanding are "principles that define what is acceptable and unacceptable in society" (IvyPanda, 2022). Law on the other hand comprises of principles that enhance and maintain morality in society.

Tim Lynch rightly states, "As the criminal law expands, there is a concomitant diminution of liberty" (2017). "Criminal law should be used only to redress blameworthy conduct, actions that truly deserve the greatest punishment and moral sanction" (Heritage Foundation). An act is criminalized based on different schools of thought.

3.1 *Paternalism*
According to the school of paternalism, criminalization ought to be based on the conception that state in its capacity as the guardian of its people, should

regulate their conduct. Under this principle the law offers protection to an impudent citizen from acting to his detriment or harming himself. It is the interference with the liberty of a person for the welfare or benefit of that person. There are different laws which come under the concept of paternalism. Laws which benefit the person who is restricted under law, like prohibition of driving under the influence of alcohol, wearing seat belts while driving, prohibition of underage smoking is called *pure* paternalism. Laws that benefit persons other than those restricted, like laws which regulate the licensing of those who practice medicine is called *impure* paternalism (Hands, 2009).

The Supreme Court of India has occasionally followed the paternalistic principle. In 1996 in *Gian Kaur v. State of Punjab* the court held that right to life did not include within its ambit the right to die. Suicide was unacceptable and attempt to suicide was criminalized under section 309 IPC which provided for imprisonment up to one year. The state instead of offering medical aid and assistance to the aggrieved person, was ready to punish him for his mental state. This application of paternalistic misconception by the state reflects its insensitivity towards the interests of its citizens.[1]

3.2 Morality

The moral school advocates the criminalization of acts that are in contravention of societal morality (Bhateja, 2019). The problem with this school of thought is that morality is defined by the majority which makes it subjective. The previous decisions of the Indian Supreme Court are reflective of such attitude. In 1985 the court in *Sowmithri Vishnu v. Union of India* held adultery to be an offence as it destroyed the foundations and sanctity of marriage; and in *Suresh Kumar Kaushal v. Naz Foundation* (2014) the criminalization of homosexuality under section 377 IPC was upheld on account of social unacceptability.

Section 497, Indian Penal Code, 1860 (IPC) which criminalized adultery initially, made it is a criminal offence punishable with five years imprisonment. The problem with the provision was that it criminalized sexual intercourse with married women and not unmarried ones. Secondly, if the husband of the married woman consented to the act of adultery, it was not an offence. Section 377 IPC criminalized homosexuality and prescribed life imprisonment or imprisonment of either description for ten years. These provisions criminalized private sexual conduct between consenting adults. The Supreme Court in *Joseph Shine v. Union of India* (2019) and *Navtej Singh Johar v. Union of India* (2018) decriminalised adultery and homosexuality respectively, thereby

---

1 Attempt to suicide has been de-criminalized under the Mental Health Care Act, 2017.

highlighting the discourse on the doctrine of unprincipled criminalization (Raj & Raj, 2018). Societal subjectivity on conceptions of morality usually leads to the exclusion of the marginalised. The furore emanating from the people against the decriminalization of adultery in the aftermath of the judgment displays the use of criminal law by society to enforce morality.

3.3 Harm Principle

The existence of criminal law is legitimised on the conception of public morality that is regarded by society as justly enforceable (Feinberg, 1965). Public morality further has two components, i.e., a theory of morally wrong acts and a theory of culpability attributing blame for such acts (Richards, 1988: 123). Societies differ in their perception of public morality. Therefore, the question arises as to what concept of morality is appropriately enforceable in a liberal society? (Richards, 1988: 123).

The classical answer is given by the English philosopher, John Stuart Mill in *On Liberty*, who postulated the 'harm principle' which attempts to provide an objective starting point for acts that should be criminalized. The most significant and critical sentence from the passage states: "the only purpose for which power can rightfully be exercised over any member of a civilized community against his will is to prevent harm to others" (Mill, 1989: 22). Mill believes that "coercion on part of the state is justified if, and only if, the acts it seeks to prevent are such as to cause harm to others, or has the potential to cause harm to others" (Srivastava). This principle was adopted by the Supreme Court of India in its 'adultery judgment' (Kishore, 2019).

The harm principle continues to evoke widespread appeal on account of its significance for contested issues like abortion, same-sex marriage, pornography etc (Smith, 2004: 8). The question however remains as to whether the principle is strong and sound enough to determine the criminalization of acts. In 1957 the Lord Wolfenden Committee recommended that consensual sexual activity between men in private should be decriminalised. This report provoked the famous Hart-Devlin debate. Lord Patrick Devlin stated that criminal law was not just for the protection of individuals but was also for the protection of society (Devlin, 1965: 22).

Devlin was of the view that the function of law was to enforce a minimum standard of morality. He believed that a society is constituted by its "common morality" or "public morality" and if a society's morality is not enforced, it will "disintegrate" (1965: 10). However, Hart realised and understood the danger of public morality and consequently argued against curtailing people's liberty to promote the moral understandings of others. He supported the harm principle (Stanton, 2022).

The concept of harm is a little vague and does not provide clear constraints on what is crime in a sense that which counts as a relevant reason for criminalisation. The question arises therefore as to whether any type of harmful conduct can be criminalized. This harm principle is unable to establish an appropriate criterion of criminalisation. We therefore turn to a more influential version of the harm principle as reformulated by Joel Fienberg. He states:

> It is always a good reason in support of penal legislation that it would probably be effective in preventing (eliminating, reducing) harm to persons other than the actor and there is probably no other means that is equally effective at no greater cost to other values.
> 1984: 26

Feinberg distinguishes between two conceptions of harm in this sense. First is a setback of an individual's interest; and second is a setback of an individual's interest that wrongs that individual (1984: 32–33). According to him it is this second category of harm that accounts for harm as a basis for criminalization (Feinberg, 1987: pp. xxvii-xxix) as only such harmful actions involve wrongful conduct. "Only setbacks of interests that are wrongs, and wrongs that are setback to interest, are to count as harms in the appropriate sense" (Feinberg, 1984: 36). This is the moral conception of harm (Holtug, 2002) that prevents the criminalization of consensual acts that harm the participants (Principle of *Volenti non fit injuria*) (Feinberg, 1984: 115–117).

According to Feinberg harm is dependent not only on 'interests' but also on certain 'pre-existing rights' (Smith, 2004: 38). Consequently, a setback to an interest is not harm unless it is wrongfully inflicted i.e., inflicted in violation of a right.

> To say that A has harmed B in this sense is to say much the same thing as that A has wronged B, or treated him unjustly. One person wrongs another when his indefensible (unjustifiable and inexcusable) conduct violates the other's right.
> FEINBERG, 1984: 34

Feinberg divides an individual's interests into "welfare interests" and "ulterior interests." Welfare interests are the higher-ranking interests which are commonly shared by all human beings and include:

> [i]nterests in one's own physical health and vigor ..., the absence of absorbing pain and suffering ..., emotional stability, the absence of

> groundless anxieties and resentments, the capacity to enjoy and maintain friendship, at least minimal income and financial security, [and] a tolerable social and physical environment.
>
> 1984: 37

An individual's interests suffer a setback when the welfare interests are missing or are damaged, which in turn leads to harm (Petersen, 2016: 361). Physical integrity and property up to a certain point constitute welfare interests. An individual requires some minimum physical well-being in order to undertake other affairs. He also requires a minimum amount of economic support to avoid debilitation. For example, preserving means of livelihood is welfare interest but owning a luxury car is not (Hirsch, 1986: 703).

Ulterior interests are more subjective in nature and therefore differ from person to person like building a house, solving a scientific problem, successfully raising a family. When these interests of those individuals are harmed, these ulterior interests suffer a setback (Feinberg, 1984: 62). However, Feinberg believes that ulterior interests should not be directly protected by law for the most part and it is primarily the welfare interests that should be protected by law (1984: 62–63).

Further not all incursions on welfare interests would amount to harm that is criminalisable. Feinberg argues that bare trespass to land is harmless in the sense that it does not harm any interest other than the property rights of the landowner on the land. Similarly, a promisee is both wronged and harmed when a breach of promise interferes with his interest in performance of the promise.

> Most such apparent examples of wrongs that are not harms to interests can be interpreted in this way. There can be wrongs that are not harms on balance, but there are few wrongs that are not to some extent harms. Even in the most persuasive counterexamples, the harm would usually be an invasion of the interest in liberty.
>
> FEINBERG, 1984: 34–35

Since it is not any harm that constitutes support of legal coercion. Feinberg believes that it is the harms that are produced by "morally indefensible conduct" that are material (1984: 215). Consequently, moral wrongs and immorality become the focus of the debate for proponents of Feinberg's harm principle (Stanton, 2022).

Such an extensive interpretation of the harm principle breaks down the distinction between wrongfulness and harmfulness. Peter Cane accordingly concludes, "Defining "harm" to include "harmless" invasion of rights merely in order to preserve the harm principle seems perverse, at the least" (2006: 43). Ironically Feinberg tries to justify the criminalization of two wrongs-trespass to land and breach of contract, that are not criminal offenses in themselves. He further states that "conduct is wrongful only when it is intentional or unjustifiable or inexcusable and is designed to violate the moral rights of others, and not otherwise" (Vashist, 2013: 84).

Therefore, one is forced to question the appropriateness of these classifications given by Feinberg. Reviewing Feinberg's opus, Gerald Dworkin wonders, "In truth, I cannot find a clear argument in Feinberg" (1999: 939). Undoubtedly Feinberg has attempted the explication of the harm principle at length, yet if one were to look for any "sustained *justification of the harm principle* as a limitation on government, one will search the book in vain" (Smith, 2004: 51) (emphasis added).

Unintentionally the issue of the proper limits of criminal law has been reduced to the debate around the harm principle. Devlin had adopted a better approach (Lacey, 1988: 98–120) by asking a non-leading question: "what factors ought to be taken into account in deciding whether conduct ought to be criminalized?" (Cane, 2006: 35). Harm is only one of such factors which seems to be an unnecessary hindrance to a clear thought process about the limits of criminal law. Non-objective harm arguments like actions inducing disgust, abhorrence, and indignation (popular morality) affect decisions on criminalisation. For example, in *Naz Foundation v. Government of NCT of Delhi* (2009) the state contended that homosexuality was wrongfully harmful since "[i]n our country, homosexuality is abhorrent and can be criminalized by imposing proportional limits on the citizens' right to privacy and equality" (para 24). Therefore, criminal law generally suffers from inadequacy of jurisprudential lucidity on the matter of criminalization wherein the harm principle is regulated and defined more so by subjective criteria like public morality (Vashist, 2013: 85). Which actions are wrong and harmful are left to be determined by the subjective notions of an overriding majority.

4   Constitutional Morality: The Idea of Justice

It takes years of practice and effort to make the principles of democracy, liberty, equality, secularism, a reality in society. Even though the Indian Constitution guarantees these principles, but a multi-cultural nation like India must constantly grapple with aspects of inequality and discrimination. Therefore, B.R. Ambedkar believed that constitutional morality was a "sentiment" that had to be "established and diffused" in India (Bedi, 2021: 36–37). He relied on the wisdom of Grote:

> The diffusion of 'constitutional morality', not merely among the majority of any community, but throughout the whole is the indispensable condition of a government at once free and peaceable; since even any powerful and obstinate minority may render the working of a free institution impracticable, without being strong enough to conquer ascendance for themselves.
>
> GROTE, 2001: 93

Public or societal morality is where the conduct of society is determined by popular perceptions. On the other hand, constitutional morality is the idea of justice transcending the notions of social acceptance. In today's times it has come to mean the substantive content of a constitution (Bedi, 2021: 39) wherein governance is carried out by the substantive moral entailment of a constitution (Mehta). Constitutional morality in Upendra Baxi's view was seen by Ambedkar as an attitude towards constitutional governance in the sense of an enlightened approach towards aspirations of the constitution regarding reform of society (2019).

Constitutional morality applies to everyone irrespective of the majority or minority status. The Constitution protects the minorities by guiding the legislative process.[2] The constitutional courts monitor such preservation of constitutional morality by ensuring conditions of human dignity and liberty. Popular, or public morality cannot guide the final decisions even in a criminal justice system. It is pertinent to mention the observations of Lord Neuberger of the UK Supreme Court:

> [W]e must always remember that Parliament has democratic legitimacy – but that has disadvantages as well as advantages. The need to offer oneself for re-election sometimes makes it hard to make unpopular, but correct, decisions. At times it can be an advantage to have an independent body of people who do not have to worry about short term popularity.
>
> 2015: para 62

---

2   No law that is violative of the fundamental rights can be enacted by the legislature as mandated by Article 13 of the Indian Constitution.

While striking down the offence of adultery, Justice R.F. Nariman held that the "archaic law" had long "outlived its purpose" (*Joseph Shine v. Union of India*, 2019: para 103). He asserted the primacy of contemporary constitutional morality over conventional and "parochial social mores." (*Joseph Shine v. Union of India*, 2019: para 87). In some ways, constitutional morality as a concept causes apprehension, as allowing unrestricted power to judges to write and rewrite the constitution making it undemocratic (Khurshid, 2020: 392). A response to this apprehension comes in the form of different judicial interpretations, where judges have tried to clarify the subject. In *Govt. of NCT of Delhi v. Union of India* (2018), Chief Justice Dipak Misra, speaking for Justice Sikri, Justice Khanwilkar and himself said that "constitutional morality" implied the "strict and complete adherence to the constitutional principles" (para 58), thereby meaning that the "spirit" of the constitution was comparable to the *basic structure doctrine* (Chandrachud, 2020: 12).

Liberal constitutional values like dignity, liberty, equality, privacy have come to define the move towards decriminalization of offences. Decriminalization based on such constitutional principles promotes a compassionate global order in which India cannot be left behind. It is not the popular morality of the State but the constitutional morality that must define the legislative process. Commitment to constitutional morality includes the guarantees of equality before law, dignity, and non-discrimination.

5 The Foresight of Constitutional Morality as a Check on Criminalization

With respect to criminal legislation, the principle which determines the "act" that is criminalized as well as the persons who may be held criminally culpable, must be tested on the anvil of constitutionality. Justice Chandrachud states that the constitutional validity of criminal laws "must not be determined by majoritarian notions of morality which are at odds with constitutional morality" (*Joseph Shine v. Union of India*, 2019: para 166).

Criminal law must be in consonance with constitutional morality. Section 497 IPC which criminalized adultery committed by women, thereby enforcing only female fidelity in a marriage was held to be an affront to the right to dignity and equality. That legislative power is driven by notions of popular morality is clear from the fact that in *Joseph Shine* (2019) the State submitted that adultery was an act which outrages societal morality and harms its members and therefore must be punished as a crime (para 266.1). Even the principle commonly advanced for legislations criminalizing same-sex relationship is that they "protect and preserve public morality" (ICJ). The Supreme Court decriminalised adultery in *Joseph Shine* (2019) and homosexuality in *Navtej Singh Johar* (2018) while basing their decision on constitutional values and constitutional morality.

Sometimes even the courts use popular opinions to legitimise public morality. The Court of Appeal, Botswana in *Kanane v. State* (2003) found "no evidence that the approach and attitude of society in Botswana to the question of homosexuality and to homosexual practices by gay men and women requires a decriminalization of those practices, even to the extent of consensual acts by adult males in private" (p. 14). The Supreme Court of Zimbabwe has also rejected the challenge to the law on same-sex conduct in *Banana v. State* (2000) and held,

> I do not believe that this court, lacking the democratic credentials of a properly elected parliament, should strain to place a sexually liberal interpretation on the Constitution of a country whose social norms and values in such matters tend to be conservative.
> ICJ, 2000

These are instances of morality based on social perceptions leading to wrong decisions.

In a society governed by liberal constitutional values like liberty, dignity, equality, and privacy it is imperative to understand the reach of constitutional values and principles. Criminalization based on constitutional morality is the first step towards achieving a compassionate democracy. Legislative actions must be grounded in the moral values of the supreme law, that is the constitution, which is more likely to protect the interests of the indefensible. Societal conceptions of morality cannot form the basis for enduring and democratic legislations. Such moral values are fleeting and change with changes in societal perceptions.

Even according to Hart morality was not a necessary condition for a law to be valid. He said that, "law is morally relevant, but not morally conclusive" (Starr, 1984: 684). He warned about the fallouts of imposing majoritarian morals: "[I]t is fatally easy to confuse the democratic principle that power should be in the hands of the majority with the utterly different claim that the majority, with power in their hands, need respect no limits" (Bittlinger, 1975: 91).

> Whatever other arguments there may be for the enforcement of morality, no one should think even when popular morality is supported by an "overwhelming majority" or marked by widespread "intolerance, indignation,

and disgust" that loyalty to democratic principles requires him to admit that its imposition on a minority is justified.

BITTLINGER, 1975: 93

Although Hart avoided the generalisation that law must be separated from morality, he believed that laws criminalizing homosexuality, "which impose a majoritarian view of right and wrong upon a minority in order to protect societal cohesion, are jurisprudentially and democratically impermissible" (*Navtej Singh Johar*, 2018: para 588).

On the other hand, Bentham's view on morality was different as he assessed it against the principles of utilitarianism. According to him, there was no need for legislators to be swayed by social morality: "ought the legislator to be a slave to the fancies of those whom he governs? No. Between an imprudent opposition and a servile compliance, there is a middle path, honourable and safe" (Bentham, 1840: 99). Adding to this Mill argued that 'disgust' could not be classified as harm and those "who consider as an injury to themselves any conduct which they have a distaste for", cannot prescribe the actions of others because such actions go against their own beliefs or views (1978: 81–82). The Supreme Court in *Navtej Johar* (2018) held:

> We are aware of the perils of allowing morality to dictate the terms of criminal law. If a single, homogeneous morality is carved out for a society, it will undoubtedly have the effect of hegemonising or "othering" the morality of minorities. ... we are inclined to observe that it is constitutional morality, and not mainstream views about sexual morality, which should be the driving factor in determining the validity of Section 377.
>
> para 594

Chief Justice A.P. Shah of the Delhi High Court in the matter of *Naz Foundation v. Govt. of NCT of Delhi* (2009) held that unlike constitutional morality, popular morality was "based on shifting and [subjective] notions of right and wrong" and while determining whether a law could be considered justified for achieving a "compelling state interest", the court must take into account constitutional morality and not popular morality (para 79).

Further is it essential to differentiate between illegality and immorality. Every immoral conduct cannot be illegal e.g., private alcoholism or simple lying. Joel Feinberg's observations are relevant, "Indeed, everything about a person that the criminal law should be concerned with is included in his morals. But not everything in a person's morals should be the concern of the law" (Raj & Raj, 2018).

Decriminalization or criminalization must be determined by the norms of the Constitution. It must be anchored in constitutional morality based on "liberty, dignity, privacy, equality and individual autonomy," (*Navtej Singh Johar*, 2018: para 564) the "relevance of divergent and dissenting opinions and ways of life, and the threat of overwhelming majoritarianism within the larger constitutional vision of social transformation" (Chaudhary, 2018). The aim of the Indian Constitution is inclusivity by ensuring dignity to every person. It is that law which holds hope for the impoverished, the marginalised and the untouchables. Articles 17 and 23 of the Constitution itself provide criminal sanctions. Untouchability, trafficking in human beings and forced labour is criminalized. Constitutional morality regulates human behaviour by criminalizing such conduct (Vashist, 2013: 93). The implications of incorporating constitutional norms are extremely relevant for the understanding of democracy, which in India is diverse, plural and hierarchical (Bedi, 2021: 46).

6 Conclusion

Amongst the various theories on criminalization, it is constitutional morality that has been the guiding force for the courts in decriminalizing conduct that should not have been criminalized. It is the constitutional values that have stood to protect people's rights and liberties from the increasing tendency of overcriminalization. The use of criminal law as a means to prohibit morally deviant behaviour has resulted in overcriminalization. It is time for the legislators to use the barometer of constitutional morality to assess the criminality of an act. Incessant criminalization degrades the quality of criminal codes and results in unwarranted punishment that ultimately jeopardises the delivery of justice (Healy, 2022). All vices cannot be categorised as crimes by the criminal justice system. Constitutional morality defined by the liberty of the people acts as a safety valve in the process of criminalisation.

Dr. Ambedkar was aware of the absence of the culture of constitutional morality amongst the Indian people. In such an atmosphere, it is the courts with the power to interpret the Constitution, that must don the role of facilitators to prevent "majoritarian excesses and the usurpation of power by the State to the detriment of constitutional ethos" (Rao: 4). When the elected organ of the State is susceptible to the desires of its voters, it is the responsibility of the courts to ensure justice through the norms of the constitution.

Although constitutional morality is important, the scope and ambit of the concept evades clarity. Hence, the apprehension that it may be subjected to the biases and perceptions of the judiciary. There is the danger of judicial overreach and violation of doctrine of separation of powers. The judges therefore, need to approach their interpretive functions with sensitivity (Healy, 2022) to evaluate the subject of criminalization of conduct with reference to constitutional morality. Latika Vashist says, "even in judges, constitutional morality is not a natural sentiment; it has to be cultivated" (2013: 92). Even though Justice Nariman interprets constitutional morality as the very "soul of the constitution" which can be found in the preamble and Part III of the Constitution (*Navtaj Singh Johar*, 2018: para 349), there is still scope for clarification of the concept. Recently, the Supreme Court in *Kantaru Rajeevaru v. Indian Young Lawyers Association* (2020) has requested for constitutional morality to be defined by a larger bench of the court (Pandey & Aanchal, 2020). Ultimately to change the face of criminal law in India lies in self-restraint exercised by both the legislature and the judiciary and exercising their powers based on constitutional values.

Bibliography

Arzt, G. (1981) *Problems of Criminalisation and Decriminalisation ofod Socially Detrimental Behaviour*. NCJRS Virtual Library. Available at: https://www.ojp.gov/ncjrs/virtual-library/abstracts/problems-criminalization-and-decriminalization-socially-detrimental. Accessed on January 04, 2021.

Bajpai, G. S. (January 11, 2019) "Invoke criminal sanctions with caution". *The Tribune*. Available at: https://www.tribuneindia.com/news/archive/comment/invoke-criminal -sanctions-with-caution-711660. Accessed on May 01, 2021.

Bajpai, G. S. and Karuna, V. (December 19, 2022) "Decriminalisation of Offences under GST". *The Hindu*. Available at: https://www.thehindu.com/business/Economy/explained-decriminalisation-of-offences-under-gst/article66279310.ece. Accessed on May 07, 2023.

Banana v. State, 4 LRC (2000) [SCZ] Supreme Court, Zimbabwe.

Banana v. State, 4 LRC (2000) Supreme Court, Zimbabwe.

Baxi, U. (2019) "Afterword: Whither Constitutional Morality? Some thoughts on Justice Dipak Misra's Enunciation". In: S. D. Rao (ed) *Reclaiming Dignity, Rights and Justice*. New Delhi: Thomson Reuters.

Bedi, S. (2021) "Constitutional Morality: Ambedkar's Progeny and India's Legacy". In: R. Singh (ed) *Ambedkar's Milestones on the Roadmap of Indian Constitution*. Gurgaon: Thomson Reuters.

Bentham, J. (1840) *Theory of Legislation*. Boston: Weeks, Jordan, and Company.

Bharadway, A. (July 29, 2020) *Is Criminal Law a Lost Cause in India?*. Outlook. Available at: https://www.outlookindia.com/national/opinion-is-criminal-law-a-lost-cause-in-in dia-news-357603. Accessed on May 01, 2023.

Bhateja, A. (December 13, 2019) *Towards a Fairer Principle of Criminalisation.* Law School Policy Review & Kautilya Society. Available at: https://lawschoolpolicyreview.com/2019/12/13/towards-a-fairer-principle-of-criminalization/. Accessed on May 24, 2021.

Bittlinger, P. A. (1975) "Government enforcement of morality: A critical analysis of the Devlin-Hart controversy". *Doctoral Dissertations 1896-February 2014.* Available at: https://scholarworks.umass.edu/cgi/viewcontent.cgi?referer=&httpsredir =1&article =2910&context=dissertations_1. Accessed on June 01, 2021.

Cane, P. (2006) "Taking Law Seriously: Starting Points of the Hart/Devlin Debate". *The Journal of Ethics, 10*(1/2): 21–51.

Chandrachud, A. (February 12, 2020) *The Many Meanings of Constitutional Morality.* SSRN. Available at: https://papers.ssrn.com/sol3/papers.cfm?abstract_id= 3521665. Accessed on July 01, 2020.

Chaudhary, S. (September 20, 2018) *Criminalisation and Privacy: Examining the State's Right to Interfere in the "Private Sphere" through imposition or lifting of Criminal Sanction.* IACL-AIDC Blog. Available at: https://blog-iacl-aidc.org/blog /2018/9/18 /symposium-criminalisation-and-privacy-examining-the-states-right-to-interfere-in-the-private-sphere-through-imposition-or-lifting-of-criminal-sanction. Accessed on November 01, 2021.

Chawla, A. (October 5, 2022) *The Burgeoning Share of Undertrial Prisoners in India's Jails.* The Wire. Available at: https://thewire.in/rights/indian-jails-undertrial -prisoners. Accessed on May 19, 2023.

Decriminalisation. International Commission of Jurists. Available at: https://www.icj .org/sogi-casebook-introduction/chapter-one-decriminalisation/. Accessed on March 01, 2024.

Devlin, P. (1965) *The Enforcement of Morals.* Oxford: Oxford University Press.

Dworkin, G. (1999) "Devlin Was Right". *William & Mary Law Review, 40*(3): 927–946.

Feinberg, J. (1965) "The Expressive Function of Punishment". *Philosophy of Law, 49*(3): 397–423.

Feinberg, J. (1984) *The Moral Limits of the Criminal Law: Harm to Others.* New York: Oxford University Press.

Feinberg, J. (1987) *Harmless Wrongdoing.* New York: Oxford University Press.

Gian Kaur v. State of Punjab, AIR 1996 SC 946 (1996) Supreme Court, India.

Govt. of NCT of Delhi v. Union of India, 8 SCC 501 (2018) Supreme Court, India.

Grote, G. (2001) *A History of Greece: From the Time of Solon to 403 B.C.* London & New York: Routledge.

Hands, B. (2009) *Paternalism and the Law.* Philosophy Now. Available at: https://philos ophynow.org/issues/71/Paternalism_and_the_Law. Accessed on July 01, 2021.

Hart Devlin Debate: Summary and Analysis. (June 19, 2022) IvyPanda. Available at: https://ivypanda.com/essays/the-hart-devlin-debate/. Accessed on May 01, 2023.

Healy, P. (August 26, 2022) *Restraint in the Criminal Law*. Government of Canada. Available at: https://www.justice.gc.ca/eng/rp-pr/csj-sjc/ilp-pji/cl-dp/index.html#note1. Accessed on July 24, 2023.

Hirsch, A. V. (1986) "Injury and Exasperation: An Examination of Harm to Others and Offense to Others". *Michigan Law Review,* 84(4): 700–714.

Holtug, N. (2002) "The Harm Principle". *Ethical Theory and Moral Practice,* 5(4): 357–89.

Husak, D. (2008) *Overcriminalization: The Limits of the Criminal Law*. New York: Oxford University Press.

Indian Penal Code, 1860 (45 of 1860).

IvyPanda. (2022). Hart Devlin Debate: Summary and Analysis. Available at: https://ivypanda.com/essays/the-hart-devlin-debate/. Accessed on March 01, 2024.

Joseph Shine v. Union of India, 3 SCC 39 (2019) Supreme Court, India.

Kadish, S. H. (1967) "The Crisis of Overcriminalization". *The Annals of the American Academy of Political and Social Science,* 374(1): 157–170.

Kanane v. The State, (2) BLR 67 (CA). (2003) Court of Appeal, Botswana.

Kantaru Rajeevaru v. Indian Young Lawyers Association. 3 SCC 52. (2020) Supreme Court, India.

Khurshid, S. (2020) "Constitutional Morality and Judges of the Supreme Court". In: S. Khurshid, et al. (eds) *Judicial Review: Process, Powers and Problems*. New Delhi: Cambridge University Press.

Kishore, P. (August 12, 2019) "Criminalisation of 'nothing': India cannot afford more criminal provisions". *Business Standard.* Available at: https://www.business-standard.com/article/economy-policy/can-india-afford-more-criminal-provisions-the-answer-is-a-resounding-no-119081200145_1.html. Accessed on May 15, 2021.

Lacey, N. (1988) *State Punishment*. London: Routledge.

Lynch, T. (2017) *Overcriminalization*. CATO Institute. Available at: https://www.cato.org/cato-handbook-policymakers/cato-handbook-policy-makers-8th-edition-2017/17-overcriminalization. Accessed on June 17, 2021.

Mehta, P. B. (2010) *What is Constitutional Morality?*. India Seminar. Available at: https://www.india-seminar.com/2010/615/615_pratap_bhanu_mehta.htm. Accessed on June 01, 2021.

Mill, J. S. (1989) *On Liberty* (2nd ed.). London: J.W. Parker and Son.

Mill, J. S., and Rapaport, E. (1978) *On Liberty*. Indianapolis: Hackett Publishing.

Muslim Women (Protection of Rights on Marriage) Act, Act 20 of 2019 (2019).

Navtej Singh Johar v. Union of India, 10 SCC 1 (2018) Supreme Court, India.

Naz Foundation v. Government of NCT of Delhi. SCC Online Del 1762 (2009) Delhi High Court, India.

Neuberger, Lord. (June 18, 2015) "Magna Carta: The Bible of the English Constitution or a disgrace to the English nation?". Guildford Cathedral. Available at: https://www.supremecourt.uk/docs/speech-150618.pdf.

Pandey, A and Aanchal. (January 26, 2020) *Constitutionalism and Constitutional Morality as a Check on Criminalisation*. NUJS Society for Advancement of Criminal Justice. Available at: https://www.nujssacj.com/post/constitutionalism-and-constitutional- morality-as-a-check-on-criminalisation. Accessed on May 01, 2021.

Pandey, A. and Aanchal (2022) "Constitutionalism and Constitutional Morality as a Check on Criminalisation". Available at: https://www.nujssacj.com/post/constitutionalism-and-constitutional-morality-as-a-check-on-criminalisation Accessed on July 01, 2023.

Petersen, T. S. (2016) "No Offense! On the Offense Principle and Some New Challenges". *Criminal Law and Philosophy, 10*(2): 355–365.

Raj, K and Raj, T. K. (September 28, 2018) "Beyond marriage and morals: State has no business seeking to control an individual's sexual expression". *The Times of India*. Available at: https://timesofindia.indiatimes.com/blogs/tracking-indian-communities/beyond-marriage-and-morals-state-has-no-business-seeking-to-control-an-individuals-sexual-expression/. Accessed on July 01, 2021.

Richards, D. A. J. (1988) "Liberalism, Public Morality, and Constitutional Law: Prolegomenon to a Theory of the Constitutional Right to Privacy". *Law and Contemporary Problems, 51*(1): 123–150.

Shayara Bano v. Union of India, 9 SCC 1 (2017) Supreme Court, India.

Singhal, N. (October 20, 2021) *The NDPS Act, Aryan Khan, & Our Ridiculous System*. Vidhi Centre for Legal Policy. Available at: https://vidhilegalpolicy.in/blog/the-ndps-act-aryan-khan-and/. Accessed on December 01, 2021.

Smith, S. D. (2004) "The Hollowness of the Harm Principle". *University of San Diego Public Law and Legal Theory Research Paper Series*: 1–62.

Sowmithri Vishnu v. Union of India, AIR 1985 SC 1618 (1985) Supreme Court, India.

Srivastava, R. (2010) "Harms' Way: Conceptualising Harm in Criminal Law". *India Law Journal,* 3(3). Available at: https://www.indialawjournal.org/archives/volume3/issue_3/article_by_raghav.html. Accessed on June 06, 2023.

Stanton-Ife, J. (2022) "The Limits of Law". In: Zalta, E. N (ed.) *The Stanford Encyclopedia of Philosophy* (Spring 2022). Available at: https://plato.stanford.edu/archives/spr2022/entries/law-limits/. Accessed on June 06, 2023.

Starr, W. C. (1984) "Law and Morality in H. L. A. Hart's Legal Philosophy". *Marquette Law Review, 67*(4): 673–689.

Statesman News Service. (December 17, 2022) "GST Council wants to decriminalise certain offences". *The Statesman*. Available at: https://www.thestatesman.com/india/gst-council-wants-to-decriminalise-certain-offences-1503139066.html. Accessed on June 06, 2023.

Suresh Kumar Kaushal v. Naz Foundation, 1 SCC 1 (2014) Supreme Court, India.

The Companies (Amendment), 2019, Act 22 of 2019.

The Heritage Foundation. Overcriminalization. Available at: https://www.heritage.org/crime-and-justice/heritage-explains/overcriminalization#:~:text=%E2%80%9COvercriminalization%E2%80%9D%E2%80%94the%20overuse%20and,greatest%20punishment%20and%20moral%20sanction. Accessed on June 06, 2023.

The Unlawful Activities (Prevention) Amendment Act, 2019. Act 28 of 2019.

Vashist, L. (2013) "Re-Thinking Criminalisable Harm in India: Constitutional Morality as a Restraint on Criminalisation". *Journal of the Indian Law Institute,* 55(1): 73–93.

CHAPTER 9

Drug Laws: The Reality and Politics of Overcriminalization

Alok Prasanna Kumar and Naveed Mehmood

1   Introduction

When one thinks of a classic example of overcriminalization, the Narcotics Drugs and Psychotropic Substances Act, 1985 ('NDPS Act') immediately comes to mind. The long title of the law itself betrays the intent to make "stringent provisions" in respect of narcotic drugs and psychotropic substances ('drugs'). Not only does the law criminalize consumption of drugs, in addition to the trafficking, sale or possession of such drugs, it loosens the strict rigours of criminal procedure to make the task of the prosecution to obtain convictions easier (Narcotic Drugs and Psychotropic Substances Act, 1985: § 37, 53A).

The draconian provisions also mean that unlike most other criminal laws, crimes under the NDPS Act have a high conviction rate relative to offences under other legislation. Data related to conviction and acquittals between 2016 and 2020 shows that the rate of convictions has remained more than 70% going beyond 80% during 2020 though the number of cases which were completed were reduced due to the pandemic (Kancharla, 2021). According to the latest data released by the National Crime Records Bureau ('NCRB'), the conviction rate for NDPS cases was 77.9% (National Crime Records Bureau, 2021: 17). To put this number in context, the conviction rate for all offences under all laws for the year 2021 was 65%, though convictions for offences under the Indian Penal Code ('IPC') were only about 51.25%.[1]

Does that however mean that India's "drug problem" is under control? Far from it. The vast bulk of accused and convicted are users. The number of cases keep increasing year on year and the vast bulk of cases under the NDPS Act are still awaiting trial (Kancharla, 2021). These statistics also hide a deeper truth about the criminal justice system which this paper will get into in the later parts. Given the data about Indian prisoners (*Mint*, 2021), it is quite likely that the people who have been disproportionately impacted by the harsh

---

1   Authors' calculations based on NCRB data indicated above.

provisions of the NDPS Act are Dalits, adivasis, Muslims and other underprivileged sections of society.

This state of affairs does prompt some questions. How did India end up with this draconian law that seems to mostly penalise drug addicts and users from underprivileged communities, to their detriment? And more importantly, beyond the broad numbers, what does enforcement of this law actually look like on the ground?

In this paper we therefore propose to examine the origins of India's current drug laws with a view to unpack the underlying assumptions of the law. To this end, we trace the history of drug legislation in India, going back to laws passed during colonial rule. This paper looks at the provisions of the laws as they were enacted in the past and the justifications that were offered for the laws, leading up to the reasons for which the NDPS Act was passed. We propose to identify the continuities and discontinuities in the legislation related to drugs in India, comparing not just the provisions of the laws themselves but also the reasons given as to why the laws were needed in the first place.

In addition, our paper also covers recent research on the manner in which the NDPS Act has been implemented. We discuss the findings of the data driven studies undertaken by the Vidhi Centre for Legal Policy ('Vidhi') in the last few years specifically covering the states of Punjab and Maharashtra. While these studies may not be representative of the implementation of the NDPS Act nationwide, they do provide important insights into the implementation of the law on the ground.

To do this, the paper has been divided into four parts, including this introduction as the first part. The second part of this paper will deal with the colonial origins of India's drug laws, specifically the origins of the two Opium Acts and the Dangerous Drugs Act, 1930 ('DD Act') which were the precursors to the present NDPS Act.

The third part of the paper goes into how the NDPS Act came into existence and how it has been implemented. In this part we will look at what the studies show us about the manner in which the NDPS Act has been implemented by the police authorities on the ground, with specific reference to the states of Punjab and Maharashtra. We argue here that the law, far from being used to reduce trafficking, is being used to punish users, turning a public health issue into a law and order problem.

The final part of the paper will summarise our conclusions on the topic where we lay out how the NDPS Act is a prime example of the problem of overcriminalization. We argue that this is a law that only victimises people who need health interventions and that the state has abdicated its responsibility by taking a law and order approach to the issue. What we call for is a larger re-imagination of the role of criminal sanction.

The data that we have used for this paper is largely from publicly available sources, including the research conducted by Vidhi.

2   Problematic Origins of Criminalization of Drug Use

When enacted in 1985, the NDPS Act was replacing a host of legislation that had existed from the times of colonial rule. Section 82 of the NDPS Act repealed the Opium Act, 1857, the Opium Act, 1878 and the DD Act, 1930. One would assume that the NDPS Act, in repealing and replacing the colonial era laws, would adopt a more constitutionally appropriate and liberal minded approach to the issue of drugs in India. However, as we argue in this paper, this might be one of those rare areas where the post-colonial legislation has proved to be worse for the rights of citizens than the colonial legislation!

In this section we will briefly cover the context in which these laws came into effect and what they provided for. What we hope to show is the changing trajectory of drug laws in India to identify the continuities and discontinuities with the NDPS Act.

2.1   *The Opium Act, 1857*

The use of cannabis and opium in India before British rule was well known and documented (Kethineni, et al. 1995: 214). Like cannabis, opium was grown for limited recreational, medicinal, ritual and ceremonial purposes. However, its status as a cash crop only grew as a result of British rule, especially given the lucrative trade with China. A second factor behind the growth of opium use in India was the de-industrialisation and pauperisation that resulted under colonial rule. This created the conditions for widespread opium addiction (Deshpande, 2009: 127). The large-scale consumption of opium also presented a lucrative source of revenue for the British government and the purposes of the initial laws, it can be seen, was to protect the British government's monopoly on the opium trade within India (Bauer, 2019).

The Opium Act, 1857 was enacted, as its preamble indicates, to consolidate and amend the law relating to the cultivation of the poppy and the manufacture of opium. One of the critical functions of the Act was to prohibit poppy cultivation and opium manufacture. However, this was not a total prohibition, and its manufacture and sale were heavily regulated. Rather, opium could be purchased from government licensed shops.

The 1857 Act prescribed the procedure for the issue of licences and mandated such licence holders to deliver the produce to government officers at established rates. Keeping in mind historical circumstances, the 1857 Act made it clear that cultivators who had licences still had the option not to engage in the cultivation of poppy and could not be compelled by any officer. In contrast to this licensing system, under Section 31, the government could allow free cultivation of poppy and manufacture of opium in any district without a licence as prescribed. It could also suspend the operation of the 1857 Act in such districts.

However, those who received advances from the government for cultivation and failed to do so were liable to a penalty under Section 10 that could be three times the amount of advances received for the land. Illegal purchase of opium from cultivators was also punishable under this law.

We may note here that there was no ban on the consumption or mere possession of opium or any other drug. The cultivation and manufacture of opium though "banned" to an extent was still permitted and heavily regulated by the government. This regulatory framework was extended in the Opium Act, 1878 which made some significant changes.

2.2 The Opium Act, 1878

The Act of 1878 was passed to establish a complete state monopoly over opium in British India, keeping in mind the enforcement difficulties that were perceived to have been faced with the 1857 Act and the revenues generated by the drug (Deshpande, 2009: 114). The 1878 Act, which also partially repealed and modified the 1857 Act, banned the manufacture, possession, sale, export, import or transport of opium, unless it was done in accordance with the 1878 Act itself. The 1878 Act also included criminal penalties for undertaking any of these activities in a manner inconsistent with the law. This law also vested with the "Local Government" the power to make rules consistent with the 1878 Act regarding possession, transport, import, export etc. of opium.

As they were originally enacted, neither Opium Acts criminalized the consumption of opium itself, or extended its reach beyond the regulation of opium cultivation and manufacture itself. In fact, the colonial government saw no reason to change the laws because of the lucrative revenue generated by the consumption of opium. The report of the Royal Commission on Opium in 1894 defended the existing regime of regulation for opium in India noting, among other things, that there is no strong local opinion in favour of prohibition and that the revenue from opium was "indispensable" for running the government (*First Report on the Royal Commission on Opium*, 1892). In recommending against a total prohibition, the report also noted that:

> From the evidence we have taken we are convinced that the great mass of Native opinion in British India is entirely opposed to the proposal, as an unnecessary restriction on individual liberty, and an interference with established Native habits and customs. "We believe that even those who are not addicted to the opium habit, and who do not belong to the races which commonly use opium as a stimulant, regard the proposal with dislike and suspicion from this point of view. The use of alcohol is admitted by all Mahomedans and, with few exceptions, by all Hindus, to be directly prohibited by their religion. On the other hand, the use of opium is generally considered to be permissible by Hindus, and by all bar a few Mahomedans in India.
>
> First Report on the Royal Commission on Opium, 1892: 64

However, it did find that smoking opium ought to be banned completely (*First Report on the Royal Commission on Opium*, 1892: 148). The nationalist movement and international opinion would prompt a change.

2.3   *The Dangerous Drugs Act, 1930*

In 1912, the world's first drug control treaty, the International Opium Convention (International Opium Convention, 1912) was signed and eventually went into effect in 1919. The treaty prohibited international trade in opium (International Opium Convention, 1912: Article 7) and urged member states to take measures to curb manufacture and sale internally (International Opium Convention, 1912: Article 6). The treaty also urged member states to limit the use of morphine and cocaine for purely medicinal and therapeutic purposes.

A second International Opium Convention was convened in Geneva in 1925 and this time India was one of the parties invited even though it was not an independent country at that time. With the intent of making a submission to the Convention, the All India Congress Committee tasked CP Andrews to come up with a report about opium consumption in Assam to submit to the Commission (Assam Congress Opium Enquiry Report, 1925). This resulted in the Assam Congress Opium Enquiry Report which, among other things, recommended sale of opium and its derivatives should be limited only to medical and scientific needs and that opium should be placed under a "Dangerous Drugs Act" within five years.

With both international opinion and public demand asking for the same thing, India's colonial government had to act – it introduced the DD Act, 1930.

In contrast with the two Opium Acts, the DD Act expanded the scope of the law to other narcotic drugs as well. The preamble also reflected India's commitment to the International Convention Relating to Dangerous Drugs, 1925

('International Opium Convention'), which sought to suppress the traffic and abuse of dangerous drugs, especially those derived from opium, Indian hemp and coca leaf. Dangerous drugs were defined to include coca leaf, hemp, opium and all other *manufactured drugs*.

The DD Act also increased the penalties regarding such operations and made them uniform across British India. The DD Act was divided into five chapters and two schedules. Chapter 2 restricted the cultivation, manufacture, import and export of dangerous drugs. Section 4 placed restrictions on the cultivation and gathering of the coca plant, the manufacture or possession of prepared opium (unless such prepared opium was lawfully possessed for the consumption of the possessor), and the import into and export from British India or tranship or sale of prepared opium. The *proviso* to this section excluded the cultivation or gathering of coca plants on the Government's behalf. Section 5 also banned the cultivation of poppy and the manufacture of opium other than in consonance with the rules and licensing requirements as prescribed by the Governor General.

Section 6 went on to limit the manufacture of any manufactured drugs other than prepared opium other than as per the rules and licensing as prescribed. Section 7 prevented the export, import and tranship of any dangerous drug, other than prepared opium, except under the rules which are to be prescribed by the Governor General in Council. The Local Government was vested with control over the internal traffic of manufactured drugs other than prepared opium and coca leaves and the manufacture of medicinal opium or preparations containing morphine, diacetylmorphine or cocaine under Section 8.

The trade of dangerous drugs obtained outside India and supplied to persons outside India was also subject to the conditions and licences granted by the Local Governments.

Two things seem to have influenced the colonial approach to law making on narcotic drugs. First there was the need to protect the monopoly over the extremely lucrative opium trade with China. This sordid part of India's history is beyond the scope of this paper but it was the underlying basis for the opium laws in India for the better part of the 19th century and into the 20th century. A second reason perhaps was the desire not to interfere with local customs and practices over the consumption of cannabis and other narcotics. However, international pressure and pressure from the nationalist movement seems to have eventually forced the British to take a tougher stance on trafficking of drugs, resulting in the DD Act.

With the adoption of the Constitution of India, the power to legislate on opium and to levy excise duty on narcotics was given exclusively to the Union Legislature by placing these subjects in List I of the Seventh Schedule. While these laws applied under what was "British India", by virtue of the Opium and Revenue Laws (Extension of Application) Act of 1950, the three laws became uniformly applicable in all the States of the Indian Union.

This was the legal position at the time when the NDPS Act was brought into force in India. However, this does not fully explain how and why the NDPS Act came into force. In order to do that, the next section explores the immediate circumstances leading up to the enactment of the NDPS Act.

3   Developments Leading to the Enactment of the Narcotic Drugs and Psychotropic Substances Act, 1985

To understand the working of the NDPS Act it is necessary to understand the backdrop in which this law was enacted by the Union Parliament. India was signatory to two conventions: the 1961 Convention on Narcotic Drugs ('the 1961 Convention') and the 1971 Convention on Psychotropic Substances ('the 1971 Convention'). These two conventions required signatory states to end manufacture, sale, traffic and consumption of drugs, except for medical use. To facilitate a gradual move, the transitional reservation clause of the 1961 Convention required that steps be taken within 25 years from the coming into force of the 1961 Convention.

Existing legislation in India did not adequately fulfil all of India's obligations under the two conventions. While the Opium Act, 1857 was enacted to remove inconsistencies between the practice and the law on cultivation of poppy and manufacture of opium (Opium Act, 1857: Preamble), the DD Act intended to centralise the control over opium, hemp, coca leaf and all manufactured drugs, and increase penalties for violations under the DD Act. Neither of the laws extended control over upcoming psychotropic substances or imposed a blanket prohibition on consumption of drugs. Violations related to cultivation, manufacture, sale etc. also attracted modest punishments, generally of up to 2 years.

The Government of India's traditionally non-interfering policy towards drug use under the colonial administration or the government of independent India, in recognition of thousands of years of medical and recreational use of narcotic substances in India, was gearing for a significant shift (Kethineni, et al. 1995). India had signed the conventions and mounting international pressure, coupled with the approaching deadline to implement provisions of the two conventions, compelled a rather hasty decision to enact the NDPS Act. In 1985, in the midst of the United States of America's "war on drugs", India joined a global system on regulation of drugs. Interestingly, this global system was a mirror image of the US's domestic policy undergoing extensive internationalisation.

Through the 19th Century, the United States Government opposed the consumption of opium and other substances. Outlawing drug use, taxing production and importation of opiates, domestic legislations such as the Opium Exclusion Act of 1909 and the Harrison Narcotics Act of 1914, among other things, recognised the growing prohibitionist sentiment in the US. However, propaganda prevalent at that time suggests the racist underpinnings of these laws – opium use by the Chinese was considered as a threat to 'American Christian morality' (Rafaeli, 2018); growing use of cocaine was tied to the African American community; and popularisation of recreational cannabis was linked to the influx of Mexican immigrants (Pagano, 2018).

As the conventions mandated eradication of even traditional and culturally ingrained use of cannabis, opium and coca leaf (Single Convention on Narcotic Drugs, 1961: Article 49) – which was socially, culturally and legally accepted in many communities, including communities in India, it perhaps marked the success of the US in influencing the world's outlook towards drug consumption.

3.1 Placing the NDPS Act within the Mandate of the Conventions

Preambles of the two conventions make it amply clear that the focus was to eliminate all forms of non-medical drug use. By referring to addiction as a 'serious evil', the 1961 convention set the tone for an ill-informed, aggressive and stigmatising approach to drug abuse and addiction. Debates on the NDPS Bill in the Indian parliament appear to be consistent with this approach.

While introducing the Bill in the *Lok Sabha* in August 1985, the Minister of State for Finance, Janardhana Poojary, underlined the deficiencies in the existing statutory framework, necessitating enactment of the NDPS Act. He stated that the existing penalties were not deterrent enough to meet the challenges posed by well organised gangs of smugglers; that provisions for controlling new drugs of abuse, such as psychotropic substances, did not exist; and that there was a need for adequate provisions to implement the international conventions that India had signed.

He also stated that the object of the Bill is to "strengthen the existing controls over drugs of abuse" and "considerably enhance the penalties particularly for trafficking offences" (*Lok Sabha* Debates, Aug 28, 1985: 193–194). Harsh punishments were seen as critical to deter trafficking of drugs. Although relatively less harsh when compared to trafficking, the approach towards drug abusers and addicts appeared to be no different.

In a debate that primarily focussed on trafficking and traditional cultivation of cannabis and opium, references to drug abuse were made only in the context of the harm they cause to the society. Phulrenu Guha, a Member of Parliament from Contai, West Bengal, underlined how everyone needs to come together to save the country from this menace (*Lok Sabha* Debates, Aug 28, 1985: 50). In fact, parliamentarians opposed nominal punishments for drug addicts and argued for harsher punishments. V. S Krishna Iyer, an MP from Bangalore South, stated that punishments should be a deterrent for peddlers as well as drug addicts (*Lok Sabha* Debates, Aug 28, 1985: 37–78). Priyaranjan Dasmunishi, an MP from Howrah, West Bengal, argued that drug users should be punished with two years of imprisonment, and that a six month imprisonment clause in the Bill was of 'no use' prisons (*Lok Sabha* Debates, Aug 28, 1985: 73). Strategies for drug demand reduction, de-addiction and rehabilitation processes were hardly discussed. As a result, the law never recognised the inherent complexities of drug abuse and consequently the problems in attempting to tackle it through criminalization.

The NDPS Act initially did not recognise the distinction between recreational drug users, addicts and traffickers. In fact, illegal possession of drugs in 'small quantities' – a term that the law did not define, could attract an imprisonment for up to one year (Narcotic Drugs and Psychotropic Substances Act, 1985: § 27). The burden of proving that such a possession was for personal consumption and not for sale also lay on the accused (Narcotic Drugs and Psychotropic Substances Act, 1985: § 27 Explanation 2). Optional diversion for de-addiction was perhaps the only consolation for addicts, that too, only after conviction (Narcotic Drugs and Psychotropic Substances Act, 1985: § 39).

The problems with this approach were flagged in the *Rajya Sabha* in 1988 and by an expert committee constituted in 1994 to "review existing provisions of the NDPS Act with regard to laying down the quantum of small quantity".

During the debate on a proposed amendment to the NDPS Act in the *Rajya Sabha* in 1988, Kamal Moraka, an MP from Rajasthan, stated that the absence of a clear distinction between addicts and peddlers was pushing addicts into prisons (*Rajya Sabha* Debates, December 20, 1988: 216). The expert committee also underlined the lacunae in the law and stated that the average addict will invariably possess quantities larger than the threshold notified by the Government and will, therefore, end up in prison (Ministry of Health and Family Welfare, 1994). While recommending decriminalization of drug use, the committee flagged the inappropriateness of criminalizing a medical disorder requiring treatment.

4 How Criminalization of Drug Use Plays Out on Ground

The current position of the law on consumption of drugs is a result of an amendment to the NDPS Act in 2001 ('2001 Amendment'). Section 27 of the NDPS Act earlier criminalized consumption of drugs, as well as possession of drugs in 'small quantities' for personal consumption. After the 2001 Amendment, possession of drugs for personal consumption was removed from the purview of section 27, and so was the reverse burden of proof. Now, whoever 'consumes' drugs like cocaine, morphine or any such substance notified by the Union Government may be sentenced to imprisonment for up to one year. Consumption of any other drug may attract imprisonment for up to 6 months [Narcotic Drug and Psychotropic Substances Act, 1985: § 27; Narcotic Drug and Psychotropic Substances (Amendment) Act, 2001: § 10].

The provision, however, does not define consumption and the process for determining consumption. Further, even though the provision attempts to create a distinction between traffickers and users – providing for comparatively less punishment to the latter – it continues to conflate the distinction between non-problematic users and problematic users or addicts. While problematic users may show addictive usage or dependence on drugs due to regular drug use, non-problematic users do not (Schlag, 2020). In its application on ground, the law criminalizes both and fails to offer any protection to addicts.

4.1 *Criminalizing the Marginalised in Mumbai*

To study the implementation of section 27 of the NDPS Act in Mumbai, Vidhi analysed data from the NCRB, the Maharashtra Crime Investigation Department and 10,669 NDPS cases disposed of by magistrate courts in Mumbai. The study (of which one of us was a co-author) showed that criminalization of drug use disproportionately impacts marginalised communities. It also exposed how loosely drafted laws can be misused to fulfil ill-conceived political objectives (Singhal and Ahmad, 2020).

Maharashtra recorded 1,081 NDPS cases in 2010, 1,368 in 2011, 1,903 in 2012 and 2,714 in 2013. In 2014, the number of cases grew by over 438% to 14,622. NDPS cases further grew to 18,979 in 2015 (*Crime in Maharashtra*, 2015: 88). Mumbai's contribution to Maharashtra's NDPS cases went from 60.8% in 2010 to 98.2% in 2015 (*Crime in Maharashtra*, 2015: 88).[2] Around 97% of the total

---

2 Mumbai registered 657 NDPS cases in 2010, 958 in 2011, 1512 in 2012, 2400 in 2013, 14274 in 2014 and 18628 in 2015. Crime Investigation Department.

arrests made in NDPS cases in Maharashtra were also made in Mumbai (*Crime in Maharashtra*, 2014: 373).[3]

Almost all of these cases were of drug use and not of trafficking. In fact, cases in which drugs were seized remained constant throughout – 444 in 2011, 440 in 2012, 405 in 2013, 546 in 2014 and 547 in 2015 (*Crime in Maharashtra*, 2015: 323). Vidhi's analysis of cases from magistrate courts in Mumbai showed that 87% of the cases of drug use involved cannabis. All of those arrested invariably belonged to deprived sections of the society – daily labourers, rag pickers, porters, among others, all of whom were either pavement or slum dwellers. Those arrested were also relatively young on average, with 52% of them being under the age of 25 and only 6% above 45 years of age.[4]

4.1.1   Questionable Adjudicatory Processes

While the police were clearly going after cannabis users on the streets of Mumbai, the adjudicatory process showed little concern towards upholding principles of fair trial. In most cases, the accused pleaded guilty, were convicted and sentenced on the same day.

In fact, of the 10,669 NDPS cases that Vidhi analysed, 10,638 (99.7%) cases went uncontested. In 9,697 or 90% of the cases, the accused was convicted. In 967 cases, the accused was either discharged or the proceedings were stopped under section 258 of the Code of Criminal Procedure ('CrPC'). In the remaining five cases, the accused was acquitted.[5]

90% of the cases in the sample were disposed of on the same day they were brought before the court. Most of the cases that took more than one day for disposal were stopped under section 258 of CrPC, leading to discharge of the accused. All such discharges were because the accused was not traceable.

Convicts were either only fined or sentenced to imprisonment, with or without fine. The maximum term of imprisonment was eight days, and the minimum was 'till rising of court'. The fines-imposed range between Rs. 100 to Rs. 8000.

---

3 In 2014, 16290 persons were arrested under the NDPS Act in Maharashtra. 15765 were arrested in Mumbai alone.
4 Of the 839 orders that Vidhi analysed, 180 orders provided for the occupation of the accused; 277 provided the addresses of the accused; and 427 provided data on age of the accused.
5 Section 258 of Code of Criminal Procedure, 1973 allows Magistrates to stop proceedings in certain cases, without pronouncing any judgement.

4.1.2 Incentivisation of Guilty Pleas

An overwhelmingly high number of 'guilty pleas' would seem to suggest that these pleas were incentivised. Even though there may not be a direct or conscious attempt, by police or courts, to incentivise these pleas, there were multiple factors that made pleading guilty an attractive proposition for the accused. These include, no or bare minimum jail terms, small fines and same day disposals. It is not clear from the data what else could have prompted such a large number of guilty pleas, especially since this trend is not seen in the context of other criminal cases.

For the accused, the cost of putting up a defence in court far outweighed the fines imposed upon conviction. This is even more true when all those accused were daily wage labourers, for whom even one day of court appearance costs dearly. In effect, thousands of people in Mumbai were made to choose between a conviction and having to go through the arduous process of a criminal trial to prove their innocence. For the accused person, whether guilty or not, pleading guilty was easier and faster.

Moreover, the system also enabled securing an easy conviction. Most of the arrests for drug use were followed by a preliminary medical assessment. Complete medical reports were never scrutinised by the police or by the courts and the prosecution relied on a mere physical examination to determine if the person was under the influence of drugs (Singhal and Ahmad, 2020).[6]

While the purpose of adjudication is to find out the truth and prevent miscarriage of justice, incentivisation of the guilty plea risks convicting innocents and has been held by the Supreme Court to be violative of article 21 of the Constitution (Kasamabhai Abdulrehmanbhai Sheikh v. State of Gujarat, 1980). Guarantees of a fair trial, presumption of innocence and the mandate to prove the case beyond reasonable doubt are pivotal to protect rights of an accused, but the processes adopted and the mechanical application of law in Mumbai exposes the subversion of these rights and consequently a fair criminal trial (Zahira Habibullah Sheikh v. State of Gujarat, 2004). Trials in NDPS cases in Mumbai showcase an apathetic attitude towards these established norms by laying no emphasis on proving a case beyond reasonable doubt. By basing conviction solely on guilty pleas, courts ignore the inherent imbalance of power and resources between the accused person and the prosecuting state.

---

6 Doctors in Mumbai informed Vidhi that they conduct a basic physical examination to determine if the person is 'under influence'. This is merely a provisional determination on which the police rely upon. A conclusive determination requires examination of blood or urine samples, which takes 1–2 months.

4.1.3 What Prompted This Arrest Spree of Drug Users?

To address the issue of rising drug abuse, Maharashtra, like other states in the country, had focussed on traffickers as well as drug users. As shown above, even though the number of consumption cases registered had always been higher than the number of cases in which drugs were seized, the ratio was never alarming. In 2013, 67% of the NDPS cases registered in Maharashtra were cases of consumption. In fact, in 2012 and 2013 the difference between consumption cases and cases in which drugs were seized was 1,463 and 2,309, respectively. However, in 2014, the difference grew to 14,076 and further to 18,432 in 2015. Over 97% of the NDPS cases in Maharashtra were registered in Mumbai and were cases of drug use. Since then Maharashtra has been booking thousands of people for drug use. So, what really changed in 2014?

It was around this time that the Government of Maharashtra, through a series of Government Resolutions, began stressing on improved conviction rates. Periodical training of prosecutors, review of pending criminal cases and appointment of special counsels, were seen as means to this end. The Maharashtra Home Department took a significant step on May 12th, 2015, by passing five resolutions focused on enhancing conviction rates. These resolutions aimed at ensuring prompt training for Public Prosecutors. The Governor (*Economic Times*, 2016) and the Chief Minister of Maharashtra asserted the importance of improved conviction rates by linking it to deterrence and crime control (*NDTV*, 2015). On the ground, this political will translate into a disproportionate increase in arrest and conviction of drug users under the NDPS Act.

In Maharashtra, the conviction rate in NDPS cases had fluctuated between 28.2% in 2010 to 64.4% in 2013 (National Crime Records Bureau, 2010: 336; National Crime Records Bureau, 2013: 336). It jumped to 92.1% in 2014 and further to 94.3% in 2015 (*Crime in Maharashtra*, 2014: 150; *Crime in Maharashtra*, 2015: 193). As a consequence of increasing conviction rates in NDPS cases, the overall conviction rates in all Special and Local Laws cases also increased. From 20.6% in 2010, it doubled to 43.9% in 2016 (*Crime in Maharashtra*, 2016: 198).

The system was, therefore, successful in using a loosely drafted law to enforce a political agenda without any concern for its adverse impact on individuals and communities.

4.2 *Criminalizing Addicts in Punjab*

As mentioned above, the 2001 Amendment to the NDPS Act led to some substantial changes in how the law imposed consequences on drug use. The 2001 Amendment also attempted to rationalise the sentencing policy for offences relating to manufacture, cultivation, transportation, and sale of drugs. Punishments for all of these offences were now linked to the quantity of drugs – small, intermediate and commercial. Marking a major shift from the earlier provisions which provided for mandatory minimum sentences of 10 years, the 2001 Amendment prescribed imprisonments ranging from up to six months to 20 years. To further facilitate diversion of addicts for treatment, section 64A was also added to the NDPS Act. It provided for affording immunity from prosecution to addicts charged with consumption or for small quantity offences.

Even though the rationalised structure was intended to distinguish between users and traffickers, and to extend a protective umbrella over addicts, its application on ground leaves much to be desired. Provisions permitting diversion for de-addiction are underused and addicts continue to be criminalized. The data from Vidhi's study on the implementation of the NDPS Act in Punjab bears this out.

4.2.1 Issues with Quantification of Drugs

Vidhi's study on working of the NDPS Act in Punjab shows that, from 2013 to 2015 no person charged with offences under the NDPS Act was sent for de-addiction by the courts in Punjab. Interestingly, judges and lawyers across districts in Punjab did not even know about provisions permitting diversion for de-addiction (Singhal, et al. 2018: 72). While lack of information about such provisions is very disconcerting, a critical flaw in the drafting of the law has practically ensured that de-addiction remains inaccessible for addicts.

As per the NDPS Act, possession of drugs in intermediate quantities may attract imprisonment for up to 10 years. Cases involving commercial quantities attract a mandatory minimum sentence of 10 years extendable up to 20 years (Narcotic Drugs and Psychotropic Substances Act, 1985: § 20–24). The law, however, does not recognise that possession of drugs in intermediate and commercial quantities may not always be for trafficking. In fact, it excludes addicts, found in possession of drugs even marginally over the small quantities' threshold, from the benefits of diversion under sections 39 and 64A of the NDPS Act.

Vidhi's research from Punjab, which was based on analysis of 13,350 NDPS cases tried by Special Courts in Punjab, shows how the different methods of quantification of drugs impact sentencing. This was particularly noteworthy in pharmaceutical preparations. Cases involving pharmaceutical preparations are, more often than not, categorised as commercial quantity cases, thus leading to mandatory minimum sentences for the offenders, including addicts. This is because of the low thresholds for such preparations and the quantification mechanism laid down by a notification issued by the Ministry of Finance in 2009 ('2009 notification') [Notification No.S.O.2942(E), 2009].

The 2009 notification amended an earlier notification that specified small and commercial quantities in relation to drugs and extended it to drugs in their different preparations and forms, such as isomeric and ester [Notification No. S.O. 1055(E), 2001]. The 2009 notification added a clarificatory note stating that the drug quantity thresholds shall apply to the entire mixture or solution of drugs and not just the pure drug content. It thus made neutral, non-narcotic and psychotropic substances, present in tablets, capsules, syrups etc. relevant for quantification of drugs.

In Punjab, in cases where the recovery was made before the 2009 notification, only the pure drug content was considered. A Special Court in Moga, in 2014, sentenced a person carrying 12,400 tablets of *reclam* (with 6 grams of *alprazolam*), 500 tablets of *diazepam* (with 2.4 grams of *diazepam*), 5,000 tablets of *lomotil* (with 12 grams of *diphenoxylate*), and 30 bottles of *recodex* (with 5.94 grams of *codeine*), to rigorous imprisonment for six months. The pure drug content for all these drugs fell within the prescribed threshold of 'small quantity', even though the weight of the recovered material was above the prescribed threshold (Singhal, et al. 2018). On the other hand, using the 2009 notification, a Special Court in Patiala, sentenced a person carrying 768 capsules of *spasmo proxyvon* (with 0.0992 grams of dextropropoxyphene per capsule), to imprisonment for ten years. Pertinently, the threshold for 'commercial quantity' of *dextropropoxyphene* is 500 grams and the accused in this case was carrying a quantity, at least five times lesser than this.

These findings reinforce the disproportionate impact of the 2009 notification, on cases involving pharmaceutical drugs. Most pharmaceutical drug cases easily qualify as commercial quantity cases, and the accused are sentenced to a mandatory minimum sentence of ten years. Further, making the quantity of drugs the sole basis for deciding on diversion for de-addiction, has ensured that many addicts are denied access to healthcare services.

In many intermediate quantity cases judges acknowledged that the accused persons are addicts. This often led to addicts being sentenced to minimal punishment, often the period already undergone during trial. While this is possible in intermediate quantity cases, it is not in commercial quantity cases, where the judge is required to impose a mandatory minimum sentence. Even then, this leniency doesn't translate into access to de-addiction services for many of these convicted addicts, since the law does not permit judges to divert intermediate quantity cases for de-addiction, neither can such cases be provided immunity under section 64A (Singhal, et al. 2018).

5   Conclusion

Looking through the history of drug laws in India, one finds that criminalization of drug use and possession is relatively recent. It is not even a colonial artefact – rather the colonial state was indifferent to the problems of drug use well into the twentieth century, preferring to defer to local sentiment and act on its own revenue considerations. During the colonial period, cultivation of narcotic crops and the opium trade with China was carefully incubated, only to be confronted by a growing nationalist movement and then by imperialist international pressure.

The law as it stands today has turned drug abuse, a public health issue into a law and order one. The blanket criminalization of drug use is rooted in a highly contestable belief that choking demand – by arresting and incarcerating consumers, will end trafficking of drugs. As a result, thousands of drug users, including addicts, are arrested every year. The system's paradoxical focus on drug users often leads to organised drug traffickers and large-scale peddlers escaping the attention of the law enforcement agencies.

While there is no evidence that incarcerating drug users addresses the problem, there is enough evidence to show that a criminal justice response to drug abuse is excessive, expensive and often discriminatory towards marginalised communities. The problem is only exacerbated by vaguely drafted provisions and misuse by law enforcement agencies.

Even as the international conventions acknowledge drug abuse as a public health issue and countries across the world move towards decriminalization of drug use, India continues to be anchored to a criminal justice response. Only a few provisions of the NDPS Act deal with treatment and de-addiction. These provisions fail to inspire state functionaries to adopt a public health approach towards people dependent on drugs. For thousands of drug users, absence of a public health approach acts as an impediment in accessing healthcare services, which include harm reduction and de-addiction. This is clear from the non-utilization of provisions in the NDPS Act for diversion to rehabilitative services and healthcare services.

It is a constitutional obligation of the state to ensure better healthcare, access to healthcare services and improve public health. Criminalizing addiction is certainly not a step-in furtherance of this obligation. India must, therefore, decriminalize consumption of drugs and possession for personal consumption. Decriminalization would ensure that a constitutionally guaranteed fundamental right to access healthcare is upheld in practice. This approach will also uphold the 'public health' premise of the international conventions and Article 47 of the Constitution of India and therefore should form the core of our outlook towards drug abuse.

Bibliography

65.90% prison inmates are from SC, ST and OBC categories, NCRB data says. (February 10, 2021) Mint. Available at: https://www.livemint.com/news/india/6590-prison-inmates-are-from-sc-st-and-obc-categories-ncrb-data-says-11612951470742.html. Accessed on May 30, 2021.

Assam Congress Opium Enquiry Report (1925) Available at: https://dspace.gipe.ac.in/xmlui/bitstream/handle/10973/32685/GIPE-006592.pdf?sequence=3&isAllowed=y. Accessed on June 09, 2021.

Bauer, R. (2019) *The Peasant Production of Opium in Nineteenth-century India*. Leiden: Brill.

"Conviction rate in Maharashtra goes up to 52 per cent: Governor". (March 9, 2016) *The Economic Times*. Available at: https://economictimes.indiatimes.com/news/politics-and-nation/conviction-rate-in-maharashtra-goes-up-to-52-per-cent-governor/articleshow/51325339.cms. Accessed on June 09, 2021.

Criminal Investigation Department. (2014) "Crime in Maharashtra 2014". *Maharashtra State*. Available at: https://mahacid.gov.in/public/uploads/file/1607074820-Crime%20in%20Maharashtra-2014.pdf. Accessed on December 20, 2021.

Criminal Investigation Department. (2015) "Crime in Maharashtra 2015". *Maharashtra State*. Available at: https://mahacid.gov.in/public/uploads/file/1607076738- Crime%20in%20Maharashtra-2015%20II%20Part.pdf. Accessed on December 20, 2021.

Criminal Investigation Department. (2016) "Crime in Maharashtra 2016". *Maharashtra State*. Available at: https://mahacid.gov.in/public/uploads/file/1606 979161-Crime%20in%20maharashtra-2016.pdf. Accessed on December 20, 2021.

Deshpande, A. (2009) "An Historical Overview of Opium Cultivation and Changing State Attitudes towards the Crop in India, 1878–2000 A.D." *Studies in History*, 25(1): 109–143.

Indian Parliament. Rajya Sabha Debates. (December 20, 1988) Available at: https://cms.rajyasabha.nic.in/UploadedFiles/Debates/OfficialDebatesDatewise/Floor/148/F20.12.1988.pdf. Accessed on December 20, 2021.

International Opium Convention. (January 23, 1912) *League of Nations*. Available at:https://treaties.un.org/doc/Treaties/1922/01/19220123%2006-31%20AM/Ch_VI_2p.pdf. Accessed on December 20, 2021.

Kancharla, B. (October 19, 2021) *Data: Pendency rate of NDPS cases in courts crosses 90% in 2020*. FACTLY. Available at: https://factly.in/data-pendency-rate-of-ndps-cases-in-courts-crosses-90-in-2020/. Accessed on December 20, 2021.

Kasamabhai Abdulrehmanbhai Sheikh v. State of Gujarat, 3 SCC 120 (1980) Supreme Court, India.

Kethineni, S., et al. (1995) "Drug use in India: Historical traditions and current problems". *International Journal of Comparative and Applied Criminal Justice*, 19(2): 211–221.

Maharashtra Crime Conviction Rate Goes Up to 42 Per Cent in BJP Regime: Devendra Fadnavis. (November 6, 2015) NDTV. Available at: https://www.ndtv.com/india-news/maharastra-crime-conviction-rate-goes-up-to-42-per-cent-in-bjp-regime-devendra-fadnavis-1240639. Accessed on June 20, 2021.

Ministry of Health and Family Welfare. (1994) "Report of the Expert Committee on Small Quantities under the NDPS Act". Government of India.

Narcotic Drug and Psychotropic Substances (Amendment) Act, 2001 (Act No. 9 of 2001) India.

Narcotic Drug and Psychotropic Substances Act, 1985 (Act No. 61 of 1985) India.

National Crime Records Bureau (2010) "Crime in India". New Delhi: Government of India. Available at: https://ncrb.gov.in/sites/default/files/crime_in_india_table_additional_table_chapter_reports/Table%204.16_2010.pdf. Accessed on August 16, 2022.

National Crime Records Bureau (2013) "Crime in India". New Delhi: Government of India Available at: https://ncrb.gov.in/sites/default/files/crime_in_india_table_additional_table_chapter_reports/Table%204.16_2013.pdf. Accessed on August 16, 2022.

National Crime Records Bureau (2022) "Crime in India". New Delhi: Government of India. Available at: https://ncrb.gov.in/sites/default/files/CII-2021/CII_2021Volume%201.pdf. Accessed on August 16, 2022.

Notification No. S.O. 1055(E). (2001, October 19) Ministry of Finance, Government of India.

Notification No. S.O. 2942(E). (November 18, 2009) Ministry of Finance, Government of India.

Pagano, A. (March 2, 2018) "The racist origins of marijuana prohibition". *Business Insider*. Available at: https://www.businessinsider.in/politics/the-racist-origins-of-marijuana-prohibition/articleshow/63140274.cms. Accessed on May 30, 2021.

Rafaeli, J. (August 13, 2018) *The War on Drugs Is Inseparable from US Imperialism*. Vice. Available at: https://www.vice.com/en/article/594j8b/how-america-convinced-the-world-to-demonize-drugs. Accessed on May 30, 2021.

Royal Commission on Opium. (1892) "First Report". London: *Eyre and Spottiswoode*. Available at: https://archive.org/details/cu31924073053880. Accessed on May 30, 2021.

Schlag, A. K. (2020) "Percentages of problem drug use and their implications for policy making: A review of the literature". *Drug Science, Policy and Law*, 6.

Singhal, N. and Ahmad, N. M. (September 8, 2020) *Criminalisation Leads To Exploitation: The Mumbai Story No One Knows About*. Vidhi Centre for Legal Policy. Available at: https://vidhilegalpolicy.in/research/criminalisation-leads-to-exploitation-the-mumbai-story-no-one-knows-about/. Accessed on May 30, 2021.

Singhal, N., et al. (2018) *From Addict to Convict – The Working of the NDPS Act in Punjab*. Vidhi Centre for Legal Policy. Available at: https://vidhilegalpolicy.in/research/2018-8-23-from-addict-to-convict-the-working-of-the-ndps-act-1985-in-punjab/. Accessed on May 30, 2021.

Single Convention on Narcotic Drugs. (1961) Economic and Social Council of the United Nations. Available at: https://www.unodc.org/pdf/convention_1961_en.pdf.

The Opium Act, 1857 (Act No. 13 of 1857) India.

Zahira Habibullah Sheikh v. State of Gujarat, 4 SCC 158 (2004) Supreme Court, India.

CHAPTER 10

The Concept of Overcriminalization in Russian Law

Daria V. Ponomareva

1   Introduction

The development strategy of domestic criminal legislation is closely connected with the processes of speciation of criminal law norms. As evidenced by the historical and legal analysis, the compositions and features of crimes are unchanged, they are modified, meaningfully transformed, determining the trends and strategies for the advancement of the entire array of norm-formation. The 21st century is no exception here, which with all certainty marked the transformation of criminal law, essentially defining a new paradigm for the development of the corresponding array of criminal law and related legal provisions.

The criminal law of the Russian Federation has its own trends of reformation. The modern period of development of Russian criminal law is characterised by such trends as the expansion and compaction of the spheres of criminal law regulation; the emergence of more fractional corpus delicti, the rapid increase in the number of special rules; expansion of criminalization due to changes in related legislation in the presence of blanket rules in the Criminal Code of the Russian Federation, as well as an increase in the number of offences with administrative prejudice.

In this chapter an attempt is made to consider one of the most rapidly developing trends: the expansion of the criminalization of certain acts (in the American legal doctrine, a special term has been adopted to designate such a trend – overcriminalization). In order to get acquainted with the implementation of this trend on the example of concrete corpus delicti, it is necessary to refer to a brief description of the system of Russian criminal law.

2   The Criminal Law System of the Russian Federation

Russian criminal law as a branch of law is divided into the General Part and the Special Part (which also reflects the structure of the only source of criminal law – the Criminal Code of the Russian Federation). The general part (Sections 1 and 2) includes the norms of criminal law, reflecting: the tasks and principles of criminal law, issues of the operation of criminal law in time, space and subjects; concept and categories of crimes; forms of multiplicity of crimes; conditions that form the basis of criminal liability (age, sanity, forms of guilt); features of criminal liability for an unfinished crime and a crime committed in complicity; circumstances precluding the criminality of the act.

In the third section – "Punishment" – the concept and goals of criminal punishment are analysed; the place and role of the general principles of sentencing, the institution of probation. The fourth section is devoted to exemption from criminal liability and from punishment in connection with active repentance; reconciliation with the victim; the expiration of the statute of limitations; a change in the situation; amnesty, pardon, etc.

Features of criminal liability and punishment of minors are considered in the fifth section: types of punishment and its appointment to a minor; application of compulsory measures of educational influence; grant of parole; statute of limitations, etc.

Other measures of a criminal law nature (compulsory medical measures and confiscation of property) are grouped in the sixth section.

A special part of criminal law includes norms defining specific crimes by their types as well as determining punishments for their commission. The system of criminal acts, in accordance with the current criminal legislation, is as follows: crimes against the life and health of the individual; crimes against freedom, honour and dignity of a person; crimes against sexual inviolability and sexual freedom of the individual; crimes against the constitutional rights and freedoms of man and citizen; crimes against the family and minors; crimes against property; crimes in the sphere of economic activity; crimes against the interests of service in commercial and other organisations; crimes against public safety and public order; crimes against public health and public morals; environmental crimes; crimes against traffic safety and transport operation; crimes in the field of computer information; crimes against the foundations of the constitutional order and state security; crimes against state power, the interests of public service and service in local governments; crimes against justice; crimes against the order of government; crimes against military service; crimes against the peace and security of mankind.

Classification of crimes. (Orazdurdiev, 2019) According to the criterion of the degree of public danger of a crime, the elements of a crime should be divided: into 1) the main and 2) additional and only then the additional elements of the crime should be divided: into 1) qualified and 2) privileged.

Qualified elements of crimes according to the degree of their qualification and increase in punishability should be divided into the following levels and given the following names, respectively: 1) qualified corpus delicti of the 1st level – the actual qualified corpus delicti; 2) qualified corpus delicti of the 2nd level – especially qualified corpus delicti; 3) qualified corpus delicti of the 3rd level – especially reinforced qualified corpus delicti; 4) qualified corpus delicti of the 4th level – heavy qualified corpus delicti; and finally, 5) skilled corpus delicti of the 5th level – especially heavy qualified corpus delicti. The above names may raise objections, since for the first time we have to deal with corpus delicti that have such numerous levels of repression and degrees of qualification.

If the main corpus delicti is defined as a set of typical features of a particular crime that characterise its average degree of public danger without features that enhance or reduce it, and distinguish it from other crimes, and are common (typical) for all crimes of this type, then under the additional corpus delicti it is necessary to understand such composition, which, while retaining the signs of the main corpus delicti, supplements it with signs that increase or decrease the degree of social danger of the crime and, accordingly, increase or decrease the responsibility of those guilty of committing it.

Privileged corpus delicti is a corpus delicti with extenuating circumstances. This is a composition in which the signs of the main corpus delicti are supplemented by circumstances mitigating the responsibility of the person guilty of the crime. The degree of public danger of such a crime is much lower than the degree of public danger of a crime containing signs of the main corpus delicti. Such composition is located either in a separate article (for example, in Article 106 of the Criminal Code "Murder of a newborn child by a mother", in Article 107 of the Criminal Code "Murder committed in a state of passion") or in a separate part of the article (for example, Part 1 of Article 108 of the Criminal Code "Murder committed in excess of the limits of necessary defence" and Part 2 of Article 108 of the Criminal Code "Murder committed in excess of the measures necessary to detain a person who committed a crime"). In order of increasing privilege, the compositions of this group can also be arranged in a certain order, as indicated above. In this case, the least privileged composition will be located at the 1st level, and the most privileged will be at the highest level.

A qualified corpus delicti is a corpus delicti with aggravating circumstances. This is a composition in which the signs of the main corpus delicti are supplemented by circumstances that aggravate the responsibility of the person guilty of the crime. An example of a qualified corpus delicti is Part 2 of Art. 167 of the Criminal Code "Intentional destruction or damage to another's property", "committed out of hooligan motives, by arson, explosion or in any other generally dangerous way, or negligently entailed the death of a person or other grave consequences" (qualifying circumstances are highlighted). The article consists of two parts, and therefore here the main corpus delicti has only one qualified corpus delicti. The degree of public danger of a crime with such a composition is much higher than the degree of public danger of a crime, the basis of which is the main corpus delicti.

If the composition, along with qualifying and especially qualifying features, provides in a separate part of the same article the third qualifying features that have a significantly higher degree of public danger than the especially qualifying features of the same corpus delicti, then such a corpus delicti should be called a composition with especially enhanced qualifying circumstances or especially enhanced qualified staff. An example of such a composition is Part 4 of Art. 158 of the Criminal Code "Theft committed: a) by an organised group; b) on a large scale". The article consists of four parts. The degree of public danger of a crime with such a composition is much higher than the degree of public danger of a crime the basis of which is the main corpus delicti, a qualified corpus delicti and a specially qualified corpus delicti.

In the event that the corpus delicti, along with some qualifying features, provides in a separate part of the same article the second qualifying features that increase responsibility for the commission of a given crime, this corpus delicti should be called a corpus delicti with especially qualifying circumstances or a particularly qualified corpus delicti. An example of such a composition is part 3 of Art. 143 of the Criminal Code "Violation of the rules of labor protection committed by a person who is entrusted with the obligation to comply with them", "caused by negligence the death of two or more persons." The article consists of three parts, the main composition of this article is endowed with two qualified offences. The degree of public danger of a crime with such a composition is much higher than the degree of public danger of a crime the basis of which is the main corpus delicti and a qualified composition of the first level of increasing punishability.

Along with qualifying, especially qualifying and especially enhanced qualifying circumstances, the corpus delicti may also provide for other more serious circumstances that increase responsibility for a particular crime. Such corpus delicti can be called a corpus delicti with grave qualifying circumstances or a grave corpus delicti. An example of such a crime is part 5 of Art. 128.1 of the Criminal Code "Slander combined with the accusation of a person of committing a grave or especially grave crime." The article consists of five parts. The degree of public danger of a crime with such a composition is significantly higher than the degree of public danger of a crime based on the main corpus delicti, qualified corpus delicti, especially qualified corpus delicti and especially enhanced qualified corpus delicti (Ivanchin, 2011: 96).

3 Examples of Criminalization (Overcriminalization) in Russian Law (Economic Sphere)

Before turning to the consideration of specific examples of the overcriminalization of individual acts in Russian criminal law, it seems necessary to refer to statistics over the past few years. The share of grave and especially grave crimes among the registered ones increased from 24.4% in 2019 to 27.6% in 2020. The share of previously convicted persons increased in the composition of criminals: from 28.3% in 2017 to 29.6% in 2019 and up to 29.9% in 2020. Over five years, the number of grave and especially grave crimes committed by organised groups or criminal communities increased from 12.1 thousand in 2016 to 17.0 thousand in 2020.

Theft remains the most common crime against property. In 2020, 751.2 thousand such crimes were included in the statistics, which is almost 23 thousand less than a year earlier. But this achievement cannot be considered a reason for pride. It is not difficult to assume that a significant part of the thieves' world, without leaving the profession, relocated to another, more profitable and safe area. There has been a marked increase in the number of thefts committed from a bank account or against electronic money. In 2020, 169.5 thousand such attacks were registered against 93.7 thousand in 2019.

The country has consistently reduced the total number of reported murders. Over the past five years, according to the Prosecutor General's Office of the Russian Federation, their number has decreased by a third (from 11.3 thousand to 7.7 thousand). If we take into account that in 2000 there were 31.8 thousand murders (with attempts) in the country, then by 2020 their number has decreased by more than four times.

The situation with cybercrime can be called the most critical. Over the past five years, their number has grown 11 times. In fact, they make up one fourth of the total array of crime in Russia. Sadly, such statistics allow, in our opinion, to talk about a complete failure in the system of countering crime operating in the field of IT technologies.

After a two-year increase, the upward movement of crime rates continued. This does not only apply to registered crime in general. According to the data for the six months of 2021, compared to the corresponding period of 2019, a negative shift within 1.0 – 1.5% affected almost all the main categories and types of crimes identified in the statistical reports, with the exception of environmental crimes, crimes committed with the use of weapons and explosives and some others. Over the same six months, the total number of cybercrimes increased by 1.5 times, including especially serious crimes by 1.7 times and serious attacks by 1.9 times (Babaev & Pudovochkin, 2021).

Crimes in the economic sphere are also showing a growing trend. I would like to dwell on this area in more detail. The legislative system of the Russian Federation is actively developing measures to prevent the concealment of funds abroad, money laundering, including those obtained by criminal means, feeding corruption and the criminal environment, for example, tax evasion and customs duties (Kudashkin, 2011: 304).

In Russia, there is a problem of criminal law pressure on the economy. It lies in the fact that actions that are part of the normal economic turnover or the result of minor errors in the economic activities of enterprises, organisations and citizens can be and are qualified as crimes. The situation when specific one-time actions that do not pose a public danger and do not entail any serious damage are considered as crimes is called excessive criminalization (overcriminalization) (Titaev & Chetverikova, 2017).

The following situations are most often unreasonably criminalized:

A) Violations of the rules of tax and accounting (for example, payment of a minor administrative fine imposed on an official from the company's account is interpreted as embezzlement);
B) Violations of the rules for working with material assets and money (improper accounting of material assets is interpreted as their appropriation, despite the fact that they did not physically move from the organisation to the employee);
C) Violation of contractual obligations (a single failure to perform the contract is treated as fraud, even if the defendant claims that the possibility of performance is lost due to objective circumstances).

TITAEV & CHETVERIKOVA, 2017

Overcriminalization becomes possible for a number of reasons. First, for crimes of a property nature, as a mandatory feature, it is necessary that the damage exceed a certain amount. However, for qualified offences of the same thefts (crimes committed by a group of persons, using their official position, etc.), the lower threshold of damage, the overcoming of which is necessary to recognize the act as criminal, has not been established. Thus, acts that cause extremely insignificant damage are criminalized. Secondly, the investigating authorities have the opportunity to ignore the position of the victim, and also not to prove the presence of intent to cause harm (often in the cases we analysed, the presence of intent was confirmed by a "cumulative evidence" without indicating specific facts that allowed the court and the investigation to come to such a conclusion). It also simplifies the criminalization of the actions of economic agents. Thirdly, a separate problem is that the law classifies many non-violent crimes as serious ones. Together, all these factors make criminal cases related to economic activity easy to investigate and beneficial to the investigating authorities in terms of formal reporting (Titaev & Chetverikova, 2017).

Excessive criminalization (overcriminalization) of economic activity causes direct damage to the country: qualified specialists receive unjustified convictions and, due to emerging restrictions, are used less efficiently in the economy, budget funds are spent on investigating such crimes. But no less significant is the indirect damage – due to fears of selective and unjustified criminal prosecution, the leaders of organisations (especially state ones) avoid using new technologies and modern management practices. Separately, it is important to note that in this way the risks of illegal (shadow) economic activity become comparable to the risks of legal activity – and this encourages entrepreneurs to move into the grey sector of the economy. In addition, this situation generates significant reputational damage for the judiciary and law enforcement agencies and creates false guidelines for the police and the investigation (instead of dealing with serious crimes, they begin to work to criminalize minor mistakes).

Firstly, in order to reduce the negative effects of the fight against crime in the economic sphere, it is necessary to establish a lower limit of damage for qualified theft offences. Secondly, it is necessary to explain to the investigating authorities, the prosecutor's office and the courts the procedure for applying Art. 24 and Art. 25 of the Criminal Code of the Russian Federation, interpreting the concept of intent to commit a crime, as well as Art. 14 of the Criminal Code of the Russian Federation, according to which actions that formally fall under the description of a crime, but do not carry public danger, which in the case of economic crimes is understood as the amount of damage, should not be considered criminal (Titaev & Chetverikova, 2017).

One of the tools to maintain economic stability and security of the state in the trading space is currency regulation and currency control, the legal basis of which is presented in the Federal Law of December 10, 2003 N 173-FZ "On currency regulation and currency control".

Articles 193 and 193.1 of the Criminal Code of the Russian Federation are aimed at combating the illegal withdrawal of capital abroad.

Under the object of crimes, responsibility for which is provided for in Art. 193 and 193.1 of the Criminal Code of the Russian Federation, are understood as public relations in the financial and economic environment, in terms of monetary circulation, which are defined and protected by the criminal law of the Russian Federation. Failure to comply with the established norms due to the public danger of the fact of a crime related to an encroachment on the financial and economic security of the state causes harm to legal relations protected by law.

Consider the theoretical and practical issues of the application of Art. 193 and 193.1 of the Criminal Code of the Russian Federation, since both articles provide for liability for committing offences in the field of currency control in the Russian Federation.

Analysing the statistical data for the previous four and a half years on cases, we can conclude that the level of crimes registered in the reporting period is variable. Taking into account the summary statistics on the number of convicts provided by the Judicial Department at the Supreme Court of the Russian Federation, it is necessary to indicate that in 2020 for committing an offence under Art. 193 of the Criminal Code of the Russian Federation, only 8 persons were found guilty, in 2019 – 17, in 2018 – 8, in 2017 – 11 (*Report on the Number of Convicts for All Offenses of the Criminal Code of the Russian Federation*, n.d.).

According to the Judicial Department of the Armed Forces of the Russian Federation, in 2020 they were found guilty under Art. 193.1 of the Criminal Code of the Russian Federation 20 people. In 2019 – 46, in 2018 – 21, in 2017 – 18. In accordance with the information of the Ministry of Internal Affairs of Russia, in 2020, 56 crimes were preliminary investigated, criminal cases that were transferred to court, followed by a guilty verdict: in 2019 – 33, in 2018 – 20, in 2017 – 30. It should be noted that in the first half of 2021 there was a significant increase in the number of criminal cases, namely, during the specified period, 58 criminal cases were brought to court (Ministry of Internal Affairs of Russia, 2020).

It is possible to assume that the positive dynamics is expressed by the process of formation of judicial practice.

As an object of the crime, established by Art. 193 of the Criminal Code of the Russian Federation, it is important to present the regulations for conducting foreign trade activities in terms of money circulation. In addition, it is fair to point out that this crime infringes on state interests in relation to foreign exchange and export policy.

It is necessary to pay attention to the similarity of the objects of the offences of Art. 193 and 193.1 of the Criminal Code of the Russian Federation.

In Art. 193 of the Criminal Code of the Russian Federation Federal Law of April 1, 2020 N 73-FZ was amended. Element of the legal norm in Part 1 of Art. 193 of the Criminal Code of the Russian Federation is supplemented with a new sign, in view of which the subject of the crime received the status of a special one, namely the commission of a crime by a person who received an administrative penalty under Part 5.2 of Art. 15.25 of the RF Code of Administrative Offences. Under Art. 193 of the Criminal Code of the Russian Federation the lower limit of criminal liability under Part 1 of Art. 193 of the Criminal Code of the Russian Federation was changed from 9 to 100 million rubles, and under

Part 2 of Art. 193 of the Criminal Code of the Russian Federation – from 45 to 150 million rubles.

Regarding these innovations, an opinion has been published in the scientific literature about the injustice regarding the crime under Art. 193.1 of the Criminal Code of the Russian Federation. Earlier under Art. 193 and 193.1 of the Criminal Code of the Russian Federation, there were identical sizes of the lower limit of a large and especially large amount: 9 million rubles, and 45 million rubles, respectively. It must be emphasised that the amount that determines the qualification of the offence under Art. 193.1 of the Criminal Code of the Russian Federation, did not change: large size – 9 million rubles, especially large – 45 million rubles. This fact allows us to think that it is necessary to unite the lower limits of the large and especially large sizes of the analysed crimes, in view of the fact that their composition and social danger are quite similar (Masterskikh, 2020).

We cannot fully agree with this statement for the following reasons. Firstly, in view of the introduction of various financial instruments and their active mass use, crimes in the sphere of credit and monetary relations are characterised by a public danger, primarily for the economic security of the country.

The danger of criminal acts that violate the currency legislation of the Russian Federation is predetermined by the fact that, in accordance with paragraphs 2, 17, 30 of Art. 67 of the National Security Strategy of the Russian Federation, approved by Decree of the President of the Russian Federation of July 2, 2021 N 400, the monetary policy is aimed at ensuring the economic security of the state and citizens, expressed in maintaining inflation at a consistently low level, in guaranteeing the stability of the national currency and the balance of the budget system, is obliged to strengthen the financial system of the Russian Federation, as well as its sovereignty, develop the national infrastructure of financial markets, increase the practice of settlements with foreign partners in national currency, reduce the transfer of assets abroad, prevent crimes in financial transactions, reduce the share of the shadow and criminal sectors of the economy, as well as the level of bribery in commercial activities.[1]

The analysed crimes have a negative impact on the guarantees of the financial security of the Russian Federation, as they attempt to comply with the order established and protected by the legislation of the Russian Federation in the field of finance and threaten the economic interests of society and the state.

---

1 On the National Security Strategy of the Russian Federation: Decree of the President of the Russian Federation of July 2, 2021 N 400 // SZ RF. 2021. N 27 (part II). Art. 535.

The objective side of the crime under Art. 193 of the Criminal Code of the Russian Federation is characterised by failure to fulfil the obligation of the subject of the crime to repatriate funds in foreign currency or the currency of the Russian Federation.

The objective side of the crime under Art. 193.1 of the Criminal Code of the Russian Federation is the performance of currency transactions for the transfer of funds to the settlement account of a non-resident with documentation confirming the fact of the transfer, which contains deliberately false information. Thus, the commission of a crime occurs in the form of an action. In contrast to evasion of obligations to repatriate funds, this crime is considered completed from the moment the amount of money is withdrawn from the current account, and the amount of withdrawn funds is determined on this date.

The crime under Art. 193 of the Criminal Code of the Russian Federation, is characterised by such a sign as a means of committing a criminal act in the form of the use of "documents containing deliberately unreliable information about the grounds, purposes and purpose of the transfer." It is worth noting that this sign, by its legal nature, has a public danger.

The use of forged documents in certain circumstances is singled out as a separate crime, for example: art. 292 of the Criminal Code of the Russian Federation on official forgery, art. 327 of the Criminal Code of the Russian Federation on the forgery, production or circulation of forged documents, state awards, stamps, seals and letterheads, and partially art. 327.1 and 327.2 of the Criminal Code of the Russian Federation.

Indicators of law enforcement activities of the customs authorities of the Russian Federation (2020) indicate that in 2019 over 31 billion rubles were transferred to the accounts of non-residents using falsified documents, and in 2020 – 14 billion rubles.

Considering the circumstances described above, it seems possible to conclude that the legislator's individual approach to assessing the social danger of the analysed crimes is appropriate.

The draft Law "On Amendments to the Federal Law "On Currency Regulation and Currency Control" with regard to the phased cancellation of requirements for the repatriation of export earnings in foreign currency for non-resource non-energy exports", being developed by the Ministry of Finance of the Russian Federation, indicates a lesser degree of public danger of a criminal act provided for Art. 193 of the Criminal Code of the Russian Federation.

When a non-resident replenishes a resident's bank account with foreign currency, this action will not be considered as an evasion from fulfilling the conditions of repatriation if the management of the organisation takes actions aimed at returning funds from other states. These actions include: negotiating, drawing up and sending claims, timely appeal to the courts and the foreign trade arbitration commission at the Russian Chamber of Commerce and Industry.

Having regard to art. 193 and 193.1 of the Criminal Code of the Russian Federation, we can conclude that there are problems with the effective application of these rules. Recent reforms do not allow these articles to function fully, the entire burden has shifted to the administrative and legal space.

The use of instruments of currency restrictions, as well as liability established for violation of currency legislation, implies an effective counteraction to money laundering. But in fact, all this is just a barrier to entrepreneurship in the Russian Federation.

In the Russian currency system, repatriation serves the purposes of formal control of settlement currency transactions, and not the purposes of the security of the movement of funds in the Russian Federation.

There are discussions in the legal community regarding the validity of the provisions of art. 193 and 193.1 of the Criminal Code of the Russian Federation. The components of crimes, in fact, do not entail the onset of significant socially dangerous consequences. The legislation of Russia contains norms on administrative responsibility for similar offences, which provide for rather severe sanctions (fines), which contributes to the protection of state interests in the field of currency control. This approach will help to find a balance in relations between business and government.

4   Conclusion

Overcriminalization is a significant part of the judicial and criminal policy that is closely connected with the unconditional influence of crime.

However, this influence is not straightforward and unambiguous. Such indicators of crime as its dynamics and social danger have an indirect impact on the state of judicial and criminal policy, which, reacting to the transformation of crime in the direction of mitigating or tightening penal practices, is subject to either political impulses or internal patterns of development and goals of functioning of the court. However, ideas about the social role of crime and its functions, with various acceptable theoretical interpretations, can set fundamentally different models of judicial and criminal policy, integrating this policy in various ways into the processes of social management.

There are the following tools to stop overcriminalization. The first is legislative. The greater severity of crimes committed with the use of official position or by a group of persons already implies a greater punishment than an ordinary crime. It seems redundant that additional penalisation of theft committed by a group of persons or using their official position, through the abolition of the minimum amount of damage for them, after which criminal liability occurs. If the waste resulted in a decrease in the tax base, then it should also be considered from the point of view of tax legislation. As for fraud for such amounts, they may entail civil or administrative liability.

The second way is related to explaining to the courts, prosecutors and investigators the rules for interpreting art. 14 of the Criminal Code of the Russian Federation, which describes the public danger of the act, and art. 24–25 of the Criminal Code of the Russian Federation, describing intent. In order to be held criminally liable, they will have to establish the fact that the situation is unsolvable solely within the framework of civil, tax or labour law and that the person had the intent to commit a crime, the existence of which can be confirmed by a plurality of criminal acts or documentary evidence (for example, correspondence of participants, from which it is clear that they are aware of the illegality of their actions) or the lack of activity or preparation for it when receiving funds under contracts or government programs in case of default and evasion of their return.

The appropriate decision of the Plenum of the Supreme Court of the Russian Federation would be an ideal tool for solving this problem. If possible – with a parallel review in the order of supervision of several dozen (or hundreds) of criminal cases in which the courts, the prosecutor's office and the investigation did not consider the requirements of art. 14, 24 and 25 of the Criminal Code of the Russian Federation when deciding whether the defendant's actions contain *corpus delicti*. Such a review would be a very good and effective signal to all law enforcement and judicial authorities.

Along with these measures, it is also necessary to take into account foreign experience, including a careful analysis of the results of the experiment in the Republic of Kazakhstan. There, a decision is made and fixed by instructive documents of law enforcement agencies that if there are documents indicating that the act belongs to civil law or labour relations (contracts, receipts, sales receipts), it cannot be the subject of criminal proceedings before it is accepted by a court decision in a civil or administrative case. Only after the issuance of a particular court decision, based on the facts established in the court session, the victim can apply to law enforcement agencies. Exceptions are made for cases in which it is necessary to establish the person who was in fact a party to these relations.

Bibliography

Babaev, M. M., & Pudovochkin, Yu. E. (2021) "Crime and Judicial-Criminal Policy". *Journal of Russian Law*, 12: 26–40.

Indicators of law enforcement activities of the customs authorities of the Russian Federation for 2019. (2020). Available at: http://customs.gov.ru/activity/pravooxranitel-naya-deyatel-nost-/informacziya-upravleniya-tamozhennyx-rassledovanij-i-doznaniya/document/224608. Accessed on December 11, 2022.

Ivanchin, A. V. (2011). *Composition of the crime.* Moscow: Prospect.

Judicial Department at the Supreme Court of the Russian Federation. (2021) "Report on the number of convicts for all offenses of the Criminal Code of the Russian Federation". *Moscow.* Available at: http://www.cdep.ru/index.php?id=79 Accessed on October 5, 2022.

Kudashkin, A. V. (Ed.). (2011) *The activities of law enforcement agencies of the Russian Federation to combat corruption: Monograph.* Academy of the General Prosecutor's Office of the Russian Federation.

McKillop, D., & Helmes, E. (2003) "Public Opinion and Criminal Justice: Emotion, Morality and Consensus". *Psychiatry, Psychology and Law*, 10(1): 210–220.

Masterskikh, E. (2020) "Another liberalization: the thresholds have been raised, and the company is no longer an organized crime group." *Banking Review (FinLegal).* 1: 9.

Ministry of Internal Affairs of Russia (2020) "Consolidated report on Russia 'Unified Crime Report'". Moscow. Available at: http://crimestat.ru/ANALYTICS. Accessed on October 15, 2022.

Orazdurdiev, A. M. (2019) "Classification of elements of crimes depending on the degree of public danger of the act". *Russian Investigator*, 8: 49–54.

Roberts, J. (2000) "Public opinion, crime, and criminal justice". *N.Y.*: 21–38.

Roberts, Julian V., and Hastings, R. (2012) "Public Opinion and Crime Prevention: A Review of International Trends". In: Farrington, D. P. and Welsh, B. C. (eds) *The Oxford Handbook of Crime Prevention.* Oxford Handbooks (online edn, Oxford Academic).

Titaev, K., & Chetverikova, I. (2017) *Excessive criminalization of economic activity in Russia: how it happens and what to do about it.* https://www.csr.ru/upload/iblock/2f3/2f3168867c73d98d581287cfe2b34836.pdf. Accessed on June 30, 2022.

Tonkonoff, C. (2012) "Las funciones sociales del crimen y el castigo: Una entre las perspectivas de Durkheim y Foucault." *Sociológica* 27(77): 109–142.

Warr, M. (1995) "Poll Trends: Public Opinion on Crime and Punishment". *Public Opinion Quarterly*, 59(2): 296–310.

CHAPTER 11

Overcriminalization by Containment without COVID: Inside Kenya's Refugee Camps

Charles A. Khamala

1 Introduction

1.1 *Criminalization of Nonconsummate Acts*

The state's security function is double-pronged. Externally, it requires safeguarding the territory from foreign invasion. Internally, it entails crime control. The latter process is society's organised response to crime (Thaman, 2004: 3). Criminal procedure prevents individuals, families, clans and tribes from taking blood revenge against perceived interference (Esmein, 1913, cited in Thaman, 2004: 4–5). By extinguishing fueds, its primary function is to establish law and order. Its secondary function is to detect incidents of wrongdoing and allocate sanctions for individual criminal responsibility. Its tertiary function of constraining officials from abusing power (*Declaration of Basic Principles of Justice for Victims of Crime and Abuse of Power*, 1985), while also economising with governmental resources is this chapter's focus. During emergencies, there is a conflict between the individual's fundamental right to liberty and the public's right to protection of health. A liberal democratic state is duty-bound to deliver both these goods. However, in normal times, the state's primary purpose is to protect the security of its citizens both collectively and individually (Hobbes, 1651/1981). The right to health is a second-generation human right which may be realised progressively [International Covenant on Economic, Social and Cultural Rights, 1966: Art. 12(1)].

The moral justification for any criminal legislation is the *wrongfulness* requirement. Nonetheless, there are principled reasons not to criminalize all wrongful and blameworthy conduct. Therefore, immorality is a necessary, but not a sufficient, reason for criminalisation. Instead for Joel Feinberg, the *harm* requirement provides the most plausible solution to wrongful conduct that is eligible for punishment. Feinberg's rendition of a liberal theory of law characterises the thesis that the only good reason to subject persons to criminal punishment is to prevent them from wrongfully causing harm to others (Feinberg, 1984: 18). However, pertaining to nonconsummate offences, liberal theory encounters problems. These are offences where 'the conduct it proscribes does not cause harm on each and every occasion in which it is performed' (Husak, 2010: 117–151, 124–125). While all jurisdictions, whether common law or civil law, include instances of nonconsumate offences, they are applied differently. Instances range across 'solicitation, conspiracy, attempt, and numerous possessory offences, as examples of inchoate crimes' (Husak, 2010: 132 fn 61). Other offences are 'defined in the inchoate mode for example, assault, false alarms, indecent exposure, forgery, deceptive business practices, self-abortion, perjury, hindering apprehension, disrupting meetings, and many bribery offences' (Husak, 2010: 132 fn 61). Confining people to prevent them from spreading contagious diseases falls within this category of incomplete crimes.

1.2   *The Presumption of Innocence*

Douglas Husak objects to a utilitarian theory of criminalization which simply increases the contents of substantive criminal law so as to 'punish innocents.' Take crimes of command responsibility. They proscribe 'being a member of a group when utilitarian advantages are gained by punishing all members of that group.' They punish being a person related to an offender in such a way that utilitarian advantages are gained by punishment. Husak concludes that '[i]nnocence is magically transformed into guilt by a simple stroke of the legislative pen' (Husak, 2009: 193). However he cautions that 'crimes should not be enacted solely on utilitarian grounds if we are serious about safeguarding the rights of persons who do not deserve to be punished.'

To protect the collective good of public health, COVID-19 laws constrain individual liberties. To the extent that the COVID-19 pandemic created an emergency situation, Kenya's liberal democratic constitution permitted constraining of fundamental freedoms to dignity (Constitution of Kenya, 2010: Art. 28), security (Constitution of Kenya, 2010: Art. 29), association (Constitution of Kenya, 2010: Art. 36), or even movement (Constitution of Kenya, 2010: Art. 39). Under emergency circumstances, the public good of security is reduced by creating crimes against spreading contagious diseases (Public Health Act, 1921). Conversely, the right to fair hearing (Constitution of Kenya, 2010: Art. 50) is non-derogable [Constitution of Kenya, 2010: Art. 25(c)]. Before being isolated or quarantined, people infected with Covid must be detected, arraigned, prosecuted and convicted [*Okiya Omtatah Okoiti v. Cabinet Secretary, Ministry of Health*, 2020: Kenya National Commission on Human Rights (Interested Party)]. Therefore, general overcriminalization problems arise regarding how much discretion is permissible to confine suspected sufferers. Who takes the decision? What test is applicable? What are the consequences for overreach by public officials and remedies available to citizens? The specific problematic issue, particularly in Africa, concerns the notion of the expanded definition of refugees under the OAU definition. This chapter shall critically analyze comparative legislative standards set out in Kenya's new Refugee Act of 2021, in response to several years of judicial interpretations of the provisions of refugee *refoulement*.

Section 2 of what follows introduces Husak's (2009) theory of domestic overcriminalization. It also distinguishes between punitive justice, which is more familiar to criminal law practitioners, and preventive justice, which is more familiar to criminologists. Section 3 explains how the abuse of coercive power to relocate refugees in the name of national security has happened repeatedly in Kenya (Khamala, 2020). Since the Al Shabaab terrorism scourge erupted over a 15 years ago, the state has attempted various means of *refouling* Somali refugees *en mass*. Such draconian measures range from relocating refugees from urban areas back to border camps (*Kituo cha Sheria v. Attorney General*, 2013; *Refugee Consortium of Kenya v. Attorney General*, 2015) to purporting to cap refugee numbers inside Kenya (*Coalition for Reform and Democracy v. Republic of Kenya*, 2015). Significantly, each of these administrative orders or legislative provisions were struck down by the courts. The most recent and emphatic example was in the case of *Kenya National Commission of Human Rights and 3 others v AG* (2017), where the court rejected the state's order purporting to close the refugee camps altogether. This chapter's hypothesis is that because in collective crime, the actual perpetration of a physical act is difficult to prove, therefore the prosecution is often tempted to develop a theory based on guilt by association to infer constructive guilt. Yet innocent people do not deserve hard treatment or censure. Blanket *refouling* orders negate the individual criminal responsibility principle that is cardinal to common law and therefore tantamount to overcriminalization. Section 4 therefore reads mischief into Kenya's Interior Cabinet Secretary Dr. Fred Matiang'i's tweet of 29 April 2020, to the effect that the COVID-19 (Restriction of Movement of Persons and Related Measures) Rules, 2020 [Public Health (COVID-19 Restriction of Movement of Persons and Related Measures) Rules, 2020] were in force within *Dadaab* and *Kakuma* refugee camps. Section 5 dissects the decision in *Okiya Omtatah Okoiti & 2 others v Cabinet Secretary, Ministry of Health & 2 others; Kenya National Commission on Human Rights (Interested Party)* (2020) which held that it was illegal and contrary to Kenya's Public Health Act (Cap. 242, Laws of Kenya) for the government to force people into quarantine without obtaining an order from a magistrate's court as required by law. Rather, a magistrate (and not an executive officer) is empowered to constrain persons who are reasonably suspected of being infected, through isolating or quarantining, for example confining them to a hospital or home. The chapter claims that the Cabinet Secretary's order that 'there shall be no movement of persons into or out of' the camps which he 'deemed to be an infected area' ("Kenya Bans Entry to Two Refugee Camps Hosting 400,000 People," 2020) violated refugees' rights to liberty and freedom of movement. Being densely populated areas, *Dadaab* and *Kakuma's* residents may have suffered catastrophic consequences if the global pandemic broke out there. Yet, on the date that the CS's contentious containment order was made, the coronavirus had not been detected inside any refugee camps. To compare the detention orders made under Kenya's COVID-19 rules, Section 6 sets out comparable criteria applicable under the UK public health legislation as a useful standard. Section 7 shows how in 2021, Kenya's Jubilee government amended the Refugees Act, seeking to empower state bureaucrats to 'legalise administrative confinement of refugees to exclusively designated residential areas or relocation away from urban areas.' In sum, this chapter critically analyses the Kenyan Interior Cabinet Secretary's Coronavirus order banning movement into and out of the refugee camps (hereafter 'cessation of movement' or 'containment' order) to assess whether or not it was necessary, subsidiary and proportionate.

2   Overcriminalization

Husak poses the following question: '[i]n virtue of what characteristics do given examples qualify as genuine instances of nonconsummate legislation' (Husak, 2009: 132)? His query is relevant to imputing indirect responsibility on third parties for doing everyday activities, which activities are not harmful in themselves, unless or until another person completes a criminal action. Such activities include intentionally exposing others to Covid 19 or other contagious diseases [Kenya's Public Health (Prevention, Control and Suppression of Covid-19) Rules, 2020]. What are the human costs incurred by violating relevant liberties? Who, if anyone, should be held accountable and what remedies are available?

2.1   *Overcriminalization and the Limits of Domestic Criminal Law*

Husak's (Husak, 2009) theory of domestic overcriminalization is based on John Rawls's hypothetical political liberal state (Rawls, 1971). Husak begins by defining punishment as hard treatment and stigma justifiably inflicted upon offenders. However, he cautions that not every statute, prosecution, conviction or *state punishment*, is justified. Beginning by assuming a right *not* to be punished, for Husak, state punishment is justifiable only for only those actions which: (1) cause nontrivial harm or are evil; and are (2) wrongful; (3) deserving of retribution; and (4) proven beyond reasonable doubt. These *constraints* on punishment, and thus on criminalization, are *internal* to the domestic criminal justice system. This chapter endeavours to extrapolate Husak's criminalization theory to evaluate Kenya's Covid 19 regulations. Most people intuitively assume that – due to their atrociousness – public health offences are inherently evil and comprise *mala in se*. They are not. Instead, this chapter shall contend that such offences may be mitigated, if not defended.

Pertinently for Husak, the constraints *external* to the criminal law reject inclusion of 'risk-prevention crimes' on grounds that they tend to arbitrarily increase criminality. Nonetheless, certain actions are regulated notwithstanding that they are neither harmful nor wrongful. Husak decries overcriminalization with respect to *mala prohibita*. He argues that modern liberal states intrude into the private sphere, thereby unjustifiably regulating individual autonomy. While Husak provides useful concepts for evaluating criminalization among liberal peoples, this chapter contends that most developing countries do not qualify as liberal, but are well-ordered, hierarchical, peoples (Rawls, 1999). Therefore, it is necessary to modify Husak's theory as applied to public health criminalization, which in this context includes punishing individuals to protect societies in emergencies. Indeed, not only is risk a cultural concept, but also, as the next section further demonstrates, criminalization of such acts is tantamount to establishing crimes of *mala prohibita* so as to over-regulate ordinary activities.

2.2 *A Critique of the Legal Moralist Theory of Criminalization*

Husak insists that retributive intuition does not require that just deserts should be inflicted by *state* punishment. Rather '[o]ur reasons to prefer the creation of an institution of state punishment to the imposition of private vengeance cannot be derived solely from the value of implementing a principle of retributive justice' (Rawls, 1971: 202). So '[w]hy should the citizens create an institution of criminal justice to do the work that can be done without the time, effort and expense?' Husak ponders. The answer is that retribution is a *necessary* but not *sufficient* reason to justify *state* punishment. Therefore, a consequentialist reason – as opposed to a naturalist justification that crime is inherently evil – is required.

According to Husak's theory of overcriminalization, although the state has a *legitimate* interest in retribution, it must have a *substantial* interest before resorting to the criminal sanction. It must overcome the costs of resorting to the criminal sanction, by overcoming three *drawbacks* of punishment:

First, the expense of our justice system is astronomical. Our penal institutions cost huge sums of money that might be used to achieve any number of other valuable goods taxpayers might prefer: education, transportation, funding for the arts, and the like. Second, our system of punishment is susceptible to grave error. Despite the best of intentions, punishment is bound to be imposed incorrectly, at least occasionally. Third, the power created by an institution of punishment is certain to be abused. Officials can and do exceed the limits of their authority, intentionally or inadvertently (Husak, 2009: 203–204). For these reasons, Kenya's Office of the Director of Public Prosecutions, albeit independent, 'shall have regard to the public interest, the interests of the administration of justice and the need to prevent and avoid abuse of the legal process' [Constitution of Kenya, 2010: Art. 157(11)].

2.3 *Who May Be Subjected to Compulsory Testing?*

2.3.1 Persons Intentionally, Recklessly or Negligently Exposing Others to Infection

Criminal procedure must balance between its search for material truth, on one hand, and refraining from violating the due process rights of suspects, on the other (Thaman, 2004: 4). To achieve this, European Enlightenment philosophers invented the idea of *mens rea* or 'guilty mind' which means that notwithstanding the perception of manifest criminality, either intention or recklessness (running a risk), should accompany an accused person's allegedly offensive act (Norrie, 1993: 14 citing Williams 1983: 73). Unless Parliament specifies the contrary, most crimes do not impose strict liability. Neither does the principle of legality permit guilt by association or the criminalization of status. Whether or not 'punishment may be imposed for something – manifest criminality, subjective criminality, (or a result such as) a harmful consequence – cannot be resolved without providing a theory of punishment' (Fletcher, 1978, cited in Husak, 2004: 761). For retribution 'simply means that punishment is justified by virtue of its relationship to the offense that has been committed' (Fletcher, 1978, 416–417, cited in Husak, 2004: 762 fn 33). In defence to a criminal charge, an accused may plead justification or excuse. For example, if he acted under provocation or out of self-defence, respectively. The presumption of innocence burdens the prosecution to prove beyond reasonable doubt that an accused intentionally, recklessly, or negligently exposed others to Covid infection. Where a suspect's identity is in issue, the state must establish that an offending act was attributable to the accused. It shall be demonstrated that Kenya's Public Health Act (PHA) presumes that a refugee, whether inside or outside a refugee camp, is Covid negative and cannot be quarantined until significant risk of infecting others is proven. Importantly, given the accused's interest in the outcome of criminal proceedings, and further because he has information which may either exonerate or implicate himself, therefore he has a right to participate in his trial (Nobles & Schiff, 2002: 28). Furthermore, he also possesses immunity from self-incrimination [Constitution of Kenya, 2010: Art. 50(2)(l)]. One may consequently choose to remain silent without any adverse inference being drawn from his decision to do so [Constitution of Kenya, 2010: Arts. 49(b) and 50(2)(i)]. This raises questions about the basis on which individuals may be subjected to compulsory testing. Can Covid tests be performed on the refugee community or only on specific individuals who may display reasonable suspicion of being infected?

The Hippocratic Oath of criminal procedure in liberal societies, is that it is 'better that ten guilty persons escape, than that one innocent suffer' (Blackstone, 1765). This chapter seeks to disabuse Kenya's Internal Security CS of German Chancellor Otto von Bismarck's misguided distortion that 'it is better that ten innocent men suffer than one guilty man escape' [Wade, 1977]. Communists employed similar repressive reasoning during the uprisings in Jiangxi, China in the 1930s that it is '[b]etter to kill a hundred innocent people than let one truly guilty person go free.' Another such refrain during uprisings in Vietnam in the 1950s went that it was '[b]etter to kill ten innocent people than let a guilty person escape' (Short, 2006: 299, 496, cited in *Blackstone's Ratio*, n.d.). In Cambodia, Pol Pot's Khmer Rouge adopted the same policy endorsing the notion that his regime 'better arrest an innocent person than leave a guilty one free' (Locard, 2005: 208–209; Werlau, 2011, cited in *Blackstone's Ratio*, n.d.).

2.3.2 The Presumption of Harmlessness

Kenya's Constitution (2010: Art. 50) enshrines the suspect's fair hearing rights. This ensures state neutrality in both citizen's and foreigner's making of economic, political, or religious choices. It is only those who resort to prohibited acts so as to alter the substantive outcomes of economic, political or social competition, that attract state criminal punishments. The presumption of innocence protects every person from decision-making influenced by irrational factors. By contrast, preventive justice concerns the presumption of harmlessness (Ashworth & Zedner, 2014: 130–132). People without previous criminal records are presumed not to be dangerous. Universal risk assessment is morally objectionable since those who have yet to offend 'enjoy the right to be presumed fee of armful intentions' (Floud & Young, 1981, cited in Ashworth & Zedner, 2014: 130). Consequently, the state is burdened to prove a reasonable basis for suspicion of innocents in order to detain or interfere with their personal security. Problematically, in emergencies where contagious diseases require detention, there may not be sufficient time to conduct a full trial. Nonetheless, an actuarial risk assessment provides a legitimate basis for profiling a suspect's characteristics (Ashworth & Zedner, 2014: 133–140). If no objective parameters are deployed to identify dangerous classes, then considerations for placing them under quarantine may invariably be contaminated by bias or unfairness. While 'the frightened man buys peace' (Riker, 1970: 371), tolerance must not only be procured from fellow citizens, but also from public officials (Scarman, 1981).[1] This chapter concerns the need to constrain rogue public officials' abuse of COVID-19 rules to detain refugees who display no significant risk of infecting anyone.

Under the Kenyan Constitution '[t]he State shall not discriminate directly or indirectly against any person on any ground, including race, sex, pregnancy, marital status, health status, ethnic or social origin, colour, age, disability, religion, conscience, belief, culture, dress, language or birth' [Constitution of Kenya, 2010: Art. 27(4)]. So as 'to adequately guard against the spread of infectious diseases' this right to equality requires magistrates to ensure that orders for the removal of persons exposed to any notifiable infectious disease are based on a certificate signed by a medical officer of health (Public Health Act, 1921: Sec. 27). Yet abuse of police power may be triggered by moral panics (Cohen, 1973). Stanley Cohen drew attention to the media's tendency to sensationalise social deviance. On hearing exacerbated news reports of apparent lawlessness, the middle classes can become outraged. They may call for the authorities to 'do something' in response. Consequently, the police may be pressured to respond by cracking down on any allegedly dangerous classes. However, instead of investigating actual criminals, they pursue stereotypical phantoms. Arbitrary arrests and detentions cause crime to increase. First, because harassment alienates the community from the law enforcement authorities. as a result, witnesses may become discouraged from reporting or testifying about incidents. The UK Scarman Report thus recommended that effective policing requires cooperation from communities who report criminality (Scarman, 1981). Second, by warehousing such innocent individuals, they associate with the criminal class. Instead of deterring potential crime, upon exposure to criminal subcultures they may suffer stigmatisation and thereby acquire jail-bird syndrome. Moral panics thus create an upward spiral effect of criminality or 'deviance amplification.' Hence high-handed policing can backfire.

The Kenyan Constitution therefore requires the National Police Service to perform their functions independently and accountably, free from corruption, while respecting for human rights (Constitution of Kenya, 2010: Art. 243). At the onset of the Covid Pandemic, the *Dadaab* and *Kakuma* refugee camps

---

1 Commissioned by the UK Government following the 1981 Brixton riots 'to inquire urgently into the serious disorder in Brixton on 10–12, April 1981 and to report, with the power to make recommendations.'

in the north-eastern and north-western regions of Kenya hosted 217,000 and 190,000 documented refugees, respectively. Predominantly with refugees from Somalia, South Sudan and Ethiopia, they accommodated undocumented individuals, some for over 20 years. Demographically, *Dadaab* had 'a quarantine capacity for only 2,000 people in place and only one dedicated COVID-19 health facility including 110 beds for more than 270,000 people' (*Al Jazeera*, 2020). Human rights groups decried the risk that these densely populated areas may suffer catastrophic consequences, if the global pandemic broke out there. However, by 29 April 2020, it had not. Nonetheless, notwithstanding that the Covid Pandemic had not broken out inside refugee camps, Kenyan media was awash with moral panics concerning a fabricated refugee-terrorism nexus. In January 2019, following the Dusitd2 Hotel terrorist attacks in Nairobi's Westlands, the government ordered the UNHCR to relocate all refugee camps out of Kenya by mid-2019 (Bhalla, 2019). It is no coincidence, therefore, that the April 2020 cessation of movement order on refugees, purporting to invoke the PHA was issued by the Internal Security Cabinet Secretary, rather than his Health counterpart. The chapter shall return to the ulterior motive behind the Interior CS's contentious containment order.

3 Contextual Factors: From *Refoulement* to Containment

3.1 *Administrative Measures* Refouling *Somali Refugees*

The Kenyan Interior Cabinet Secretary's April 2020 Covid order directing the cessation of refugees' movement is illustrative of a pattern of containing refugees on frivolous grounds. As explained elsewhere, previously, the state had been unable to link any specific refugee with a crime, terrorist act or property crime (*Coalition for Reform and Democracy v. Republic of Kenya*, 2015; Khamala, 2019: 28). Consequently, mass expulsion, relocation or confinement orders were default positions, after the Director of Public Prosecutions failed to identify any specific offence to charge a particular refugee with. Neither did the Director of Criminal Investigations procure any evidence of 'individual criminality.' Nor did the authorities accord suspected refugees with an opportunity to defend themselves against any serious criminal allegations or at all. Instead, the state routinely responded by 'doing something' about the public's 'fear of terrorism' being sensationalised in the media.

The 1951 UN Refugees Convention constraints Member State Parties from *refoulement* (United Nations Convention relating to the Status of Refugees, 1951: Art. 33). It provides that states should not return persons escaping from any country where they face serious threats of persecution to their lives or freedom based on their race, nationality, ethnicity, political opinions or social group. The test provides that *refoulement* is only permissible in two circumstances. These are: where such refugee is reasonably regarded either as threatening national security or as committing a serious crime [United Nations Convention relating to the Status of Refugees, 1951: Art. 32(2)]. Not even in an emergency may the right to a fair hearing be derogated from [Constitution of Kenya, 2010: Art. 25(c)]. As explained above, Kenyan courts have conclusively held that relocation is tantamount to *refoulement*. Indeed, if a *refoulee* is actually tortured, the *refouler* may be complicit in such crime against humanity. An analogous question is whether the COVID-19 pandemic constitutes an emergency which justifies Cabinet Secretary Matiang'i's April 2020 cessation of movement out of refugee camps where no Covid infection has been reported.

High Court Judge Joseph Mativo's judgement in the landmark 2017 KNCHR case laid down the above *non-refoulement* test (*Coalition for Reform and Democracy v. Republic of Kenya*, 2015; Khamala, 2015). In that case, the Court nullified the government's camp closure directives as unconstitutional, since Somali refugees confined to camps were not necessarily creating 'fear of Al Shabaab' in the country. Earlier that year, the Court of Appeal affirmed the refugee's freedom of movement and right to dignity (*Attorney General v Kituo Cha Sheria & 7 others*, 2017). Subsequently, in January 2019, following the Dusitd2 Hotel terrorist attacks in Nairobi's Westlands, the Kenya government ordered the UNHCR to relocate all refugee camps out of Kenya by mid-2019 (Bhalla, 2019). Once again, however, the state did not demonstrate reasonable belief that all refugees posed any national security or serious crime danger. Notwithstanding that the 2019 blanket closure order ignored the KNCHR precedent, no legal challenge was brought to quash it. Remarkably, Wood (2019) recognizes that the expanded definition's scope and meaning is not self-evident and requires interpretation. Perhaps it may be argued that conditions in Somalia have substantially changed, such that refugees no longer fear persecution there? Or perhaps the refugees may be secured inside safe havens across the border on the Somalia side? Apparently, series of judicial protections culminating in the Dusitd2 incident triggered 2019 camp closure orders. They were followed by the Refugees Act's agenda of confining refugees in camps designed to prevent terror attacks, despite derogation of refugees' constitutional rights to equal liberty and free movement. Applying the KNCHR precedent, the question becomes: what are the consequences, following the judiciary's introduction of an unjustifiably high standard of proving 'reasonable belief,' rather than requiring mere 'reasonable suspicion,' to justify *refoulement*? The high standard of proof effectively prevents state authorities from implementing mass *refoulement*. Arguably, one unintended consequence is therefore that to circumvent such judicial activism, the executive co-opted the legislature to legalise mass refugee containment in an attempt to enhance the Interior CS's powers under the 2021 Refugees Act.

3.2 Refugees as a Problem Population: Labelling is Discriminatory, Disproportionate and Unnecessary

It is useful to define some new provisions affecting refugees (including asylum seekers) under Kenya's amended Refugees Act (2021). Of relevance to this chapter, first, '"asylum" means the protection granted to a person in Kenya who is outside his or her country of nationality or habitual residence, who is fleeing persecution *or serious harm or for other reasons*.' Second, "Asylum seeker" means a person seeking protection in Kenya in accordance with the provisions of this Act but whose application has not been determined. Third, '"refugee," not only includes an asylum seeker (Refugees Act, 2021: Sec. 2), but also, in pertinent part, such person who:

> owing to external aggression, occupation, foreign domination or *events seriously disturbing public order in either part or whole of his or her country of origin or nationality* is compelled to leave his or her place of habitual residence in order to seek refuge in another place outside his or her country of origin or nationality [Refugees Act, 2021, Sec. 3(1)(c) (emphasis added)]

The Act aims to give effect to the UN Convention (United Nations Convention Relating to the Status of Refugees, 1951) the OAU Protocol Relating to the Status of Refugees and the OAU Convention (OAU Convention Governing the Specific Aspects of Refugee Problems in Africa, 1969) [Refugees Act, 2021, preamble (emphasis added)]. Finally, the 1969 OAU Convention provides that 'refugee' shall:

> *also* apply to every person who, owing to external aggression, occupation, foreign domination or *events seriously disturbing public order* in either part or the whole of his country of origin or nationality, is compelled to leave his place of habitual residence in order to seek refuge in another place outside his country of origin or nationality. [OAU Convention 1969, Art. 2 (emphasis added)]

Gurr's conceptualization of public order comprises 'manifestations of social disorder that are the objects of concerted public efforts at control' (Gurr, 1976: 9, cited in Lacey, et al. 2003: 114). In using the idea of public order, or disorder, we raise the question of whose view of order 'public' order is. For instance, relative to institutionally accepted or imposed standards of public disorder as threatening to the stability and authority of the state. Nicola Lacey and her colleagues ask whether 'public order' presupposes a consensus. Or does it assume the existence of political power to impose a particular conception of order? Who is to say whether a noisy picket line constitutes legitimate expression or an affront to public order (Lacey, et al. 2003: 115)? Another concern about public order relates to the behaviour of groups who do not conform to modern conventions about lifestyle, not only pastoralist communities, or even squatters, homeless persons or the internally displaced whom local authorities do not provide spaces for living, but for this chapter's purposes, refugees or asylum seekers. Violence is associated with marginalized protesting groups which seek to agitate for space to exist or civil liberties has been castigated as 'subversive,' 'unpatriotic' or even 'communistic,' or 'dissidents,' and 'terrorists' (Waddington, 1992: 29, cited in Lacey, et al. 2003: 125). It is thus necessary to determine whether the definition of who is a refugee, is broad or narrow in Kenya. The narrow, linguistic approach under the UN Refugees Convention, is limited to persons fleeing political persecution [United Nations Convention relating to the Status of Refugees, 1951: Art. 1; Refugees Act, 2021: Sec. 3(1)(a)]. By contrast, Wood observed that the 1969 OAU Convention (Organization of African Unity Convention Governing the Specific Aspects of Refugee Problems in Africa, 1969) was necessary because the key drivers of displacement have changed from colonial and minority rule to intra-state conflict, political instability, and increasingly, natural hazards, disasters, and the effects of climate change. This evolution spawned the OAU's broader or expanded, humanitarian definition. She decries the notable dearth of case law or institutional guidance on the expanded definition's terms. She notes that 'the Kenyan government's 2016 attempt to close Dadaab refugee camp and force the return of hundreds of thousands of Somali refugees provides one salient example of the hostile protection environment now faced by refugees in some African States' (Wood, 2019: 300). This chapter therefore questions whether Kenya's Interior CS was entitled to subjectively consider the Covid pandemic as comprising an 'emergency' by invoking the Public Order Act in order to deny refugees a right to a Covid test before containing them. Or should his Health counterpart have first established 'reasonable grounds' for suspecting that a particular individual was infected with the coronavirus before regarding him or her as posing a threat to the health of others? Ultimately, in a constitutional democracy, executive discretion is subject to judicial review. 'The High Court has supervisory jurisdiction over the subordinate courts and over any person, body or authority exercising a judicial or quasi-judicial function' [Constitution of Kenya, 2010: Art. 165(6)]. This chapter concludes that the blanket cessation of movement order labelling refugees as COVID-19 positive was discriminatory, disproportionate, and unnecessary. First, because out of Kenya's then 384 recorded coronavirus infections (*Kenya Records 129 COVID-19 Recoveries*, 2020), none were inside any refugee camp. Second, because less restrictive measures, such as testing, social distancing or wearing protective clothing, may prevent danger to public health. Third, because there are no 'reasonable grounds' for preventing uninfected persons from moving from one Covid-free place to another.

4 Challenging Kenya's Public Health Act and COVID 19 Rules

In *Okiya Omtatah Okoiti & 2 others v Cabinet Secretary, Ministry of Health & 2 others; Kenya National Commission on Human Rights (Interested Party)*, Okoiti petitioned the High Court on various grounds. First, that 'the Cabinet Secretary, Ministry of Health … forced persons required to go into compulsory quarantine for public health protection to pay for their upkeep yet the law requires the State to foot their bills with some individuals having had their period of compulsory quarantine un-procedurally and unfairly extended' (*Okiya Omtatah Okoiti v. Cabinet Secretary, Ministry of Health*, 2020: 1–2, para 1). Second, that the Health CS 'exceeded his powers to make regulations under Section 36 of the PHA by purporting to create criminal offences and penalties which is a preserve of the Parliament' (*Okiya Omtatah Okoiti v. Cabinet Secretary, Ministry of Health*, 2020: 1–2, para 1). Third, that 'none of the Regulations issued or purportedly issued under Section 36 of the PHA define what COVID-19 is, despite the disease caused by coronavirus 2 (SARS-CoV-2) being new and previously unknown both in law and as a health concern thereby making them vague and legally unenforceable.' Okoiti sought, *inter alia*, several declarations two of which are pertinent. One, that without order of magistrate, the administrative decision to quarantine citizens at various facilities and forcing them to pay for their own upkeep was 'contrary to Section 27 of the PHA and it contravened the constitutional imperative of the rule of law under Articles 10 and 47(1), tenet that they were not subjected to public participation and to parliamentary scrutiny and approval' (*Okiya Omtatah Okoiti v. Cabinet Secretary, Ministry of Health*, 2020: 2, para 3). Two, that '[t]he Government should refund in full the money each and every person who it quarantined was forced to pay for their upkeep'.

Supporting Okoiti, fellow activist Khelef Khalif was aggrieved that isolation centres lacked 'sufficient number of beds, food and other essential basic human needs required by the standards of health within the laws of Kenya.' Furthermore, that simultaneously some individuals had 'been forcefully quarantined without reasonable cause or probable infection of the COVID-19 virus and/or without prior testing to confirm the status of the individuals in relation to the COVID-19 virus' (*Okiya Omtatah Okoiti v. Cabinet Secretary, Ministry of Health*, 2020: 3, para 4). The co-petitioner lamented that isolation facilities were 'in poor degradable conditions contrary to the constitutional provisions.' Moreover, that '[s]ection 27 of the PHA provides that in the case of an epidemic and a health official concludes' or suspects that an individual is infected, then 'the local authority is mandated to incur all costs relating to the treatment of such persons throughout their isolation' (*Okiya Omtatah Okoiti v. Cabinet Secretary, Ministry of Health*, 2020: 3, para 5). Finally, Khalif decried the fact that 'the power of the CS to mandatorily require asymptomatic carriers of COVID-19 virus provide specimens for investigations and examination without the carrier's consent raises plausible legal questions of infringement of constitutional rights and freedom including the right to property, right to freedom and security of the person, human dignity and privacy' (*Okiya Omtatah Okoiti v. Cabinet Secretary, Ministry of Health*, 2020: 3, para 6). He therefore sought declarations for 'equal protection of the law, human dignity and right to safety and security as constitutionally enshrined' (*Okiya Omtatah Okoiti v. Cabinet Secretary, Ministry of Health*, 2020: 3, para 7), as well as injunctions to restrain the government from violating sections 27 and 36 of the PHA. Significantly, the activist demanded that those who were being forcefully quarantined and/or isolated without sufficient reasonable cause or prior testing justifying their quarantine and/or isolation against their right and freedoms 'should be released unconditionally' (*Okiya Omtatah Okoiti v. Cabinet Secretary, Ministry of Health*, 2020: 3, para 7).

In rebuttal, the government argued that it was 'entitled to act on the basis of precautionary principle to contain the spread of the deadly COVID-19 virus and in view of the emergency circumstances occasioned by the rapid spread of the virus, the need for immediate action to prevent and control the spread of the same, public consultations was not feasible prior to the publication of the rules' (*Okiya Omtatah Okoiti v. Cabinet Secretary, Ministry of Health*, 2020: 4, para 10). Furthermore, the state claimed 'that the precipitate measures that the rules seek to implement were undertaken within the context of necessity which is permitted in law within the context of prevailing circumstances.' On disposing of the case, Judge Makau issued a declaration dated 3 December 2020, 'that the decision to quarantine members of the public at various facilities *without an order of magistrate* and forcing them to pay for their upkeep is contrary to Section 27 of the PHA and is thereby unconstitutional'

[*Okiya Omtatah Okoiti v. Cabinet Secretary, Ministry of Health*, 2020: 27, para 152 (emphasis added)]. This was because 'the local authority of the district (state) where the isolated person is found, has the solemn constitutional and statutory duty to provide health care services to the people and this includes but is not limited to shouldering the quarantine costs' (*Okiya Omtatah Okoiti v. Cabinet Secretary, Ministry of Health*, 2020: 25, para 144). Moreover, it was held that the African Charter on Human and Peoples' Rights (The Banjul Charter) proclaims that 'every individual shall have the right to enjoy the best attainable state of physical and mental health' [*Okiya Omtatah Okoiti v. Cabinet Secretary, Ministry of Health*, 2020: 25–26, para 138, citing African (Banjul) Charter on Human and Peoples' Rights, 1981: Art. 16, & International Covenant on Economic, Social and Cultural Rights, 1966: Art. 12(1)]. However, citing procedural technicalities, the Judge declined to 'order that the government should refund in full the money each and every person who it quarantined was forced to pay for his/her upkeep.' Nonetheless, the Judge observed that the Constitution is further amplified by Section 5(1) of the Health Act, 2017 which provides that 'every person has the right to the highest attainable standard of health which shall include progressive access for provision of promotive, preventive, curative, palliative and rehabilitative services' [*Okiya Omtatah Okoiti v. Cabinet Secretary, Ministry of Health*, 2020: para 135, citing Constitution of Kenya, 2010: Art. 43(1)); Health Act, 2017: Sec. 5(1)]. Even individualised quarantine orders contravene the section 27 of the PHA which provides that:

Where, in the opinion of the medical officer of health, any person has recently been exposed to the infection, and may be in the incubation stage, of any notifiable infectious disease and is not accommodated in such manner as adequately to guard against the spread of the disease, such person may, on a certificate signed by the medical officer of health, be removed, *by order of a Magistrate and at the cost of the local authority of the district where such person is found*, to a place of isolation and there detained until, in the opinion of the medical officer of health, he is free from infection or able to be discharged without danger to the public health, or until the Magistrate cancels the order [Public Health Act, 1921: Sec. 27 (emphasis added)].

By comparison, concerning the April 2020 containment order that this chapter addresses, the relevant official who issued the cessation of movement order to refugees was the CS Internal Security, and not even the CS Health, leave alone a magistrate. Therefore, it is assumed that his decision was based on ulterior public security motives, rather than legitimate public health concerns.

5 Applying Public Health Criteria to Evaluate Refugee Confinement under Covid Rules

5.1 *Comparative Judicial Decisions*

This section compares relevant refugee vis-à-vis human rights jurisprudence from South Africa and the European Court of Human Rights. The South African Supreme Court of Appeal invalidated the South African Home Affairs Department's closure of the Cape Town Refugee Office, since such closure decision would render the making of applications for temporary permits inaccessible to asylum seekers (*Scalabrini Centre, Cape Town and Others v. Minister of Home Affairs and Others*, 2017; Lenaola 2019: 344–5). More recently, the South African Constitutional Court upheld a High Court of South Africa decision declaring sections of the Refugees Act (1998) constitutionally invalid to the extent that they provide that asylum seekers who have not renewed their visas within one month of the date of expiry, have abandoned their applications (*Scalabrini Centre of Cape Town and Another v. Minister of Home Affairs and Others*, 2023). In a groundbreaking judgment in 2014, South Africa's High Court held that refugee status decision makers who fail to consider refugee status under the OAU expanded refugee definition's scope and terms commit an error of law reviewable by the courts (*Radjabu v Chairperson of the Standing Committee for Refugee Affairs and Others*, 2014); Wood, 2019, 302). Regarding the unique threat that the pandemic created, we know that Covid sufferers may be asymptomatic and therefore do not necessarily manifest illness (Oran & Topol, 2020). Moreover, there is no evidence that the government actually tested each and every refugee to ascertain their health condition, leave alone that each or even any refugee was found to be infected with the coronavirus. Hence in light of the expanded refugee definition and further applying the *KNCHR* precedent, we can conclude that the CS's April 2020 order purporting to effect 'blanket' cessation of movement was arbitrary, discriminatory and for that reason null, void and unconstitutional. Second, because less restrictive measures, such as testing, social distancing or wearing protective clothing, may prevent danger to public health, therefore the impugned cessation of movement order was excessive.

Given that at the time of the order, no refugee currently within the refugee camps suffered from Covid, on what basis did the CS Interior find that they were a danger to public health? Consider the landmark case of *Enhorn v Sweden* (2005). Enhorn suffered from an infectious disease which he transmitted to another man. Swedish law listed HIV/AIDS as a public health threat. To stem the spread of infectious diseases under national public health law the court ordered his compulsory isolation. Although the order extended over a period of almost seven years, his actual deprivation of liberty lasted only 18 months. Nonetheless, Enhorn complained of unjustifiable infringement of this right to liberty. The European Court of Human Rights agreed that his compulsory isolation was not a last resort. Because his liberty was at stake, attention should have been paid to less restrictive means of protection. 'The Court made a stand against deprivation of liberty in case of arbitrary acts of authorities that mainly resonates uneducated public hysteria' (*Sweden Violated Human Rights by Compulsory Isolating HIV Positive Person*, n.d.).

Applying this precedent to the Kenyan 2020 containment order, in its response to the *Okoiti case* it may be argued that the government raised a necessity defence. Importantly, as shown in the preceding section, the High Court held the quarantining orders unconstitutional because they were not pursuant to a magistrate's order. It follows that even assuming that it was necessary to encamp refugees by a cessation of movement order, such order could not be made by an executive officer without judicial imprimatur. Moreover, applying the subsidiarity and proportionality principles under UK public health law, the least restrictive means of protection should be deployed. Otherwise, even sufferers from TB are at risk of involuntary detention (*Example 1: Defining the Grounds for Compulsory Isolation of a Patient with an Infectious Disease*, 2004).

Third, the Interior CS's cessation of movement order would be void because there are no 'reasonable grounds' for preventing uninfected persons from moving from one Covid-free place to another. On one hand, notwithstanding the usually busy Easter weekend, outside the boundaries delineating Nairobi, Mombasa, Mandera, Kilifi and Kwale Counties which were locked down, undiagnosed individuals remained free to travel to Covid affected regions across Kenya (*COVID-19: Kenya Bans Travel in and Out of Nairobi, Other Areas*, 2020). On the other hand, rampant Covid infections and deaths justified a presumption that people in Eastleigh at Nairobi or Old Town of Mombasa, were contaminated and thus presented a degree of risk of harm to human health (Kabale, 2020). Therefore, medical evidence supported locking down such Covid-infected zones. In light of the manifestly high Covid rates detected in the above said constituencies, no public-spirited citizen moved to court to challenge the administrative lockdown orders. Conversely, containment inside Covid-free refugee camps was irrational. Even if Covid infections were at that date thought to be lethal as there was no vaccine or cure, its grave consequences could be discounted, considering the statistically insignificant risk the coronavirus posed to most healthy people, even if one suffered from it. According to scientific evidence at that time, '[t]he case-fatality rate for COVID-19 varie[d] markedly by age, ranging from 0.3 deaths per 1000 cases among patients aged 5 to 17 years to 304.9 deaths per 1000 cases among patients aged 85 years or older in the US. Among patients hospitalised in the intensive care unit, the case fatality [wa]s up to 40%' (Wiersinga, et al. 2020). Moreover, '[a]pproximately 5% of patients with COVID-19, and 20% of those hospitalised, experience severe symptoms necessitating intensive care. More than 75% of patients hospitalised with COVID-19 require supplemental oxygen' (Wiersinga, et al. 2020).

Given Kenya's past counter-terrorism *refoulement* attempts, CS Matiang'i's unilateral *anti-Covid* April 2020 order unreasonably containing refugees in overcrowded camps, not only constituted a threat to their own health. It also unconstitutionally violated their rights to liberty and movement. On 6 July 2020, ignoring the coronavirus cases surge, President Uhuru Kenyatta lifted Nairobi's, Mombasa's and Mandera's 90-day lockdowns, having freed Eastleigh, Kilifi and Kwale 30-days earlier. Confoundingly, by 20 July 2020 despite the Interior CS's April 2020 cessation order, within the refugee camps, there were '2,510 confirmed COVID-19 cases and two deaths, eight in *Dadaab* and two in *Kakuma*' (*Kenya Situation Report, 21 Jul 2020 – Kenya*, 2020) out of the total number of 13,771 confirmed cases in Kenya. Apparently, the Interior CS's cessation of movement order had little impact in preventing infection of the refugee population. Instead, it effectively confined them at locations where the disease spread was intensified.

By comparison, in *Rus v Romania* (No. 2621/21) the applicant saw the cause for Covid infection in his conditions of detention, in particular the overcrowding. He complained of being infected with the COVID-19 virus while incarcerated. The European Court of Human Rights gave notice of the application to the Romanian Government and put questions to the parties under Article 3 (prohibition of inhuman or degrading treatment) and Article 35 (admissibility criteria) of the European Convention on Human Rights ("Factsheet – COVID-19 Health Crisis," 2022).

5.2   Limitations

Initially, the Kenyan Interior CS's order was reported by the media and apparently announced by way of a tweet. Hence its existence is shrouded in doubt and uncorroborated by official documents. Second, throughout the Covid period, regulatory orders were issued for 60 days at any given stretch. There are no indications of whether the cessation of movement order was officially extended beyond June 2020. Third, because the Courts were closed for long durations of time at the outset of the pandemic, it was difficult for aggrieved persons to challenge the cessation of movement order. Indirectly, but nonetheless arbitrarily labelling refugees as COVID-19 positive was discriminatory, disproportionate and unnecessary. Inadvertently, by scaling down judicial operations during COVID-19, Chief Justice David Maraga further frustrated people contained in 'uninfected' refugee camps from accessing legal representation and to courts. To partially alleviate exclusion of litigants, electronic filing of court cases was introduced to Nairobi courts in June 2020, but not permissible in other regions.

6 Lessons from the United Kingdom's Public Health Act

A comparative statute providing a normative standard by which to evaluate quarantine orders is useful. The UK's Public Health Act provides for preventive justice through compulsory orders relating to people suffering from a set of legally notifiable conditions such as tuberculosis, cholera, leprosy, typhoid, fever meningitis, and malaria (Ashworth & Zedner, 2014: 200). Since these conditions could present a significant risk of causing serious harm to people, a justice of the peace (a judicial not an executive officer) is empowered to make a compulsory order in increasing levels of severity. From the mildest to the most severe intrusiveness, they escalate by requiring testing, constraining movement, and imposing the wearing of protective clothing, through to detaining, imposing quarantine or isolation. For persons of no fixed abode, a quarantine order would amount to being committed into the custody of a home or hospital. Given the tremendous violation of human rights upon detention or containment of persons suffering from contagious diseases or who are mentally disordered, this creates cause for considerable concern.

According to Andrew Ashworth and Lucia Zedner, 'it is insufficient to simply say … people taking action without a patient's consent must attempt to keep to a minimum the restrictions they impose on the patient's liberty, having regard to the purpose for which the restrictions are imposed' (Ashworth & Zedner, 2014: 220–221, citing UK MHA and Code). They therefore criticise the UK Mental Health Act and Code for failing to accord sufficient weight to the fundamental nature of the right to personal liberty. Instead of respecting rights, the constraining power tilts towards a flexible justice system 'which proceeds by a crude model of balancing that can easily be made to give public protection priority over individual rights' (Ashworth & Zedner, 2014: 222). Four reasons underpin Ashworth and Zedner's critique of public health laws. First, it is essential to ensure that the list of contagious diseases contains only those conditions that can do serious harm to the well-being of others so long as they are untreated. Using an overly-broad concept creates concerns regarding its malleability in the context of sometimes indefinite deprivations of liberty. Second, the legislature's failure to insist on a suitably targeted form of harm is worrisome. The UK MHA opaquely references 'the prevention of harm' or 'protecting other people from harm' but does not specify the type of harm which is to be prevented. Deprivation of liberty should require 'serious physical or psychological harm' (Ashworth & Zedner, 2014: 222). Third, the magnitude of risk to which the public is exposed should be significant risk of serious physical or psychological harm (Ashworth & Zedner, 2014: 222). Fourth, 'ineradicable uncertainties about the evidential foundations on which judgments can be made identifying the levels of risk (of serious harm) required' are bound to remain. Nonetheless, Ashworth and Zedner emphasise that 'the fundamental right to personal liberty must be respected.' Therefore, only as a last resort 'in cases where there is a strong reason to believe that there is a significant or substantial risk of serious physical or psychological harm,' may deprivation be justified. Where the pre-conditions for detention are met, they conclude that risk-reductive treatment should be offered to those deprived of their liberty for preventive reasons (Ashworth & Zedner, 2014: 222). They recommend monitoring of detention so that it is for the shortest possible period. Moreover, the detention criteria should not only be applied on admission, but throughout one's detention period in relation to decisions concerning release and recall. Ultimately, considering invasion of fundamental rights, detention conditions should be as normalised as possible (Ashworth & Zedner, 2014: 223).

7 Emergent Confinement Powers Proposed under Kenya's 2021 Refugees Act

Securing any state's own citizens from harm is its first responsibility, before rescuing refugees. Kenyan domestic law provides that: 'The general rules of international law shall form part of the law of Kenya [and] Any treaty or convention ratified by Kenya shall form part of the law of Kenya [Constitution of Kenya, 2010: Art. 2(5) & (6)]. By dint of the Victim's Declaration:

States should periodically review existing legislation and practices to ensure their responsiveness to changing circumstances, should enact and enforce, if necessary, legislation proscribing acts that constitute serious abuses of political or economic power, as well as promoting policies and mechanisms for the prevention of such acts, and should develop and make readily available appropriate rights and remedies for victims of such acts (*Declaration of Basic Principles of Justice for Victims of Crime and Abuse of Power*, 1985: Art. 21).

Consequently, in 2019, the Jubilee government proposed amendments to the Refugees Act (Refugees Act, 2006), seeking to empower state bureaucrats to relocate refugees *en mass*. Kenya's new Act (Refugees Act, 2021) on one hand, seeks to regulate resettlement and integration of refugees with the host communities. On the other hand, incorporating the jurisprudence on using less restrictive measures when relocating refugees, the Commissioner must consider 'any special needs or conditions that may affect' his or her protection and safety before requiring 'any refugee within a designated area to move to or reside in any other designated area' [Refugees Act, 2021: Sec. 31(1)]. Confinement orders may be made by the Commissioner for Refugee Affairs who shall 'work with the national and county Government authorities within and around the designated areas to ensure the protection of the environment and the rehabilitation of areas that had been used as designated areas' (Refugees Act, 2021: Sec. 30). For purposes, *inter alia* of control of designated areas:

The Cabinet Secretary shall make rules for the control of designated areas and, without prejudice to the generality of the foregoing, such rules and directions may make provision in respect of all or any of the following matters:

(a) the organisation, safety and discipline and administration of a designated area;
(b) the reception, transfer, settlement, treatment, health and well-being of refugees. [Refugees Act, 2021: Sec. 32(a) & (b)]

Nonetheless, the benefit of the *non-refoulement* right 'may not, however, be claimed by a refugee or asylum seeker (of) whom there are reasonable grounds for him or her being regarded as a danger to the national security or public order of Kenya' [Refugees Act, 2021: Sec. 29(2)]. This chapter has critically analysed the extent that these proposed amendments are likely to deny this particularly vulnerable population their right to be presumed innocent before being punished even during emergency times. In the context of public health, there are several question. One is whether the Interior CS is entitled to subjectively construe the Covid pandemic as comprising a security 'emergency' by invoking the Public Order Act (1950) in order to deny refugees a right to a Covid test before containing them. Or should his Health counterpart establish 'reasonable grounds' for suspecting that an individual is infected with the coronavirus before regarding one as posing a threat to the health of others? Second, does the expanded, humanitarian definition apply to Somalis who are reluctant to return to Somalia because of drought? Third, is climate change an event 'seriously disturbing public order' that merits their continued displacement? There seems to be no temporal limitation to that criterion. Theoretically, refugees seeking protection may also claim to be entitled to provision of amenities that give them a better life in future such as employment and education. The generalized nature of the OAU Convention's enumerated refugee-producing events – external aggression, occupation, foreign domination and events seriously disturbing public order – is said to make the refugee definition better suited to large scale population displacement and situations of mass influx. The narrow definition limited to persons fleeing political persecution is tantamount to overcriminalization of refugees by receiving countries whose police may be prone to moral panics motivating refugee expulsion or containment for ulterior motives. Wood applies this evolutionary approach to the definition to terms such as 'occupation' and 'aggression' to numerous situations in Africa including Kenya's 2012 incursion into Somalia and the presence of Rwanda in the DRC, border disputes between North and South Sudan, and Morocco's occupation in Western Sahara (Wood, 2019: 313).

The OAU Convention's expanded refugee definition's refugee-producing event 'events seriously disturbing public order' is arguably the expanded definition's most contentious component, owing to its potential breath and concerns that represents a potential 'blank cheque' to would be refugees (Wood, 2019: 317). This is important for interpretation, since 'the key-drivers of displacement have changed from colonial and minority rule (at the time of adoption of the 1969 Convention's adoption) to intra-State conflict, political instability, and increasingly, natural hazards, disasters, and the effects of climate change' (Wood, 2019: 311). Hence '[o]ne means of ensuring the treaty's enjoining effectiveness in a changing environment is via an "evolutionary" approach to its interpretation. Evolutionary interpretation rejects the quest for "originalism", or the idea that a treaty's meaning remains static at the time of its drafting and mandates instead that a treaty be interpreted in light of the context in which it now applies' (Wood, 2019: 311–12).

8   Conclusion

To what extent did domestication of the 1969 OAU Convention under the amended Refugees Act (2021) suggest that the legislature intends to incorporate an evolutionary interpretation of who a refugee is, into Kenya's refugee law and practice? Before 2021, Kenya's executive frequently attempted to expel or relocate Somali refugees *en mass* in pursuit of the 1951 UN Refugee Convention's narrow definition. What do such earlier repressive experiences of the Kenya government's non-compliance with its *non-refoulement* obligations under international refugee law indicate about its COVID-19 strategy in relation to refugees? Past *refouling* administrative orders indicate that when faced with public outcries to 'do something' to control the perception of the rising global health pandemic, the CS Interior either lacked proper legal advice or was bereft of political will to respond within the confines of the rule of law.

Previously, Somali refugees were *refouled* in the guise of 'terrorists' and 'criminals.' Judicial requirements of high standards of proof before *refouling* refugees may be instructive. Subsequently, the same refugees were labelled as 'COVID-infected' to justify confinement to refugee camps. The PHA requires that the CS's declaration that the April 2020 Public Health Rules which restricted movement out of refugee camps, would require reasonable belief of COVID-19 infections, before subjecting refugees or camps to cessation of movement. By extension, it is unreasonable to base preventive health orders declaring any individual, group or area as being infected on subjective whims. Labelling and treating refugees as COVID-19 positive without a magistrate's order was discriminatory, disproportionate and unnecessary. First, because out of Kenya's then 384 recorded coronavirus infections, none were in either refugee camp. Second, because less restrictive measures, such as testing, social distancing or wearing protective clothing, may prevent danger to public health. Third, because there are no 'reasonable grounds' for preventing uninfected persons from moving from one Covid-free place to another. Refugees adversely affected by the blanket cessation of movement order suffered violation of their constitutional rights to dignity and security and their freedoms of association and movement. Notwithstanding the containment order, thousands of the encamped even contracted Covid, thus compromising their health. The principles of false imprisonment under tort law entitle them to claim compensation for injury and losses incurred. In 2021, Parliament introduced novel provisions imposing the use of less restrictive measures in line with the expanded refugee definition. Indeed: 'In its interpretive role, a court may identify gaps in the law' (Lenaola 2019: 347). This move to decriminalize refugees may be attributable to adopting the Court's evolutionary approach in the *Kituo* and *Kenya National Commission on Human Rights* cases. Nonetheless, in March 2021, Kenya's Interior Ministry ordered the closure of *Dadaab* and *Kakuma* sprawling camps that host 410,000 refugees from neighbouring Somalia and gave the UNHCR two weeks to present a plan to do so ("Kenya Orders Closure of Two Refugee Camps, Gives Ultimatum to UN Agency," 2021).

Bibliography

African (Banjul) Charter on Human and Peoples' Rights. (*June 27, 1981*) Organization of African Unity. Available at: https://au.int/sites/default/files/treaties/36390-treaty-0011_-_african_charter_on_human_and_peoples_rights_e.pdf. Accessed on June 30, 2022.

Ashworth, A. and Zedner, L. (2014) *Preventive Justice*. Oxford: Oxford University Press.

Attorney General v Kituo Cha Sheria & 7 others, Civil Appeal no. 108 of 2014 [2017] eKLR.

Bhalla, N. (March 29, 2019) *Kenya orders closure of Dadaab refugee camp this year, according to leaked U.N. document.* Reuters. Available at: https://www.reuters.com/article/us-kenya-refugees-somalia-idUSKCN1RA1FN. Accessed on June 30, 2022.

Blackstone, W. (1765) *Commentaries on the Laws of England.* Oxford: Clarendon Press.

Coalition for Reform and Democracy v. Republic of Kenya, Pet. No. 628/2014 & 630/2014 (Nairobi H.C. 2015) Nairobi High Court, Kenya.

Cohen, S. (1973) *Folk Devils and Moral Panics: The Creation of the Mods and Rockers.* London: Paladin.

Constitution of Kenya, 2010.

COVID-19: Kenya bans travel in and out of Nairobi, other areas. (April 6, 2020) Al Jazeera. Available at: https://www.aljazeera.com/news/2020/4/6/COVID-19-kenya-bans-travel-in-and-out-of-nairobi-other-areas. Accessed on June 30, 2022.

Oran, D. P. & Topol, E. J. (2020) "Prevalence of Asymptomatic SARS-CoV-2 Infection: A Narrative Review". *Annals of Internal Medicine*, 173 (5). Available at: https://doi.org/10.7326/M20-3012.

Declaration of Basic Principles of Justice for Victims of Crime and Abuse of Power. (1985) United Nations General Assembly. Available at: https://legal.un.org/avl/ha/dbpjvcap/dbpjvcap.html#:~:text=29%20November%201985.-,The%20Declaration%20of%20Basic%20Principles%20of%20Justice%20for%20Victims%20of,Victims%20of%20abuse%20of%20power%E2%80%9D.

Ekins, E. (2016) "Blackstone's Ratio: Is it More Important to Protect Innocence or Punish Guilt?". In: Ekins, E. (ed) *Policing in America: Understanding Public Attitudes toward the Police.* The Cato Institute. Available at: https://www.cato.or g/policing-in-america/chapter-4/blackstones-ratio. Accessed on June 30, 2022.

Esmein, A. (1913). *A History of Continental Criminal Procedure with Special Reference to France.* Translated by Simpson, J. Boston: Little, Brown and Company.

Enhorn v Sweden 41 EHRR 643 (2005) European Court of Human Rights.

Example 1: Defining the grounds for compulsory isolation of a patient with an infectious disease. (March 11, 2004) Health and Human Rights Resource Guide. Available at: https://www.hhrguide.org/2014/03/11/example-1-defining-the-grounds-for-compulsory-isolation-of-a-patient-with-an-infectious-disease/. Accessed on June 30, 2022.

Factsheet – COVID-19 Health Crisis. (2022) European Court of Human Rights. Available at: https://www.echr.coe.int/Documents/FS_Covid_ENG.pdf. Accessed on June 30, 2022.

Feinberg, J. (1984) *The Moral Limits of the Criminal Law 1: Harm to Others.* New York: Oxford University Press.

Fletcher, G. P. (1978) *Rethinking Criminal Law.* Boston: Little, Brown and Co.

Floud, J. & Young, W. (1981) *Dangerousness and Criminal Justice.* London: Heinemann.

General Assembly Resolution 2200 (XXI). (December 19, 1966) *International Covenant on Economic, Social and Cultural Rights*. Available at: International Covenant on Civil and Political Rights – A/RES/21/2200 A Annex 2 – UN Documents: Gathering a body of global agreements (un-documents.net). Accessed on June 30, 2022.

Gurr, T. R. (1976) *Rogues Rebels and Reformers*. London: SAGE Publications.

Hobbes, T. (1981) *Leviathan*. London: Penguin Books.

Husak, D. N. (2009) *Overcriminalization: The Limits of the Criminal Law*. Oxford: Oxford University Press.

Husak, D. N. (2010) *The Philosophy of Criminal Law: Selected Essays*. New York: Oxford University Press.

Husak, D. (2010) "Crimes Outside the Core" *Tulsa Law Review* 39:4 755–780.

Kabale, N. (September 18, 2020) *Lockdown in Eastleigh, Old Town as COVID-19 cases shoot to 582*. Business Daily. Available at: https://www.businessdailyafrica.com/bd/news/lockdown-in-eastleigh-old-town-as-COVID-19-cases-shoot-to-582-2288882. Accessed on June 30, 2022.

Kenya bans entry to two refugee camps hosting 400,000 people. (April 29, 2020) Al Jazeera. Available at: https://www.aljazeera.com/news/2020/4/29/kenya-bans-entry-to-two-refugee-camps-hosting-400000-people. Accessed on June 30, 2022.

Kenya National Commission of Human Rights v. AG, Const. Pet. No. 227/2016 (2017) Nairobi High Court, Kenya.

Kenya orders closure of two refugee camps, gives ultimatum to UN agency. (March 24, 2021) Reuters. Available at: https://www.reuters.com/article/uk-kenya-refugees-idUSKBN2BG1MA. Accessed on June 30, 2022.

Kenya Records 129 COVID-19 Recoveries. (April 30, 2020) Ministry of Health. Available at: https://www.health.go.ke/kenya-records-129-COVID-19-recoveries-nairobi-wednesday-april-29-2020/. Accessed on June 30, 2022.

Kenya Situation Report, 21 Jul 2020 – Kenya. (July 22, 2020) ReliefWeb. Available at: https://reliefweb.int/report/kenya/kenya-situation-report-21-jul-2020. Accessed on June 30, 2022.

Khamala, C. A. (2020) "When Rescuers become Refoulers: Closing Kenya's Refugee Camps amid Terrorism Threats' and leaving vulnerable groups out in the cold". *Africa Nazarene University Law Journal*, 8(1): 1–29.

Khamala, C. A. (2019) "Oversight of Kenya's Counter Terrorism Measures on Al-Shabaab". *Law and Development Review*. 12(1): 79–118.

Kituo cha Sheria v. Attorney General, Pet. No. 19/2013 & 115/2013 (2013) Kenya High Court, Kenya.

Lacey, N., Wells, C. & Quick, O. (2003) *Reconstructing Criminal Law: Text and Materials* (3rd edn). United Kingdom: Cambridge University Press.

Lenaola, I, (2019) "The Role of African Courts in Promoting Refugee Rights" *International Journal of Refugee Law*, 31 (2/3): 343–348.

Locard, H. (2005) *Pol Pot's Little Red Book: The Sayings of Angkar.* Chang Mai: Silkworm Books.

Nobles, R. & Schiff, D. (2002) *Understanding Miscarriages of Justice: Law, the Media and the Inevitability of Crisis.* Oxford University Press.

Norrie, A. (1993) *Crime, Reason and History: A Critical Introduction to Criminal Law.* London: Weidenfeld and Nicolson.

Okiya Omtatah Okoiti v. Cabinet Secretary, Ministry of Health, Pet. No. 140/2020, 128/2020 & 28/2020 (2020) Nairobi High Court, Kenya.

Organisation of African Unity Convention Governing the Specific Aspects of Refugee Problems in Africa. September 10, 1969. Organisation of African Unity. Available at: https://au.int/en/treaties/oau-convention-governing-specific-aspects-refugee-problems-africa

Public Health Act, Cap. 242, Laws of Kenya (1921).

Public Health (COVID-19 Restriction of Movement of Persons and Related Measures) Rules (2020).

Public Order Act, Cap. 56, Laws of Kenya (1950).

Radjabu v Chairperson of the Standing Committee for Refugee Affairs and Others (8830/2010) [2014] ZAWCHC 134; [2015] 1 All SA 100 (WCC) (September 4, 2014).

Rawls, J. (1971) *A Theory of Justice.* Cambridge: Harvard University Press, Belknap Press.

Refugee Consortium of Kenya v. Attorney General, Pet. No. 382/1014 (Nairobi H.C. 2015).

Refugees Act, No. 13 of 2006, Rev. Ed. 2012, Cap. 173. Laws of Kenya [2006].

Refugees Act, No. 10 of 2021 (2021).

Riker, W. H. (1970) "Public Safety as a Public Good". In: Rostow, E. V. (ed) *Is Law Dead?* New York: Simon and Schuster.

Rus v. Romania (No. 2621/21). European Court of Human Rights.

Samow Mumin Mohamed v. Cabinet Secretary, Ministry of Interior Security and Co-ordination, Pet. No. 206/2011 (2014) Nairobi High Court, Kenya.

Scalabrini Centre of Cape Town and Another v. Minister of Home Affairs and Others (CCT 51/23) [2023] ZACC 45; 2024 (4) BCLR 592 (CC); 2024 (3) SA 330 (CC) (12 December 2023).

Scarman, L. S. B. (1981) *The Scarman Report: The Brixton Disorders 10–12 April 1981: Report of an Inquiry.* Penguin: Harmondsworth.

Short, P. (2006) *Pol Pot: Anatomy of a Nightmare.* New York: Henry Holt and Company.

Sweden Violated Human Rights by Compulsory Isolating HIV Positive Person. (n.d.). ILGA Europe. Available at: https://new.ilga-europe.org/resources/news/latest-news/sweden-violated-human-rights-compulsory-isolating-hiv-positive-person. Accessed on June 30, 2022.

Thaman, S. (2004) *Comparative Criminal Procedure: A Casebook Approach.* Durham: Carolina Academic Press.

The Public Health (Prevention, Control and Suppression of Covid-19) Rules, 2020.

United Nations Convention relating to the Status of Refugees. (December 14, 1950) *United Nations General Assembly*. Available at: https://treaties.un.org/pages/View DetailsII.aspx?src=TREATY&mtdsg_no=V-2&chapter=5&Temp=mtdsg2&clang =_en#:~:text=The%20Convention%20was%20adopted%20by,Nations%20on%20 14%20December%201950. Accessed on June 30, 2022.

Waddington, D. (1992) *Contemporary Issues in Public Disorder*. Routledge.

Wade, J. W. (1977) "A Uniform Comparative Fault Act: What should it Prove?". *University of Michigan Journal of Law Reform*, 10: 220.

Werlau, M. C. (2011) *Che Guevara Forgotten Victims*. Washington, D.C.: The Free Society Project.

Wiersinga, W. J., et al. (2020) "Pathophysiology, Transmission, Diagnosis, and Treatment of Coronavirus Disease 2019 (COVID-19)". *JAMA*, 324(8): 782.

Williams, G. (1983) *Textbook of Criminal Law* 2nd ed. Stevens & Sons Ltd.

Wood, T. (2019) "Who is a Refugee in Africa? A Principled Framework for Interpreting and Applying Africa's Expanded Refugee Definition". *International Journal of Refugee Law*, 31 (2/3): 290–320.

Index

abortion   46, 144, 149, 196
accountability justification   120
Act   7, 11, 13, 19, 20, 21, 22, 23, 24, 25, 26, 27, 28, 29, 30, 31, 32, 33, 34, 37, 38, 43, 79, 80, 89, 101, 103, 108, 109, 113, 116, 117, 119, 126, 127, 128, 130, 131, 133, 134, 135, 138, 140, 141, 142, 143, 146, 147, 148, 160, 161, 162, 163, 164, 165, 166, 167, 168, 169, 170, 171, 172, 173, 175, 176, 178, 180, 181, 196, 197, 198, 200, 202, 204, 205, 206, 207, 209, 210, 213, 214, 215, 216, 220, 221
   Bihar Prohibition and Excise Act, 2016   19, 21, 23, 27, 32
   Canadian Charter of Rights and Freedoms   105, 113
   Constitution of Kenya, 2010   196, 200, 201, 202, 204, 207, 209, 214, 218
   Coroners and Justice Act, 2009   138
   Criminal Code of the Russian Federation   182, 188, 189, 190, 191, 192, 193, 194
   Criminal Financing Act, 2017   89
   Criminal Tribe Act   79
   Dangerous Drugs Act, 1930   164
   Dowry Prohibition Act, 1961   146
   Harrison Narcotics Act of 1914   170
   Indian Evidence Act, 1872   108
   Information Technology Act, 2000   119, 127
   Jan Vishwas (Amendment of Provisions) Act, 2023   7, 13
   Muslim Women (Protection of Rights on Marriage) Act, 2019   7, 19, 30, 31, 146
   Narcotics and Psychotropic Substances Act, 1985   20
   National Security Act, 1980   134, 135
   Opium Act, 1857   165, 169, 181
   Prevention of Crime Act (1908)   38
   Public Health Act, 1921   196, 202, 209
   Scheduled Castes and the Scheduled Tribes (Prevention of Atrocities) Act, 1989   7
   UK Prison Act (1898)   38
   Unlawful Activities Prevention Act, 1967   131, 146
   Uttar Pradesh Prohibition of Unlawful Conversion of Religion Act, 2021   19, 20, 21
addiction   22, 23, 26, 165, 170, 171, 176, 177, 178
administrative confinement   198
administrative prejudice   182
adult prisoners   38
aim of criminal law   73, 74
All India Muslim Personal Law Board   30
antinomies   5, 8, 75
archaic law   154
arrest   28, 31, 46, 86, 89, 119, 131, 175, 201
Bill   30, 33, 101, 170, 171
burden of proof   11, 20, 21, 27, 72, 79, 89, 90, 97, 99, 105, 106, 107, 108, 109, 172
   Ei incumbit probatio qui dicit, non qui negat   104
   foundational facts   20, 90
   legal burden   20, 89, 90
   reverse burden   12, 19, 21, 27, 90, 106, 107, 108, 109, 110, 172
   reverse burden of proof   21, 27, 106, 107, 108, 109, 172
cannabis   95, 165, 168, 170, 171, 173
censure   4, 13, 18, 46, 197
child pornography   46
citizenship   9
civil society   50, 57, 58, 59, 67
Codification   14, 16, 91, 94
colonial   5, 11, 79, 128, 136, 137, 142, 164, 165, 166, 167, 168, 169, 178, 206, 216
colonial outlook   11
colonialism   5
commendable behaviour   46
condition of legality   53
condition of proportionality   53
Constitution, the   1, 14, 19, 22, 27, 28, 29, 30, 91, 113, 126, 128, 130, 155, 157, 158, 161, 168, 174, 179, 209
   Article 14   29, 30
constitutional governance   153
constitutional morality   2, 9, 11, 24, 76, 144, 145, 152, 153, 154, 155, 156, 157, 158

constitutional norms   145, 157
constitutional order   183
constraints   8, 75, 76, 78, 97, 100, 101, 150, 198, 199, 203
   internal and external constraints   75
   moral constraints   76
contagious diseases   196, 201, 213
conviction   23, 27, 38, 45, 89, 111, 129, 139, 163, 171, 174, 175, 179, 180
corpus delicti   182, 183, 184, 185, 193
counterterrorism   10, 44, 47, 49, 55, 58, 62, 63, 64, 65
Covid-19   218, 219
   cessation of movement order   203, 207, 209, 210, 211, 212, 217
   Coronavirus   198, 221
   isolation   208, 209, 210, 213, 218
   social distancing   207, 210, 217
   testing   13, 201, 207, 208, 210, 213, 217
crimes against military service   183
crimes against the peace and security   183
criminal law   1, 2, 3, 4, 5, 6, 7, 8, 9, 11, 12, 17, 18, 19, 24, 44, 45, 46, 47, 48, 49, 50, 52, 53, 54, 56, 57, 58, 59, 62, 63, 64, 71, 72, 73, 74, 75, 76, 77, 78, 79, 80, 81, 82, 83, 84, 85, 86, 87, 88, 89, 90, 95, 96, 98, 99, 102, 103, 104, 106, 112, 127, 138, 144, 147, 149, 152, 154, 156, 157, 158, 163, 182, 183, 186, 187, 188, 196, 197, 199
   aims and functions   71, 73, 74
   boundaries of criminal law   9, 74, 75, 77
   core functions of criminal law   46
   executive criminal law   80
   General Part   182
   Implied limitations   56
   limits of criminal law   72, 152
   political theory   36, 75
   Russian criminal law   12, 182, 186
   socio-political milieu   74
   Special Part   3, 91, 182
criminal liability   16, 93
criminalization
   aims and functions of criminal law   71, 73, 74
   composite theory   72, 79
   institutional form   8
   justificatory principles   77
   master theory of criminalization   75
   right not to be criminalized   76
   unprincipled criminalization   72, 76, 149
   utilitarian ideals   73
criminalized onion   101, 102, 117
culpable wrongdoers   74
cultural bias   71
currency control   188, 189, 192
currency legislation   190, 192
cybercrime   119, 186

Dalits   7, 164
dangerousness   40, 73, 89
de-addiction   171, 176, 177, 178
decriminalization   8, 9, 13, 14, 76, 91, 95, 144, 147, 149, 154, 155, 158, 171, 178
decriminalize   7, 13, 178, 217
defamation   136
deficit discourses   40
definition of crime   73, 76, 82
delinquency   40
democratic society   54, 107, 120, 136
derogation   54, 55, 69
deserved punishment   72, 74
designated area   215
detention orders   135, 137, 138, 198
detenu   134, 135, 137, 138, 139, 140
deterrence   71, 102, 175
deviance   10, 202
dignity   83, 104, 131, 153, 154, 155, 157, 183, 196, 204, 208, 217
dissent   7, 111, 119, 121, 122, 123, 124, 125, 126, 127, 133, 136, 137, 138, 140, 142
drug consumption   11, 170
   commercial quantities   12, 176, 177

ease of doing business   9, 13, 74, 87
ease of living   9, 13, 74, 87, 88
embezzlement   56, 187
emergency powers   51, 52, 61, 62
endangerment law   45, 64
entrepreneurship   12, 192

fair and reasonable notice   80
fair trial   50, 54, 57, 58, 173, 174
fault requirement   5, 72, 79, 88
   common intention   83
   maliciously   83
forced labour   157
free speech   11, 120, 122, 125, 126, 127, 128, 130, 136, 137, 142

INDEX 225

freedom of association 54, 59, 138
Fuller 72, 78, 79, 82, 84, 92
   clarity 58, 63, 78, 83, 157
   congruence between official action and declared rule 78, 84
   constancy 78, 83
   generality 78, 79, 215
   legality 51, 53, 57, 59, 63, 64, 72, 78, 81, 83, 107, 200
   no contradictions 78
   non-retroactive laws 78
   possibility of compliance 78
   promulgation 78, 80
fundamental right 1, 21, 30, 51, 128, 136, 138, 153, 178, 195, 214

habitual criminal 37, 38
harm principle 3, 4, 11, 18, 73, 74, 145, 149, 150, 151, 152
harmfulness 151
hazard law 64
hegemony 5, 7
homosexuality 39, 46, 145, 148, 152, 155, 156
human rights 1, 2, 10, 44, 45, 46, 47, 49, 50, 51, 52, 53, 54, 55, 56, 57, 58, 59, 60, 61, 62, 63, 64, 67, 68, 87, 100, 101, 106, 119, 129, 134, 138, 202, 210, 213

ignorance of law is not an excuse 80
imperialist 178
inchoate offences 73, 77
increased regulation 12
Indigenous peoples 10, 35
individual autonomy 157, 199
individual criminal responsibility 13, 47, 195, 197
individuality 121
Industrial Schools 37
internal armed conflict 54
international human rights law 10, 44, 47, 57, 59, 60, 61, 64
international law 10, 44, 47, 48, 50, 51, 52, 62, 214
   1961 Convention on Narcotic Drugs 169
   CERD 66
   customary and treaty law on human rights 62
   Declaration of Basic Principles of Justice for Victims of Crime and Abuse of Power, 1985 195, 214

Human Rights Committee 47, 128
International Convention against the Taking of Hostages 49, 67
International Covenant on Economic, Social and Cultural Rights 195, 209, 219
International human rights law 51
Siracusa Principles 54, 61, 69
the 1971 Convention on Psychotropic Substances 169
international terrorism 44
   counterterrorism laws 44
   United Nations Global Counter-Terrorism Strategy 50, 51, 69

John Stuart Mill 3, 17, 121, 149
judicial procedures 6
justice delivery mechanism 11

lack of consent 108
law enforcement 2, 12, 45, 46, 61, 84, 85, 87, 144, 178, 188, 191, 193, 194, 202
law enforcement agencies 61, 84, 178, 193, 194
law making 2, 81, 168
   participative criminal law making 81
lawlessness 125, 202
law-making 29, 31
legal moralism 74
legal obligation 146
legal paternalism 3, 18
legislation 7, 37, 40, 48, 49, 50, 51, 52, 55, 57, 59, 61, 62, 63, 64, 65, 83, 84, 96, 97, 102, 103, 133, 134, 150, 154, 163, 164, 165, 169, 182, 183, 190, 192, 193, 195, 198, 214
legitimacy of punishment 4
legitimate violence 49
liberal constitutional values 155
liberal critique 10
liberal theory of criminal law 5, 75
liberalism 10, 36
   authoritarian liberalism 36
liberty 1, 2, 19, 21, 24, 31, 44, 45, 49, 53, 54, 83, 86, 104, 105, 120, 121, 126, 131, 132, 147, 148, 149, 151, 152, 153, 154, 155, 157, 167, 195, 198, 204, 211, 212, 213, 214
liberty justification 120
licensing 148, 166, 168
Lok Sabha 30, 170, 171
love jihad 19

Macaulay   14, 16, 17, 73, 80, 91, 93, 94, 128
Maharashtra Crime Investigation
    Department   172
mala prohibita   199
mandatory public consultation   80
marital rape   145
mens rea
    common law presumption of
        mens rea   90
mens rea requirement   5, 73, 82, 90
Michel Foucault   10, 35, 42
    conduct of conduct   37, 38
    counter-conduct   38, 39, 40, 41, 42
    governmentality   38
    power and freedom   38
    revolts of conduct   38
minimal impairment   53
moral blameworthiness   73, 88
moral offences   73, 77
moralism   3, 18, 74

national security   9, 53, 59, 88, 133, 134, 197, 204, 215
nationalist movement   168, 178
necessity principle   79, 87
negative liberty   120, 121
negligence   5, 185
Nirbhaya judgement   9, 19
nomadic communities   80
nonconsummate acts   195
normative theory   2, 3, 8, 13, 44, 71, 75, 77, 78, 79, 95
nullum poena sine lege   81

offensive act   200
otherness   5
over-criminalization   1, 8, 9, 74, 85, 87

pandemic   135, 163, 196, 198, 203, 204, 206, 210, 212, 215, 216
penal law   75
penalties   12, 18, 83, 84, 145, 166, 168, 169, 170, 207
Policing   37, 42, 218
poppy   165, 166, 168, 169
positive moral judgement   60
predispositions of police   74
Preparatory crimes   46
presumption of harmlessness   201

presumption of innocence   9, 11, 19, 20, 72, 79, 95, 97, 103, 104, 105, 106, 107, 108, 109, 110, 111, 112, 113, 144, 174, 200, 201
preventive detention   81, 89, 119, 133, 134, 135, 136, 137, 138, 139
preventive function   45, 71
preventive justice   13, 197, 201
prima facie   58, 107, 128, 130, 131
principle of necessity   50, 78, 87
principled criminalization   6
principles of legality   57, 72, 78
prisons   39, 145, 171
probation officers   37
proportional and deserved punishment   72
prosecutors   2, 6, 45, 74, 76, 79, 84, 103, 175, 193
prostitution   46
public danger   183, 184, 185, 187, 188, 190, 191, 193, 194
public health approach   12, 178
public morality   2, 9, 17, 18, 149, 152, 153, 155
public opinion   7, 8, 9, 29, 77, 85
public order   59, 126, 127, 134, 136, 138, 145, 183, 205, 206, 215, 216
public wrongs   74, 81
punishment   4, 6, 9, 12, 13, 17, 18, 22, 23, 24, 29, 45, 46, 49, 51, 56, 73, 74, 75, 78, 81, 82, 83, 86, 87, 88, 89, 97, 98, 102, 108, 109, 111, 144, 145, 147, 157, 172, 183, 193, 195, 196, 198, 199, 200
    community service   86, 88
    confiscation of property   86, 183
    death penalty   56, 86
    deprivation of liberty   54, 86, 211
    deserved   4, 72, 74, 75, 79, 88, 97
    fine   7, 13, 19, 22, 23, 29, 30, 86, 88, 147, 173, 187
    freezing of bank accounts   88
    harsher punishments   171
    imprisonment   13, 23, 28, 45, 56, 85, 86, 88, 147, 148, 171, 172, 173, 176, 177, 217
    justification of   4, 45, 152
    probation   37, 86, 183
    punishment of thoughts   46
    punitive compensation   86, 88
    severity of   46, 89, 193
    unjust punishment   111
punitive justice   197
punitive measures   3, 77, 86, 87

quarantine   13, 197, 202, 207, 208, 209, 213

radicalisation   57, 58
Rajya Sabha   133, 171, 179
rational and autonomous individual   73
reasonable restrictions   22, 126, 127
reasonable suspicion   201, 204
recklessness   5, 200
refouling   13, 197, 216
refugee camps   13, 197, 198, 202, 203, 204, 211, 212, 213, 217, 219
Regulatory criminal laws   12
regulatory oversight   12
rehabilitation   31, 171
Religion   19, 20, 21, 34
   Buddhism   123, 143
   Christianity   123
   Islam   124
   Sanatan Hinduism   123
remote harms   73
retribution   4, 198, 199, 200
   culpability-based retributivists   73
right to life   2, 48, 49, 52, 105, 148
right to security   49, 52, 53
risk management strategies   40
rule of law   1, 18, 46, 50, 52, 64, 78, 84, 207, 216
Russian criminal law
   crime rates   87, 186
   crimes in the economic sphere   187
   privileged   184
   privileged corpus delicti   184
   qualified corpus delicti   183, 184, 185
   qualified elements   183

sanctions   18, 19, 47, 51, 58, 78, 86, 87, 88, 97, 99, 100, 103, 144, 145, 146, 147, 157, 158, 192, 195
security   7, 9, 13, 31, 45, 47, 48, 49, 52, 53, 55, 56, 59, 61, 62, 72, 86, 88, 89, 105, 126, 133, 134, 141, 151, 183, 188, 190, 195, 196, 197, 201, 204, 208, 209, 215, 217
Security Council   49, 50, 57, 68
sedition   7, 11, 128, 129, 130, 133, 137, 138, 140, 142, 143, 146
sentencing   6, 28, 29, 38, 39, 111, 175, 176
   indeterminate sentencing   38, 39
   mandatory minimum sentence   176, 177
   preventative intervention   40
Seventh Schedule   168
severity of crimes   193
social deviance   202
social work   40, 41
socially dangerous   192
Somali refugees   13, 204, 206, 216
southern criminal law   6
Special Part   3, 91, 182
spousal violence   25
strict liability   5, 45, 73, 77, 82, 88, 89, 90, 200
substantivist approach   109

theory of criminalization   2, 3, 5, 6, 8, 71, 72, 73, 74, 75, 77, 78, 79, 80, 86, 196
traditional criminal law   12
traffickers   171, 172, 175, 176, 178
trafficking of drugs   168, 170, 178
travaux préparatoires   53
treatment   4, 9, 85, 171, 176, 178, 197, 198, 208, 212, 214, 215
triple talaq   7, 11, 30, 31, 32, 33
   Talaq-i-biddat   9

unconstitutional   22, 23, 30, 119, 127, 135, 145, 146, 204, 208, 210, 211
under-criminalization   9, 74, 95
Union Legislature   168
utilitarianism   17, 156

war on drugs   169
wrongfulness   3, 97, 151, 195

www.ingramcontent.com/pod-product-compliance
Lightning Source LLC
Chambersburg PA
CBHW060950050426
42337CB00053B/3846